WORKS AND DAYS

EDITH COOPER

From a drawing by Charles Shannon, R.A.,
in the Birmingham Art Gallery.

Frontispiece

WORKS AND DAYS

FROM THE JOURNAL OF
MICHAEL FIELD
EDITED
BY T. & D. C.
STURGE MOORE

LONDON
JOHN MURRAY
ALBEMARLE STREET
W

First Edition . . . *1933*

CONTENTS

ILLUSTRATIONS

INTRODUCTION

BY
SIR WILLIAM ROTHENSTEIN

MARGARET WOODS once wrote of the hopeless-
ness of conveying, to those who have never
known it, the colour and depth of a rare personality ; as
though mariners suddenly saw, rising to the sea's surface,
some strange creature, hitherto unseen by human eyes,
resting for a few moments in the light of the sun before
sinking ; and on their return to land, speaking of the
wonder they had seen, found unheeding ears.

I believe these extracts from the Michael Field's
journals will give to those who never met these two poets
in the flesh, an inkling of the complex, vivid charm of
their characters. I see them in my mind's eye, Michael
stout, emphatic, splendid and adventurous in talk, rich
in wit ; Field wan and wistful, gentler in manner than
Michael, but equally eminent in the quick give and take
of ideas. But how to pass on to others their shining
comments on people, on books and pictures, and on
human experience—an impossible task ! Both were endowed with an ecstatic sense of beauty—of the loveliness of the visible world, and in addition a sensitiveness
to the subtleties of art and poetry which inspired them
with a perception of the touching poetry which clings to
all material things. Even later, when their views of life
changed, and love of God came before all else, it never
lessened their delight in man's gracious handiwork, or

in generous giving and receiving.   With so much beauty
to occupy them, they had no time for, and no patience
with, the meaner objects which too many men and women
pursue.   For their poet's integrity must be kept bright
and spotless, as everything about them, furniture, silver,
china, was to be kept.

For those they deemed traitors to the realm of the mind
they were without mercy.   So, for all their hero-worship
of George Meredith, when they found he could fall below
the conduct they expected, from him as from others,
friendship with him became impossible.   How observant
these shy ladies were of " the fine shades," their account of
their visits to Box Hill, here given, well shows.   Indeed,
it would seem as though those who live remote from their
fellows see most clearly what goes on in the world, both
good and evil ; as the abstemious man preserves the most
sensitive palate.   Yet there was nothing of the blue-
stocking in Michael Field.   What Edmond de Goncourt
said of the artist's nature—" Chaste de corps et libertin
d'esprit "—could be aptly said of these ladies.   Even
after they became converts to Rome, and a new devotion
absorbed them, and disciplined their lives, their smiling
gaiety remained.   So indeed did their wit, and their
enjoyment of that which their rich talk inspired in their
friends.   I know nothing so exhilarating as wit bubbling
up from an exquisite nature.   Always there comes a sense
of discomfort at talk, be it never so brilliant, which is not
rooted in charity.   It was this radiance springing from
inner illumination which gave such value to their friendship.   Indeed I never left their company without seeming
to tread on air.   Yet woe to one who fell short of their
expectations.   More than one reflection of their scorn
appears in their journal.

I first met these remarkable ladies at the Dutch Gallery

in Brook Street, where, with Charles Shannon, I was for
the first time, in London, showing drawings and lithographs. At this time (1894) they impressed me as æsthetic
ladies, Ruskinian in their enthusiasm for Italian painting,
little attracted by the realistic aims of the nineties. They
were at once charmed by Shannon's sanguines and silver
points ; it was only in the subjects of my drawings, Pater
and Verlaine especially, that they found an interest. I
accompanied them several times after this to picture
galleries. We had in common a love of Rossetti, and the
exhibition of his work at the New Gallery drew from
them such subtle understanding as made me eager to
introduce them to Ricketts and Shannon. Then for a
few years they vanished from my ken. When we came
together again, I was to find their sympathies broadened
and more human. To their friendship for me was added
an affectionate relationship with my wife, which was
continued to the end. They came to stay with us at
Hampstead more than once ; each time elaborate arrangements were made for their attendance at early mass ; a
pony carriage would be ordered, and departure and
re-arrival at the house was of the nature of a cere-
monial.

Of the younger of the two ladies, Miss Cooper (Field),
Charles Ricketts has left a noble record in a sensitive
miniature. That Charles Shannon should not have
painted Field is surprising, for from her he formed a
type which appears often in his paintings. Michael,
whose poet's nature appeared only in her flashing eyes,
was no good subject for portraiture. At her earnest
desire I made a drawing of Field when, alas, her hold
on life was of the slenderest. But since little has been
written of Michael Field, perhaps I may be allowed to
repeat an impression printed elsewhere.

"The Paragon, the Michael Field's house at Richmond, was an 18th-century house, with a garden running down to the river. In the living-rooms the furniture was of satinwood, chosen by Ricketts, and on the walls hung Shannon's lithographs, and prints by Ricketts and Sturge Moore, exquisitely mounted. Ricketts and Shannon gave to mounting and framing the care which only Eastern artists give as a rule. There were always choice flowers, lovingly arranged, and in a large cage cooed a pair of doves. Field, wan, a little drooping, with large eyes, clear forehead and sensitive lips, looked the poet she was; Michael, stout, with a high colour, masterful, protecting, was the active, managing spirit of the Paragon. Field again looked the poet in any dress she wore; but dress, like everything else, must for long be discussed and pondered and finally ordered from the modiste with elaborate directions. But most important were the hats. Once a year a visit was paid to Kate Reilly, a Dover Street milliner, and imperial hats were chosen; purple with superb feathers, that drooped over Field's small ear, and waved proudly above Michael's head. But these poetesses were fiery ladies. There were grass borders in the gardens of their minds on which one must never tread. For they were both ardent converts to Roman Catholicism and they gave all the wealth of their imaginations, their entire obedience, and somewhat, I fancy, of their worldly wealth to what was for them the only true church. And what a rich fantasy was theirs; what lightning play of mind, and how they valued the same in others! They knew but few people, but from these few they expected—everything, all they had to give. They were imperious ladies, these exquisite poets, Michael especially. They knew the value of their friendship ; if they gave it, it must be with both hands ; but those to whom they gave must be worthy of their trust every moment, whether in their company or out of sight and hearing."

On reading the extracts selected by Mr. Sturge Moore from the journals regularly kept by Michael Field, there comes again a poignant sense of the beauty of these two indomitable spirits. The last chapters surely prove that the long hierarchy of Saints in the Catholic church has not ended ; and I long, as when reading Haydon's autobiography, for more extended extracts. Happily the original journals exist and Mr. Sturge Moore, in whose care they were left, is not likely to show the criminal callousness of Tom Taylor. If the gifts of these two great ladies receive the recognition they deserve, there may well be a demand for further material from this rich quarry.

EDITORS' PREFACE

KATHERINE BRADLEY and Edith Cooper, who wrote under the pseudonym of Michael Field, having appointed me their literary executor, left me instructions to open, at the end of 1929, their journal entitled *Works and Days*, to read it and then to publish so much and whatever parts of it I might think fit; and to supplement it from bundles of letters written by or to them at the time.

The following volume is a first selection from this material. Chronology has been disregarded where it would have interfered with the continuity of interest. A few biographical details should then be of help to the reader.

Katherine Bradley, the daughter of a tobacco manufacturer, was born on October 27th, 1848, at Birmingham. Her elder sister Emma married J. R. Cooper, a merchant settled at Kenilworth, in 1860, where Edith was born in 1862. Two years later Mrs. Cooper had a second daughter, Amy, an event which left her a permanent invalid. Then Katherine and her widowed mother moved in to look after the little family. She was sixteen or seventeen; and so began the long association which only ended with Edith's death in 1913.

Katherine was ardent for knowledge, corresponded with Ruskin, and went to Newnham, Cambridge, for a summer vacation course, and to the Collège de France, at Paris. Here she fell in love with the brother of a

French friend. He was considerably older than her and before their intimacy had time to ripen, he died. Though this event was long passed when the diaries begin, there is an entry every year on the anniversary of his death, witness to the scar that this tragedy had left on her life.

By this time Edith was growing up and the family had moved to Bristol, where aunt and niece entered into the life of the University with great zest, enthusiastically supporting the more advanced ideas, women's suffrage, anti-vivisection, etc., at debating societies. They also studied literature and art. Before many years they were visiting the picture galleries of Europe and following Bernhard Berenson's lectures, making a close friend of him and later of his wife.

In 1875 Katherine had published a volume of verse, *The New Minnesinger*, by Arran Leigh, and in 1881 *Bellerophon*, by Arran and Isla Leigh, appeared, their joint work. But this was kept secret from their friends, and they never considered either of these books as worthy of Michael Field, though some of Edith's contributions to the second were re-published in the posthumous volume *Dedicated*. *Callirrhöe and Fair Rosamund* (1883) was the first book to bear this pseudonym, for which they gave various reasons at different times. They were prolific in nick-names, for themselves and others; but as the years went by Katherine became Michael, and Edith, Field or Henry; this last by Michael, either drawn out into Hennery or shortened to Henny.

After the first flush of acclamation their work was treated with ever-increasing coldness by the literary world, and there is no doubt that the discovery that Michael Field was no avatar of " Waring," but two women, was partly responsible. The tragic deaths of Edith's father and mother combined with Edith's ill-health to estrange

them from the " little London " which ferments around
the newest reputations.

I hope to publish shortly another book centring round
their friendship with the late Charles Ricketts, R.A., who
with his friend Charles Shannon, R.A., became " The
Artists " for the writers of these pages. Ricketts had
written them a letter of vivid admiration after reading
their *Tragic Mary*; slowly and at shortening intervals the
friendship between these pairs of fellow creators ripened,
till on the death of Mr. Cooper in 1898, Ricketts insisted
on their leaving the bourgeois house at Reigate and coming to Richmond. " The Artists " found them a house,
Shannon doing the measuring to convince them that they
could fit in. And the two homes dedicated to art were,
for a year or so, less than ten minutes' walk from one
another. Then " the painters " moved to Lansdowne
House, Holland Park, " not too near, to avoid familiarity,
not too far for intercourse " with the poets.

At No. 1, The Paragon, the eighteenth-century doors
and mouldings were painted white, the walls of the small
room to the right on entering were silver. Here Edith
worked ; and here, to Ricketts' intense disapproval, choked
down out of respect for affectionate piety, was installed
a mantelpiece by her father, whose hobby had been wood-
carving, in which he was extremely accomplished, but
conformed to Swiss taste. Yet the birds, flowers and
fruits were perhaps conscious of Ghiberti's, though the
panels and their placing were outrageously not Florentine. There were two Hiroshigi prints in this room and
several lithographs by Shannon. In the slightly larger
room, which opened through folding doors, out of this,
they received. Conversation would be interrupted by
the over-loud cooing of doves, whose cage had then
to be removed to the small glass-house that opened

through the right-hand french-window. The furniture was eighteenth-century satinwood, severely elegant rather than florid, all chosen or at least approved by " The Artists." Shannon's lithographs, dignified, for the first time, with gilded frames of beautiful proportions, made walls, distempered a warm grey, exquisite ; among them hung two of Ricketts' *Hero and Leander* woodcuts and a drawing of two heads of wild garlic ; later this room was papered with a narrow white and silver stripe.

On the dainty, polished table-tops stood several pieces of white porcelain and rare glass, or old plate, and a tangle of necklaces or other jewels were displayed with artful carelessness. But above all there were flowers in this " Sun Room." Edith's choice and arrangement of these, Ricketts regarded as beyond comparison finer than any he had met with. The afternoon sunshine flooded through the windows, while the ceiling was always alive with reflections from the river. For the view embraced a most lovely reach of the Thames, leading to the stone arch of Richmond Bridge. Huge elms and cedars stood in luxuriant meadows opposite ; these have since been improved away by those whose eyes do not discover beauty. These rooms, if small, were exquisite, and the house, which showed but two stories and retreating attics to the Petersham Road (not then invaded by hideous motor traffic), had at least six above the garden, which sloped down to the tow-path, from which a fairly high wall closed it. The roses, though abundant, always failed to veil a wire-net cage for their large dogs, Whym Chow and Music the Bassett hound, who redecorated its level floor only too frequently. This touch of the Zoo was at least as much out of keeping as the carved mantel-piece, but the piety which maintained it was even less to be reasoned with.

My first memory of these ladies is dining at the Paragon in 1901, while staying at 7, Spring Terrace during the absence of " The Artists " on the Continent—" house-dogging for them " they called it. I had met Michael at the Sangers' six months before, but my memory of that is a quite empty ghost. Their manners, though a second nature, were more elaborate than any I had encountered, and intimidated me. Michael, who was grey-haired and overflowing with indisguisable human nature, soon put me at my ease, even her tantrums could be easily understood ; but for years the admired Henry kept me uneasy. Being the larger of the two, her pallor, dignity, ill-health and reserves of intellect frustrated even her sweetly-smiling advances ; yet in the end I was to have closer touch with her thought than with Michael's impulsiveness. They insisted on evening dress, and clothes I wore so rarely were a barrier in themselves.

The wainscoting of the stairs and of the tiny downstairs dining-room was apple green. Here the walls were covered with gilded canvas on which hung a small round mirror and the sketch for Ricketts' lovely *Tobit and the Angel* now in the Birmingham Gallery ; his *Jacob and the Angel*, now in the Ashmolean, hung in the little adjunct to this room, which supported the small glass-house above. In this adjunct Michael worked. Both were industrious and as a rule did not exchange a word between 9 a.m. and 1 p.m. ; they took their profession with extreme seriousness. Long before, the one seventeen the other thirty-two, while making beds in their old house at Kenilworth, they had dedicated their lives to poetry.

> It was deep April, and the morn
> Shakespeare was born ;
> The world was on us, pressing sore ;

My Love and I took hands and swore
Against the world, to be
Poets and lovers evermore,
To laugh and dream on Lethe's shore,
To sing to Charon in his boat,
Heartening the timid souls afloat;
Of judgement never to take heed,
But to those fast-locked souls to speed,
Who never from Apollo fled,
Who spent no hour among the dead;
Continually
With them to dwell,
Indifferent to heaven and hell.

And in them I, who then had been but eight years old,
touched a fellow-feeling in regard to poetry which was in
many ways more intimate than I could feel with Yeats or
even with Binyon. Yet there remained regions into
which I could not follow even them; and they were, I
know, disappointed in me, so profoundly solitary are we.

Joy is born and dies in an hour
And we to homely pain return.

However, the frequent evenings I passed with them were
a very great and delightful addition to my life, and I have
been happy to find, by these journals, that my pleasure
was reciprocated.

In 1907, after having been much tossed by " winds
of doctrine," they found a haven in the Roman Church.
A few years later both poets were stricken with cancer.
Miss Bradley, the second victim, concealed the fact till
after her fellow's funeral. Though suffering agonies,
she had spared Edith the cruelty of knowing that her feet
were to be followed on the path of pain.

Works and Days contains the record of their thoughts

and actions, and the draft of much of their poetry. It
consists of twenty-six vellum-bound folios of the size of
office ledgers, one for each year from 1888 to 1914. I
could not possibly have dealt with these alone. My son
has taken upon his young shoulders not only the
laborious deciphering of the often baffling script, with
the indexing and general preparation of the work, but
has helped me sort and group the extracts, and becoming
himself an ardent appreciator, has discovered much that
might have been overlooked.

This book opens with chapters that have already
appeared in *The Cornhill Magazine*. Let me therefore
now repeat what I then wrote :

To prepare readers for a plunge back into the eighteen-
eighties, I would remind them that the characteristics of
that age are not yet so quaint and dear as those of Boswell
or of Pepys. We must expect to laugh, but our laughter
will not quite so easily blend with love and respect, and
yet I fancy that in the end few readers of these diaries can
fail to become both friends and admirers of the authors,
who have a most engaging vitality and are without any
notion of the reflections that will now seem most obvious.
With all their conventionality, they are simplicity itself,
as open as children, while their own characters and minds
and those to whom they introduce us, are of a force and
dignity to have created respect in any age. We must also
remember that Katherine Bradley was thirty-nine and
Edith Cooper twenty-three, when the first letters to
Robert Browning begin, a few years before the diary, he
being then in his seventy-seventh year. Mrs. Browning
had been wooed and saved some forty years earlier,

and her works were still idolized, though she had
been dead more than twenty years, before he came
on these young poetesses. To him, in many unhoped-
for ways, they must have been the past returning.
His own work was again studied and pored over by
a most distinguished poetess. He was reading verse
which he admired and behind which he discovered
exceptional gifts of refinement and goodness. Indeed,
Katherine Bradley was the same age as Miss Barrett when
he had first met her. This situation so unique, so mira-
culous in the happiness it created, must be realized by any
reader who wishes to avoid misreading intimate touches,
which occurred naturally to people with those manners
and beliefs and this unheard-of relation to one another.
At first he alone knew that they were the authors of
Michael Field's *Callirrhöe*, etc. The guests they met at
his table were unaware that these ladies were "the new
poet."

CHAPTER ONE

ROBERT BROWNING

Correspondence between Robert Browning and Michael Field

WARWICK CRESCENT,
July 7, 1883.

DEAR MISS COOPER,

You have been very good and patient with my poetry and I thank you heartily. I thank you also for your kindness in sending the review itself. I ought to mention the Hebrew title is an imaginary one, the words meaning only "a collection of many fictions."[1] I profit no less by your ingenuity. The second translation is correct, "From Moses to Moses, etc."

Pray believe me, dear Miss Cooper, yours with much regard,

ROBERT BROWNING.

STOKE GREEN,
May 7, 1884.

DEAR MR. BROWNING,

The same Edith Cooper who ventured to send you a review of *Jocoseria* last year, is daring again. Repeti-

[1] See note to Jochanan Hakkadosh, *Jocoseria*.

I

tion is born of Encouragement. The kind letter with which you accepted the review is answerable for the intrepidity of this second attack on your kindness. This time I send you a book—partly mine—plays—the first fruits of thought spent by a new labourer on the vineyard of human life.

If you will taste the fruit, it will not have been grown in vain.

Yours with deep respect,

EDITH COOPER.

WARWICK CRESCENT,
May 28, 1884.

DEAR MISS COOPER,

I should be glad to know—since it is *you* whom I address and must thank—how much of the book that is " partly yours " is indeed your own part; it is long since I have been so thoroughly impressed by indubitable poetic *genius*; a word I consider while I write, only to repeat it, " genius." The second play is brimful of beauty; in thought and in feeling, admirably expressed; I think I see often enough the proof of youth and perhaps haste; but the great promise is not promise only; there is performance in an extraordinary degree. So with the first play; it recalls, to its disadvantage in certain respects, the wonderful *Bacchæ* of Euripides; and the deaths are dealt thickly about, in hardly an artistic fashion; but the scene between Machaon and the Faun [1] would compensate for almost

_____
[1] *Callirrhöe and Fair Rosamund.*

any amount of crudeness and incompleteness, which probably will not be so observable when I read both poems again, as I mean to do. Meanwhile accept my true congratulations and believe me,

Yours sincerely,

ROBERT BROWNING.

STOKE GREEN,
Postmark *May* 29, 1884.

DEAR MR. BROWNING,

Such words as yours give more abundant life: to expend it in higher, more reverent effort is the only true gratitude possible. As to myself and my part in the book—to make all clear to you, I must ask for strict secrecy. My Aunt and I work together after the fashion of Beaumont and Fletcher. She is my senior, by but fifteen years. She has lived with me, taught me, encouraged me and joined me to her poetic life. She was the enthusiastic student of the *Bacchæ*. Some of the scenes of our play are like mosaic-work—the mingled, various product of our two brains. The Faun scene is mine. I was just nineteen when, with joy mixed with a dreary sense of woe, the conception came to me. *Emathian* is also almost wholly mine and much of *Margery*. I think if our contributions were disentangled and one subtracted from the other, the amount would be almost even. This happy union of two in work and aspiration is sheltered and expressed by " Michael Field." Please regard him as the author.

If we are united in our poetic work, so are we also

in our true admiration and earnest study of your works. The book was really sent by both, though a kind letter from you last year to me, gave me, it was judged, the privilege of writing to you.

Still hoping, doubting that I can make you feel what your letter has been to me, I remain, dear Mr. Browning,

Yours with deep respect,

EDITH COOPER.

WARWICK CRESCENT,

May 31, 1884.

DEAR MICHAEL FIELD,

I shall indeed have help in being suffered to so address you; I receive this moment, from a person I met at dinner last night, the critique in the *Spectator*, of which I heard for the first time in your letter. It is sent because of my saying, with a notion that I was the actual discoverer, "There is a new poet." My acquaintance replied, "You mean Michael Field,"—and here comes the very style and title anticipatively accorded—most justly. I should like to add a word or two to what I hastily wrote on the supposition that I was the discoverer. I read both poems again, only to confirm my opinion of the extraordinary clearness of the evidence, that genius runs through it all, like your "starry serpent of torch-light," now fully emerging, now sufficiently divined. I did not at the first hasty reading of the first part of *Callirrhöe*, do justice to the originality of the poem; what seemed fine and true at first sight, approved itself even more unmistakably so, when twice laid to head and heart. I am far from wanting to add a sort of poor grace to this recognition of mine, by assuring you, what is not hard to believe, that it is unfortunately seldom indeed, that with the best will in the world, I am able to say anything beyond a natural thanks for the books of verse, which imply a compliment if not a kindness by their visitations : I was not prepared for veritable poetry in your case. And as for the sense of gratitude one is bound to have, when made aware that there is liking for works of one's own in the same way, it stands actually as hindrance to what may resemble a payment in kind. But I count on your understanding this and more. The critique is capital in the main ; and timely above all things. Don't be frowned out of that scene,[1] which is quite your own, and decisively original, and consonant with a deeper " naturalness," than friend Hutton ever had experience of ; in the main however he sees the points and speaks to them. Now go and prosper! I wanted to say (I remember) that you may depend on your secret—as to the divided authorship, and the rest —being kept by me—who am very unnecessarily apprised that the difference in age between such relatives need not be considerable : I think the most beautiful woman I ever saw was two years older than myself, and for all that my very Aunt—my grandfather having married a second time in middle life.

Yours most truly and with renewed congratulations,
ROBERT BROWNING.

[1] The Faun scene.

STOKE GREEN,
Sunday even., 23 Nov., 1884.

Spinoza with his fine grasp of unity says : " If two individuals of exactly the same nature are joined together, they make up a single individual, doubly stronger than each alone," i.e., Edith and I make a *veritable Michael*. And we humbly fear you are destroying this philosophic truth : it is said the *Athenæum* was taught by you to use the feminine pronoun. Again, someone named André Raffalovich, whose earnest young praise gave me genuine pleasure, now writes in ruffled distress ; he " thought he was writing to a boy—a young man . . . he has learnt on the best authority it is not so." I am writing to him to assure him that the best authority is my work. But I write to you to beg you to set the critics on a wrong track. We each know that you mean good to us : and are persuaded you thought that by " our secret " we meant the dual authorship. The revelation of that would indeed be utter ruin to us ; but the report of lady authorship will dwarf and enfeeble our work at every turn. Like the poet Gray we shall never " speak out." And we have many things to say that the world will not tolerate from a woman's lips. We must be free as dramatists to work out in the open air of nature—exposed to her vicissitudes, witnessing her terrors : we cannot be stifled in drawing-room conventionalities. In Clifton we have made a desperate fight for the freedom of our privacy ; and yesterday, to my joy, Edith was asked by a friend to read a sonnet in the *Spectator* I wrote a fortnight ago, on Fawcett ; " by Michael Field—a Bristol man ! " That is victory here

. . . meanwhile in London ? Oh, with a word you can persuade the critics you have been tricking them : the heart of the mystery is not plucked out. Besides, you are robbing us of real criticism, such as man gives man. The Gods learn little from the stupid words addressed to them at their shrines : they disguise ; meet mortals unsuspecting in the market-place and enjoy wholesome intercourse.

We want to listen, like that old poet of yours, who sat quite still and knew all that happened. But you will divine all this and more. As women we trust to lead a quiet life, deepening as the years roll on. That deep nook in Michael's nature where the Faun plays—you, our Father Poet, will help to keep free from tourists' prying feet ?

In respectful entreaty, I am faithfully yours,

KATHERINE BRADLEY.[1]

STOKE GREEN,
Nov. 27, 1884.

DEAR MR. BROWNING,

I seem to remember that I wrote to you in my own name as a woman. I trust you overlooked that in your reply. I do not care to speak to you again of our relations to our work : on one point, however, your misapprehension is so serious that I cannot keep silent. I did not speak of combating " social conventions." It is not in our power or desire to treat irreverently customs

---

[1] Browning's reply to this letter is missing and was probably destroyed at the time.

or beliefs that have been, or are, sacred to men. We hold ourselves bound in life and in literature to reveal —as far as may be—the beauty of the high feminine standard of *the ought to be*. What I wrote was, "we cannot be stifled in drawing-room conventionalities." By that I meant we could not be scared away, as ladies, from the tragic elements of life.

I am sorry I should have to explain this to you.

Faithfully yours,

KATHERINE H. BRADLEY.

STOKE GREEN,
June 7, 1885.

DEAR MR. BROWNING,

The words that you wrote to me when I sent you *Callirrhöe*, made the chief joy I had in the little white book of last year. Its somewhat larger successor I venture to send you as a witness of my true gratitude, and I hope you will read it without thinking of the authors' pseudonym, only of the pleasure and encouragement you gave them, by your right generous praise and recognition.

Sincerely yours,

EDITH COOPER.

I find the book cannot reach you till Tuesday. *The Father's Tragedy* is all my own with the exception of Emmelino's song.

WARWICK CRESCENT,
June 8, 1885.

MY DEAR MISS COOPER,

The " little white book " caused the day on which I
first became acquainted with it to become "a great
red-letter day "; and every after reading has procured
me one delight the more—there is the truth. How glad
I was to hear that a second book was about to appear,
you ought not to doubt—nor do you, I will believe.
What I said on an impulse concerning *Callirrhöe* was
less, I am sure, than I should have managed to say had
I waited a little; but I wanted to speak first—and was
anticipated all the same, as I found in a day or two.
The post brings also a most welcome invitation from
my dear friend Miss Swanwick, to meet you (" you "
being in the dual number) next Saturday. You shall
then lay an injunction upon me as to what I shall say
and not say, if the matter of authorship is mooted : and
pray be assured that I shall act just as loyally as lovingly
—to the best of my powers, at least. All success attend
you—beginning with a conviction that you have done
your fine powers justice !

ROBERT BROWNING.

CHRISTCHURCH VICARAGE, BLACKHEATH,
June 15, 1885 (p.m.).

DEAR MR. BROWNING,

We ask leave to tell you—for we could not speak
at all on Saturday—of the happiness it gave us to be
with you. Your belief in us will go on, literally all our

days through, goading us and yet keeping us patient in our labour. We shall always "remember and understand." If you should find any tricks of style, any individual mannerisms, that break the unity of our work, will you be a critic as stern as you have been disinterested ? We love our work too earnestly to be hurt by any educating severity. This you will know. Hoping that we may some day meet again.

Very sincerely yours,
EDITH COOPER.

June, 1885.

. . .[1] Well, it is over and gone. We went in the morning to the Grosvenor [Gallery], where we saw the portrait of the old dear. . . . As soon as I entered the drawing-room [Miss Swanwick's]—alas, among many faces—I at once recognised the old poet. True, he does not look the poet, there is no magnetic charm and little change of expression. He is rather stout, with a blank brow, strange flat-looking eyes, that flash nothing out when he is showing his " worldly soul side " ; and that are quietly deepened when the other soul side is turned towards you. A smile in which serenity and geniality meet in steady balance ; no ancient and hoary splendour of beard and hair, both rather London-dust-coloured. A man whose emotional nature is commanded and reproved by a vast desire for knowledge, marked seriousness and worldly wisdom. Yet it was a moment in our

[1] Letter from Edith to her Cousin Fanny.

KATHERINE BRADLEY   EDITH COOPER

MICHAEL   FIELD

lives when he stood fondling our hands, with a touch that conveyed what he could not speak, then said, " How nice it is to have you standing one on each side of me."

He next explained how impartial a·critic he was ; how early he judged our work as literature. Then he spoke of his son, and how, like the dear father, he discovered his art gift in Millais' studio.

Then came lunch, old Canon Bell, Benson a rising young actor with strange, mobile features, Mrs. Bruce and daughter, etc., besides the inspired-looking hostess, who sat with old prophetic eyes, just under the Cumaean Sibyl. This lunch was very dull. Afterwards our father poet at once joined us and talked of Chatterton (for whom he has a strange admiration) and Shelley. When we parted he took our hands with firm, secret pressure, gently fondling them as he wished us all success and regretted he could not meet us again. I believe he would have kissed us had it not been for the public, who must have been astonished as it was. Of course we dared not talk much betraying talk. The book was on the table.[1] Ah ! he was gracious and fatherly. As we parted he said he wished he had met us under happier circumstances and left us the benediction of his belief [in us]. Indeed we love him devotedly. . . .

[From two separate papers and a letter of Edith's to her mother. Edith is for the moment St. Mark and Katherine Bradley St. Matthew, but since the two gospels overlap considerably, the best passages of each

[1] *The Father's Tragedy.*

have been welded together. The gospel according to St. Matthew is headed, " To Blow up the World."]

Gospel according to St. Mark

May 18, 1886.

Crown the old gentleman !

We arrived at Warwick Crescent just before one o'clock. It looks on a canal. We rang. The door was opened by a man, not a slave in livery. . . . I caught sight of a white head and standing figure through the door. . . . In another moment our hands were clasped with tender fervour by the old poet. He dragged us almost vehemently forward to an ugly, but most kind-looking lady, in brown, with white cap, bunched with pinky and claret-coloured ribbons. Her reception of us was most warm ; never loosing my hand [Edith], she took me to a seat and we talked of many things. Close to me, under a heap of books was *The Father's Tragedy*, black with use. We descended to lunch. " Tell Mr. Robert to come." And then we were astonished by the entrance of a veritable curly ball, most grotesquely ugly. A jocund youth of thirty, who seems to find life delightful and tragic writers and suicides especial food for mirth . . . dear little woolly bear " Pen," as his father calls him, joining in full of amusement and mockery and seeming to realise that we thoroughly belonged. Enjoying too, Edith said, our artistic gold and green dresses. Then the old poet began a tale.—Listen, you tragic dramatists !—An old Venetian gentleman had three daughters and one son. One day the girls got on board a steamer for the Lido ; it was evening and the steamer was the last. The captain warned them to return to the boat in time ; but they never came. He waited, but at last went his way. The girls were found drowned ; purposely, for most careful directions were found as to the disposal and use of their things. The sentry at the Lido said that he saw them, but thought they were spirits. One of the girls when kissing her father, before starting, noticed he wanted a button to his coat and quietly replaced it. It seems there was a governess in the house, to whom the brother began to pay addresses, and who gave herself mighty airs. The brother had spoken unkindly to the sisters and told them three times they must leave the house, if they took such a bitter view of the case. After he had spoken for the third time, they prepared for death. We felt we were sitting at table with the author of *The Ring and the Book*, as we listened to his delightful unravelling of motives and sentiments in this sad story of an event which had taken place while he was at Venice. A new poem was evolved before us, that only wanted writing. In the middle of the meal he suddenly exclaimed : " We do not often have dramatists to see us. I feel with Dr. Johnson, who so revered tragedians, that when letting them out, he always announced that there was *one step*." During lunch letters came and were received with the same eagerness as at Stoke. One was from Archdeacon Denison, asking Mr. Browning to meet O. W. Holmes (the 9th invitation). He said, " Should you like to meet Mr. Holmes ? " " He must be an interesting man."

Our old poet, giving Sim [1] a hearty pat on the shoulder, said, "There are more interesting persons than Wendell Holmes. I am for the tragic writers." We went up-stairs again and saw a curious inkstand of a Falstaffian swordsman, which Beddoes gave to Barry Cornwall. Then the old gentleman took us into a little room where stood pictures by his son. . . . Here we heard the tragic story of Rossetti's marriage. On return to the drawing-room, we told about Swinburne's letter. "He is very generous," said the old poet, "not that anyone need be generous to you." When we moved to go, he proposed that we should first visit his study. Miss Browning kissed us and said humbly, "You will not forget us?" Mr. Browning, "If I hear that you are in town and do not let me know, I shall be deeply offended."

The room where he lives as a poet is small, with red curtains and two plain book-cases filled with old books; over the mantelshelf is an Italian picture, there is a cast of Dante, some portraits, some vigorous studies of peasants (I should say by Pen) and a picture of Pen at his easel. There is a large chair with a screen at its back, a large desk, very worn, old, quantities of ink, etc., and in a black case worked in leather, the new poem. He let us glance at the MS., running on a

---

[1] A nickname for Miss Bradley, not, as I had supposed, short for Simaetha, but as I learn from Miss A. Trusted, for Simiorg, a fabulous, Eastern bird, mentioned in *Vathek* and *Thalaba* as endowed with reason or "all knowing"; it had seen the world destroyed at least three times. Miss Bradley often spoke of herself as the "all-wise bird" or "fowl" or used as signature the sign Y.

beautiful stream of penmanship.   He showed us a most
humorous sketch that Rossetti took of Tennyson reading
Maud to Mrs. Browning.   Then out of a drawer came
the very book, bought for ninepence on a Florentine
bookstall (white vellum, with a mixture of print and old
letters) on which *The Ring and The Book* was founded.
We held it in our hands, he translated to us here and
there.   He said how he had sent it to three novelists,
but they could do nothing with it.   So one fine morning
he determined to work at it and began his poem.   " You
could have done it," he said ; when we protested, he
added, " not in my way."   He showed us the first book
he bought as a boy, Mrs. Hemans' *Commonplace Book*
. . . his wife's Hebrew *Bible*, with notes in her own
hand, even on *Leviticus*.   He showed us the wooden box
in which lie all the Beddoes MSS. (a genius whose work
we must read) . . . the first book which Landor bought
and which he finally gave to " his best friend Robert
Browning "—a Catullus.   Then he showed us all the
tiny classics at which his wife worked, full of her notes
and still breathing her love.   He had been telling us
that they never knew anything of each other's work till
it was finished.   " We had better things to talk about
than our work."   Taking up a little *Euripides*, he said,
" She would join my name to hers in all the books that
belonged to her, she would have nothing of her own—
it was very pretty of her.   This explains what I meant
by better things."   And there was " Robert " put in front
of " Elizabeth."   When he thought I asked if he approved
of writing together, he said, " Yes, if you are two
sympathetic souls.   I live lonely—I have never had help

of this kind—lonely from my son. Here is my new
poem—my sister has not heard a single word of it."
Word was made of his wife, " Do you care for her ?
I hope so," he said, giving me [Edith] such an emotional
push that he nearly hurt me. . . . Then we said farewell—he said, " If you don't let me know when you are
in town, I shall think you have taken to chloral " (referring to Rossetti). At the door he paused, " Well, I
should always think poets the most glorious things in
the world." Then taking my hand, " You are beginning
where I am leaving off." Then putting an arm round
us, a fatherly kiss. " My blessing will not do you any
harm. God bless you." He took us to the gate, and
we left him with tears in our eyes, of joy and yet regret
that he is so old, though his age is as noble as that to
which Rabbi ben Ezra looked forward. Now you have
heard all. Nothing that ever happened to me is so
precious as those few moments of parting [Edith].
There was not an inch of difference in the devotion of
the old gentleman to one or the other [Katherine]. He
was tenderness itself, he could not have been more
loving . . . of his humility, of his expressive tenderness
—Oh, he deserves *The Sonnets from the Portuguese*—I
cannot speak. I [Katherine] never loved him till to-day,
now I love him dearly. . . . Oh ! love. I give thanks
for my Persian : ¹ those two poets, man and wife, wrote
alone ; each wrote, but did not bless or quicken one
another at their work ; *we are closer married*.

[On March 22, 1887, Katherine Bradley and Amy

¹ Persian (cat) = Puss = Edith.

Cooper, Edith's younger sister, went to see the Brownings, who were just about to leave their house in Warwick Crescent for De Vere Gardens, Palace Gate. Edith was unable to come up to town owing to the ill-health of her parents, and they both write to her describing the visit.]

March 23, 1887.

[1] . . . I will tell you at once about our visit. Miss Browning was alone in the drawing-room when we arrived, and received us as warmly as any old friend could. . . . The old gentleman has never liked De Vere Gardens. He came there as a widower with his little boy, to be near Annabel Barrett, his wife's sister, who had settled in the neighbourhood, and—this amused me much—it would be near Paddington, when the boy should go to Oxford. Directly after tea had come, the old dear himself appeared, " You here ! " he exclaimed and came warmly forward to Sim, then greeting me.

Little Elsie had been greatly excited, when we told her the night before that we were going to see the great poet. She wanted him to have her love, and to be told that she had learnt one of his " pieces." Just before we started she gave us twopence to buy a nice bunch of violets for him. At infinite trouble we did this, and secured a lovely bunch (for a shilling, but we do not tell her this) ; and Sim gave it, almost at once, to him, giving her words, " Please give them to Robert Browning." He was delighted, " We don't get flowers every day. Elsie—is that the name of the lady who gave me the violets ? I must write her a little note." And down

[1] Letter from Amy to Edith.

he went and stayed some minutes, writing this beautiful little letter, so beautiful that one can hardly bear to read it—

MY DEAR ELSIE,

It was very kind and good of you to send me those violets. I will keep them alive as long as possible, and long after they are dead, I shall remember you affectionately, as you must remember

Your new old friend,
ROBERT BROWNING.

The little maid fully appreciates the honour and slept with the letter under her pillow, though what child could see all that it contains !

[1] Pussie [2] when it was not babbling of Pussie was babbling of Puss.[3] But it can really only shake its head for joy, to think what he was, of his warm, fondling tender manner and watchful, loving eyes. "I want to strip you of all these things," he exclaimed—but wonder as to what would become of the " heapy hair " kept me from unbonneting . . . then I told him all about *A Cup of Water* and Pussie ; [4] and what Pussie would make of it and how he was to like it, " I'll look to like, if looking liking move " (get the right quotation).[5] In the midst of the talk, when my hand was ungloved for tea, he caught it vehemently and exclaimed, " And you do the lyrics." Truly love, I would fain put back the clock thirty years,

---

[1] Letter from Katherine to Edith.   [2] Amy.   [3] Edith.
[4] Edith.   [5] *Romeo and Juliet*, I. 3.

and be loved by Robert Browning in his glorious manhood.   He always thinks of you when he loves you—
not, I am sure, of any pleasant sensation to himself ; he
seems full of rejoicing in one's spirit.   I told him all
about the Sapphics,[1] and how we meant to do no more
harm than George Herbert, when he took a text from
the Holy Writ and wrote a hymn thereon, and I especially
warned him the metres were of the plainest.   " All that
I can do with my poor scholarship, shall be done," he
said, with evident deep interest in the project.   I doubt
whether the old gentleman can do much for them ; but
I feel that I must write one or two for him, I love him
so.   When he brought Elsie's letter, I told him I should
be jealous, if the lady to whom I was bearing it were
not much younger than I, and he said, attacking me in
his sudden way, " Oh, you have quite enough letters
from me."   When I added, no : Michael had.   I had
only received two ; he added, " Well, you have only to
write and say you are in town, and you will receive a
note saying, ' Come to-morrow.' "   And yet, P., it went
to my heart, to feel somehow the matureness of age about
him.   The whole of the mighty intellect is there, but
it seems as if one had to climb a high tower to it ; and
the dear old gentleman was sleepy and tired.   I rather
grieve to think of Kensington, he will be too much
harassed.   He is so glad to hear that we are working ;
Puss, we will have fine times with him in Paradise. . . .

. . .[2] He talked about Tennyson ; he told the Laureate
that he ought not to have made the hero of the first

[1] *Long Ago*.   Published 1889.   [2] Amy.

Locksley Hall the speaker of the second.   It would spoil
the joy in the first for future young readers. . . .   He
took Sim on his arm downstairs ; in the hall he turned
to me and said, " I have not talked to you much," and
warmly pressed my hand.   He watched me a good deal
and asked Sim, did this lady do anything ?   He seems
very old, though bright, one feels a little difficulty in
making him understand.   I felt as though I had known
him for years.   He looked very tired and I fear he goes
out too much. . . .

[1] We found the drawing-room at Palace Gate full of
flowers.[2]   Under one of Pen's statues, in a pale-blue roc's
egg, were our carnations.   Mr. Browning came in, greeting us as his " two dear Greek women."   He opened
ὦ τέκνον a feint of kisses.   Ardently then and afterwards,
he spoke of the Sapphics, expressing interest in Tiresias,
which he himself had once thought of treating.   When
I remarked that I wished he had treated it, he said, " No :
it ought to be treated by a woman."   He said to Edith,
that he liked the second series of poems even better than
the first, and prophesied that they would make their mark.
But he refuses to write a preface.   We must remember we
are Michael Field.   Again he said, " Wait fifty years."

[July 4, 1888.   There are entries by both Edith and
Katherine.   They have been mingled to give a con-

[1] Katherine.   May 9, 1888.
[2] Browning's birthday was on May 7.

secutive narrative; where necessary the writer of a particular phrase or paragraph is indicated.]

It was on Monday, after a midsummer of cold, heat and thunder, rain and blight—we asked to go to Palace Gardens. Ah, but we were happy—deep mowing grass of happiness was ours. Three poets together—conventionality and ceremony put away—we shaped life divinely —and talked of poets, past, present, and to come. It is wonderful to watch the "Old's" serene, pondering, almost awed gaze at P.[1] The young face responds frankly, the trembling hands hid from sight and no colour on the quiet face, while I glow and thrill like a sunset.

Miss Browning made a long crowing noise of joy and astonishment when we entered—fresh from the pouring rain. He too, when he came in, did not know whether to thank us or not. At lunch we talked of, "Whoever wakes in the city,"[2] and they both seemed pleased with my genuine appreciation of the poem. After talk of Ruskin, "A very attaching man," Matthew Arnold, etc., the "old" grew meditative an instant and then said, "What would the world be without such people as Matthew Arnold, Ruskin, and Michael Field?" I said he must not put Michael's name with such names as these. But he stoutly maintained that he had been disinterested in the discovery as in the case of Matthew Arnold. His limitless belief in us is appalling. What indeed is so appalling as the "Be ye therefore perfect" of love?

---

[1] Puss = Edith.   [2] Mrs. Browning?

There was wonderful, passionate praise of the Char-
treuse and its precious liqueur, which Edith tasted—a
golden drink full of the piercing flavours of many good
creatures of God.   Our talk was much of de Musset;
all his life he had regretted not being present at his discourse at the Academy.   His wife went; he had an
engagement and did not give it up.   " Such a man—it
would have been worth while to see him, even for three
moments."   Matthew Arnold had told him that at sixty-
two he hoped to give up the inspectorship and devote
himself to poetry.   Devote himself to poetry at sixty-
two! it seemed a strange notion, " when one thinks of
the flowery, bowery, bewigged sort of person a poet is
usually conceived to be."   Our good host covered our
plates with strawberries, telling us at the same time of
the Italian imprecation, " May he want sugar to his strawberry ! "   After lunch he drew us both down beside him
on the sofa, in the drawing-room, and would not let us
go, even when the kind Miss Browning dropped a lot of
books from the book-shelves, where she was searching
for some French volumes for us.   He held us tight, and
by and by read us some of the loveliest little poems of
de Musset, very quietly, with a low voice, full of " recueillement " and now and then a brief smile at some
touch of exquisite playfulness.   When he heard we were
writing prose, he said, " take care you do not derogate."
I asked what models should be taken for prose comedy.
He was not much for models :—" Prick it out yourself.
Trust yourself."   He promised me [1] to play, the next
time we meet him, some of Galluppi's *Toccatas*.   Think

[1] Edith.

of hearing them played by the poet, who has opened to us all their reserves of pity, of dreariness, their notes of far-off festivity and regret. At last he was forced to go ; he hoped we should come again, " under happier auspices." We could not be so happy when he had gone. We stayed and talked with Sarianna about Pen and his father.

He is always the poet with us ; it seems impossible that he goes behind a shell of worldly behaviour and commonplace talk, when he faces society, yet so it is. In his own room, in his study, he is Rabbi ben Ezra, with his inspired, calm, triumphant old age. His eyes rest on one with their strange, passive vision, traversed sometimes by an autumnal geniality, mellow and apart, which is beautiful to meet. Yet his motions, his touch, are full of impetuosity and warmth, and contrast with his steady outlook and his " grave, kindly aspect."

[1] I went to see my vivid old damask rose, Miss Swanwick. We spoke of *Long Ago* and the old gentleman. She told me how once at dinner he had said to her, " I wish you could have known her.[2] . . . It was something for fifteen years to have the society of such a woman, and I valued it ; for while we were at Florence, I never left her for an evening." He spoke to Miss Swanwick of the *Sonnets from the Portuguese*. " It seems to me, that if I had written such sonnets, they would have burnt a hole in my desk," she said. But the poets had been wedded two years, before Elizabeth Barrett placed them in her husband's hands. Then, had he consulted his own feel-

[1] Katherine.   [2] Mrs. Browning.

ings, he would have kept them sacred from the light, but he remembered he was the guardian of his wife's genius —and bade her publish them. Choosing this sublime old maid for this deep confidence of his nuptial life, is a sign of the old gentleman's fine faculty for selection— the fool or insensitive person never looks where he is talking. On Tuesday February 12 we went to De Vere Gardens to lunch. The poet was dissatisfied with his own moods and the psychic entertainment he could give us. But he was infinitely sympathetic over *Long Ago*. He spoke to me of the tragic largeness of the lyrics. As he bore us down to lunch, he stopped us before Pen's *Dryope* [1] and said it had been worthily sung, referring to Edith's " There was laughter soft and free." We showed him the archaic head of Sappho.[2] Miss Browning could not forgive the smirk ; but the old gentleman looked at it with thoughtful consideration. " If I were an artist, I should like to paint what the artist strove to express but could not. For instance the firm, round chin shows that this is a young face, and the smirk is an attempt to reproduce a sweet smile, and the great eyes show that he was struck by the beauty and size of Sappho's eyes—that he felt them beautiful. . . ." He also said of the third batch of Sapphics, that they seemed much better to him than the others—there was certainly no falling off.

Yesterday, Friday April 26, 1889, we had our first in-formal, friendly lunch at De Vere Gardens. The April sunshine was continuous and splendid. Mr. Brown-

[1] *Long Ago*, p. 111.   [2] Reproduced on the cover of *Long Ago*.

ing took up the seated Sappho [1] and began to read the fine Greek MS. After lunch, a Miss Heaton called ; though extremely quiet, she had the faculty of rekindling old images and pictures. Once, Mr. Browning had been, for one week, in the same house as the Duchess of Cambridge ; she, wishing to be gracious to him, asked " And how is Mrs. Browning ? " " That was years after I had lost her." Such a story as this justifies Matthew Arnold's description of the British aristocracy as barbarians. Anent public speaking and dinners, he referred to the occasion when Talfourd's *Ion* was issued. Landor and Wordsworth were present, and the health of the youngest poet present was drunk—that youngest being Robert Browning, then twenty-two. It was evidently much to him, to have these great poets drinking his health. He will never respond for literature ; but once at the Temple, unexpectedly, allusion was made to him which demanded response, and he contrived to make an adequately pretty speech, I fancy. He alluded to Spenser's

" Where whylome went the templar knights to byde
Till they decayed through pride " ;

to Shakespeare's red and white rose scene, in the gardens, *Henry VI*, Part I, Act ii, Scene iv ; to Charles Lamb's old benchers in the Temple.

After the caller had gone, I sat on a low stool and told him the plot of *Carloman*. (His eyes looked like Corot's pools in their gravity and stillness.) He listened gravely, feeling and realising the problem. He said he would

[1] The frontispiece to *Long Ago*. A reproduction of the figure on the well-known vase at Athens.

read some lines an admirer had sent him to judge—we should judge them—the letter was of the usual kind, written in grief after bereavement. In his youth, Mr. Browning had belonged to a glee-club, under the management of the parish clerk. They sang a poem of Tom Moore's in which occurred the line : " And flowers . . . gathered in Heaven." To save the morality of the piece, for the flowers were to garland a lady's brow, the old clerk substituted, " . . . gathered in a wood." Browning mournfully remarked that we must say the admirer's verses were gathered in a wood. Then we spoke of joy, not grief, being the heart of literature. He told us that once he had heard a barrel-organ playing a tune that went exactly to a chorus of Aristophanes'— chorus in Plutus (Cario and the chorus bring up the rear in antic dance), of which he gave us the delicious, balmy lilt. Then as we were twisting up the branches of the seven-branched candlestick (the staircase) to the bedroom, we heard his soft touch at the piano. But he would not be persuaded to play to us on our return. This was a blessed day—he was genially contemplative of the past— and beholding it seemed to find it very good. We were glad of the visitor, she led to talk undisturbed. We have so much to tell him, there is clash and convulsion. I felt, when he talked to Miss Heaton, that he is used to serenely dominate the society he enters. He will not engage himself to go again to Venice : he has been nine times, and appears to cling to his wide, rich palace rooms at home.

[The Private View of the Academy, 1889.] [1] On Friday morning, Edith and I started for Kensington,

[1] Edith.

for my new dress of blond fawn, and a little before noon we were in the Academy. . . . In the afternoon, in a dense crowd, I caught sight of him. He turned quickly and we hastened together. He introduced the fair Venetian, his daughter-in-law. Later we encountered, just as [Fairfax ?] Murray was drawing my attention to a beautiful, nude figure of a girl with a lyre, which he called an Egyptian Sappho. He dragged me by the arm, and stood gazing at it, with and by me, full of many thoughts. Then he turned with me to a bronze by a friend of his ; careful, " but not such beautiful work as the other." He looked across at P.[1] (His glance is a travelling and a passage.) When we parted, we recognised that he was proud to manifest to the world that we were his friends, and we believed in him, in the deep scriptural sense.

[Mrs. Cooper was dying.] [2] I shall never forget the silent grace of our friends' welcome. No crowing chant from Sarianna,[3] and the old gentleman behind, so silent that I hardly knew he was in the room—their hearts were as muted bells, full of soft rejoicing—quieted by perfect sympathy. Afterward, when with tender impatience Mr. Browning said we had enough of that—with reference to the details of illness at home—he enquired about the book [4]—and a fine conversation began. . . . He would certainly have the book. " Ah, Mr. Browning, you will not care so much for the song book—it is not Greek." " Try me," was the emphatic response. I began to talk of Mrs. Carlyle, " No, you would not have

---

[1] Edith.   [2] Katherine.   [3] Miss Browning.
[4] *Underneath the Bough.*

liked her much, though I know of no one who could
have been more safely trusted with her. She would have
tried to pick holes in you. . . . She had a fine forehead,
black eyes, deep brown complexion " (not a happy nose,
from the old gentleman's description), " and black hair."
Miss Browning told indignantly how a Keats had been
lent to her, and she had found it " the work of one who
had over-eaten himself with cake." . . . When Edith
told how I had a friend, who I knew spoke ill of me, yet
whom I continued to like, the Poet said, " I do not care
what people say of me, but I do not like them to speak
against those I love." His bearing was majestic and
animated, the occasion of wonder in me. Even then,
though I did not know it, he was awaiting the *Athenæum*,
containing words of his to Edward Fitzgerald,[1] so appal-

[1] To Edward Fitzgerald.

I chanced upon a new book yesterday :
I opened it, and where my finger lay
  'Twixt page and uncut page, these words I read
—Some six or seven at most—and learned thereby
That you, Fitzgerald, whom by ear and eye
  She never knew, " thanked God my wife was dead."

Ay, dead ! and were yourself alive, good Fitz,
How to return you thanks would task my wits :
  Kicking you seems the common lot of curs—
While more appropriate greeting lends you grace :
Surely to spit there glorifies your face—
  Spitting—from lips once sanctified by Hers.
The Athenæum. July 8th, 1889.

This has been re-published in the *Week End Book* of the Nonesuch
Press.

ling that after we had read them, our spirits lay as dead
at his feet for three days. It was as if we had been playing
fearlessly about the thunder-guarded throne, and discovered that therefrom a fiery shaft had been that instant
sped. . . . It is precious to the world that there should
be such passion in it, such fidelity, such undeviating
remorseless wrath. What championship ! It was as if
Fitzgerald had exposed and profaned his dead. One
hears the groan with which he covers away such sorrow
—ere he falls on the injurer with Swift's masterly stroke.
Suddenly from being shut away in our dull bit of Surrey,
we felt ourselves removed to the white central point
of London life—to the mid-edge of intensest passion
there.

[A conversation with William Sharpe.] . . . Talk
came up on the close confidential relations between
Browning and his sister. He so feared the turbulence
of his own nature, that all his correspondence passed
through her hands, as a safeguard against such expression
as might stir up newspaper warfare. When he wrote
the unfortunate [1] lines on Fitzgerald, he sent them
secretly to the post by his servant, and Sarianna had the
triumph of convincing him that her supervision was
wiser than his impulse. They lived, said Sharpe, in
comradeship.

[2] We arrived at De Vere Gardens at about three

[1] Fitzgerald's remark occurred in a private letter. The real
offence was its publication after his death and before Browning's.
[2] Edith.

o'clock ; he was out, his slippers announced it to anxious
Sarianna.   She was indefatigable in talking time down.
. . . We saw a photograph from Watts' head of him,
not conceivably like.   Also one taken by Groves, his old
manservant ; once a little ploughboy, who rang the even
bell for [Canon] Knox Little, two years, not forgetting
it in work or play.   While in service he got artistic hints
from Pen, and the impulse to become a photographer
from Smiles' *Self Help*.   Tea came at four-thirty and the
Botticelli table had our two disconsolate cups on it.
Then he came—haste about his white hairs ; Mrs. Orr
had promised to drive him home, there had been a delay.
His love sped to us through movement and words.   We
told him his picture had been with us.   When he heard
that mother would like to see it, although destined for
another, he gave it to Sim zealously.   " There, you shall
have it."   Sarianna also gave up her photo.   " Go, write
your name properly as I have done," said her brother.
It is a good likeness, but the cap is an ugly erection of
flowers.   " She is not wearing anything like this pretty
cap," he said, and touched the nice grey thing, with its
peach and grey ribbons.   When Sim said she was pleased
he liked it, he answered it was well the compliment had
been to the right person.   He had just whispered,
" Qu'elle est belle," to Mrs. Orr in comment on the maid
at a friend's house.   Mrs. Orr stayed behind him a
minute, to please mistress and daughter with a poet's
comment on one of them, and was dumbfounded to learn
her mistake, when she joined him with the question,
" Which was it ? "   This he told with amused eyes and a
little shake of his beard.   He was wroth—yes faith,

heartily—at the ill-natured review in the *Spectator*.[1]   He hoped it was not that which kept us from issuing a new edition.   He was concerned and fearful lest we had suffered.   I assured him, *No*—I was nearly slain by a review in the *Athenæum*, when I was but a child, after that I had never been hurt by any judgement ; it had killed such sense of pain entirely.   He told us of his own youthful disappointments.   *Pauline* had been reviewed generously by Alan Cunningham in the *Athenæum* ; when *Paracelsus* came out, the young author was sure of notice, and only had two lines in " Recent Verse " ! Browning evidently dislikes unsigned articles and the fluctuating criticism on an author's successive works. What respect he feels for the *Spectator* (" well known for its Puritanism ") is due to the unanimity of its appraisements, from the influence of one mind.   This brings it nearer to the ideal of continuous criticism and responsible signature.   One year one man, the next another, reviews an author's books—hence the perplexing contradictions of their fate.   *Long Ago* was no longer on the table, it had been lent to Mendelssohn's grandson, a poet, restive, " foolishly," under the classical tuition at Balliol. Browning wrote to him, to charm him into willingness to work for knowledge honours, while he had the precious opportunity.   The young man called, and *Long Ago* was lent to him, to teach him the uses of Greek learning ! " Sarianna was not gracious and did not want to let it go." Indeed, the dear soul was bleating after it.   When we spoke of returning some books, her brother exclaimed derisively, " Are you afraid of Sarianna ? "   He assured

[1] *Long Ago.*

us solemnly that he had never been able to say, that he could have done better work if he had had the opportunity—throughout life he had been blessed with good conditions for work.   As we passed *Dryope*, he said his daughter thought χελώνη,[1] the most beautiful poem in the book.   "Yes," said Sarianna, "the simple creature had *Long Ago* for the sake of those lines."   Our friends have no idea where they will spend their holidays—he is hard to stir.   "I should like to take you two to Venice, and show its beauties to you—that would be an inducement."   Pen and his wife love hospitality.   "I am not like that," mused the old poet.   "I am not hospitable in their sense.   I don't mind dining with thirty or forty people every evening and it's done with.   But I do not like to bring them into my inner circle.   I like a few people immensely and want to have them with me."   So much for the outside of our converse, "the rest is silence."   Oh! Hamlet, love is holier than death and as unalterable.   N.B. The "Old" likes caraway cake.

[2] It was delightful to learn that Hindoos care greatly for his poems, and that great numbers of Hindoo examinations in English are set from them.   His new book is to be called, *A New Series of Jocoseria.*[3]   It is all ready, only a manuscript to be made.   "But I am more interested now in what other people do, than in what I do myself," said our old friend sadly.   We shall never ask him to play again; the music is still in his head, but the hands no longer execute—"Perhaps when some good

[1] *Long Ago*, p. iii.   See note, *Pen's Dryope.*
[2] Katherine.   [3] Eventually *Asolando*.

day comes that will never come." We cannot bear to think that age has stiffened the hands. But he will go on writing, he hopes, till the end; to cease would be to him true death. I told how we never wrote a song, without thinking how he would react to it, and how we hoped to have finished a bookful before he returned. And he sighed piercing sighs, full of warm new grief—not youth's sighs—age and death so close—and parts of life still so sweet. And he begged us to come again soon. He did not like saying good-bye. Even on our way to " Mrs. Muggins " he would like us to come in and have bread and cheese with him ! . . . When I said we should not go home that night, he said, " Worse things might happen than that he should have us to stay with him."

He spoke of the sons of great men ; he had met the sons of Wordsworth, Coleridge, Southey, Shelley and Burns—the latter at Carlyle's. He was rewarded after he had left the room (he had sung one of his father's songs) by, " Can this be the son of Burns ? " Many of Burns' letters cannot be printed. One was brought to Carlyle, apparently in Mr. Browning's presence ; Carlyle shook his head and said, " Oh no, this must never be published."

Oh ! De Vere Gardens—our New Place, Stratford.

[Mrs. Cooper had died on August 19, 1889.]

[1] Llannie has just sent us the news of our poet's illness. Sim has gone through the dark, with letters and a tele-
[1] Edith.   December 12th, 1889.

gram.   Is this year going to bereave us again—yet again,
O God ?   I should have more hope, save for our last
meeting ;   he was so gentle—as autumn is before dropping ;   presageful, penetrative gentleness, which has
somewhat of remembrance in the manner and the look.
He said of our song book, " Try me " ;   shall we never
hear the caressing voice give judgement and praise ?   It
will half kill our poetry and make all the deep parts of
our love memorial, which means that the value of life
strikes the ground and is over (at least as the young
estimate it).   His kiss comes to my lips again, as I think
of him—that seal of his comprehension of one's woman-
hood—flawless in stamp, tender with knowledge, warm
as all action is that is divine and reverent.   Perhaps he
will die and never think of us.   He " dared to hope " last
spring that we loved him.   As I hoped to have my
mother's smile before she fell asleep—I hope he will think
of us.   I have always loved him with deep communion
of spirit—Isaiah's " way of Holiness " seemed to span
the air that divided us, and we walked thereon without
speech, without fear.   *Prospice !*   He is no longer " near-
ing the place "—he is there.   It makes me stiff, till I
think of the beyond, and her breast, that " soul of his
soul." [1]   She was a woman, a poet.   His coming will be
all gain to her—To him !—can I wish that he should die,
as I did for my Darling's blessedness ?   Perhaps there is
a remote strength in me that could say yes—but it is
very far away among the hills.   He is so great, I am
tearless as I write of him—the moment I slip back into
myself, the tears burn.

[1] See Browning's *Prospice.*

He wrote for us—

> "I have heard a team
> Of swans, so deathward chanting breast the stream."

I wonder if his last hours will be harmonic, if they will have glory and impulse.

How strange, in spite of weeping I feel cold. Sim returns. The *Telegraph*, in a review of *Asolando* says that, by the most recent reports, he is recovering. The new poems are dedicated to Mrs. Arthur Bronson—the rest is silence once again. Ah, I remember, she is his old friend of Asolo.

" Set me as a seal upon thine heart, as a seal upon thine arm : for love is strong as death : jealousy is cruel as the grave : the coals thereof are coals of fire, which hath a most vehement flame. Many waters cannot quench love, neither can floods drown it ; if a man would give all the substance of his house for love, it would be utterly contemned." [1]

He has written of a kiss—

> "Good night, God bless you, Good-bye ! "

[2] We went, with the dark rain in our faces, to the reading-room, just after nine. As I left the house, I recalled the drear, lightless morning of our darling's death and felt strange and braced. At first we could find no news. Sim went to *The Times*. She said in a slow whisper, " It is all over." I read ; my breath was quick

[1] *Song of Songs*, Chap. VIII, verses 6–7.
[2] Edith.

with pain and tears. . . . Our telegram would reach Venice this morning. No words could contain the shadow of my love for him—they could bring me to his thoughts, that is all—yes, all, love cries with intolerable hunger. I hope he thought of us, but such hope is a vital kind of despair. His death was a perfect thought of God's. How I wish that I had been less proud when away from him and trusted more in his friendship. But my love was so great, it fortified itself with walls against weakness or mere familiarity. When I was with him, all my nature issued and was free to his touch and his eyes. Reserve with me must be as utterly broken as the rock by the stream, when I love indeed and am close to the beloved one.

[1] . . . He is gone evergreen to God—full of courage and energy, to that great world of thought and love. We could not have willed for him a more perfect death— dying on that Thursday, for which you were waiting so breathlessly—able to receive the welcome given to his new book ; and passing at the close of its birthday, to the resumption of all that is vital in our past that we call Heaven.

. . . I have been praying : what he has done, what gives him Westminster Abbey, in so far as it is given him by the English people, is this, he has given them access to the spiritual world, quite apart from Revelation—he has shown them the deep things of Revelation as in *Karshish*, but he has found new pathways to God. . . .

[1] Katherine.

¹ January 1st, 1890. Burial of Robert Browning at the Abbey (yesterday).

Flashes of impression

The face of Richard, his servant, demure and pondering many things—the face that has met us at our Palace Gate so often, or looked helpless at the free, energetic entertainment our host gave us at his table. The sight was condensed pain—remembrance in travail of still-born sobs.

Next, the " blind plunge down " of the tolled bell to wreck the heart's earthly love—cruel, cruel ! Then the great hush—human breath waiting, withdrawing itself from the air, becoming a reserve power, tragic and perceptible. The great expectation was motionless ; while the mist kept steady and dense above the arches.

At last the labouring movement of the coffin—so small, octagonal, hung with softest purple, crossed with violets —dark some, and some dim ; wreathed with sprays of the tender, milky lilac of the season. It lay before the golden altar, reverend in stillness—a stillness which strikes the eyes more than that of the rocks, that may never be moved.

The pall well-nigh brushed us as the coffin was carried past to Poets' Corner. I had never heard " Earth to earth, ashes to ashes, dust to dust," said over a human body : the voice that so said, dropped like sharp gravel, syllable by syllable, on my love—the suffering was torture. All the old days, so brave and fulgent, rose up and seemed to listen to their doom with inexpressible

¹ Edith.

passion.   Mortality turns round on mortals, outraging
its subjects and making what is common to them and it
an insult.   The cleavage of Atropos' shears, could it be
heard, would be as nothing to that sentence of grit and
mould.   It is the " leave not a wrack behind " of Earth's
life—friendship in dear rooms, meetings, hand-clasps,
kisses. . . .   O poor lips of those who stay behind ; eyes
that can behold no more with a frank outward vision—
the senses shattered as organs of love !
    One burst of relief came :

> " O God, our help in ages past
> Our hope for years to come " :

its elemental music and the words antique as David—full
of the fading and vanishing typified by the cruder soil
cast on the coffin, yet strong in confidence that we dis-
solve to be gathered the surer into the breast of that
" Soul of the soul."   We, the living, on the rim of the
New Year—a black crowd, minute under the great walls
and roof of the Abbey—we sang as we looked forward
into the future : above us, just above the clustered singing heads, stood larger figures, fewer, white with solemn
whiteness—the company of the sculptured Dead, in silent
calm attesting the unison of the Past with the Prophetic
Present in lifting that mighty hymn to the " ineffable
Name."   Next the soft, pained arousing silence itself at
the first notes of the Dead March and the muffled thunder
of it like a far-off avalanche among the stony heights of
the Tower and Transepts.   Just at the bitterest moment,
when " Earth's old life " was given to the dust, the sight
of Ben Jonson's sturdy front was a beacon of triumph to

overwhelmed faith. He was buried upright, with the
ruddy head erect, for resurrection. To my wet eyes his
fecund person, rich, enmeshed with actual vitality—" O
rare Ben Jonson "—was a dramatic comment on despair,
forsworn belief—square set against every kind of annihi-
lation. What mattered the hollow masks hung from his
tablet? They were null, were naught. Last of all, the
crunch of the sod under the black carpet as we pressed
quietly to the spot—and the black-lined grave, close
round its treasure : one look, a long second of looking
. . . and the oaken coffin only a gleam amid the blue
flash of violets. " Forever and forever farewell " was
put on my mouth to say voicelessly, and I turned away,
with a last, unseen kiss, from the *mortal*.

Dirges and lulled music (" He giveth his beloved
sleep ") were not for him, who asks to be greeted with a
cheer; nor crape-enveloped women, nor old men in
their nonage (Canons, vergers, etc.), nor trivial singing-
boys : still less the row of vivid press-men under the
altar-rail, note-book in hand—typifying in their very
position the sacrilege of the times—its form and present-
ment. He would have said once more :

> " Outside should suffice for evidence :
> And whoso desires to penetrate
> Deeper must dive by the spirit-sense—
> No optics like yours at any rate ! "

In the nave, among the people—the disciples—we
should have felt the world less with us, and the Living
Risen One nearer. The artists, men of letters and women
of fashion were chill and curious : awe only fell as the
bearers carried their freight, " famous, calm and dead "

under the lantern, where the body rested. The tick of
a workman's hammer, on the outside of the Abbey, pre-
ceded the organ, when Purcell's music began its exquisite,
premonitory wail, the whole standing assembly bent one
way—and forward. We caught an early train home—
the mist had risen ; Thames looked pleasant.

[At Miss Swanwick's.] [1] Here are some of her [Miss
Swanwick's] memories of the " Old." She once saw
him angry to fierceness, when he told how he and his
wife had promised that they would communicate each
with each after her death, if it were possible—and yet a
medium dared say she spoke to *him*. It was a sacrilege
against love. Miss Swanwick asked his opinion of Walt
Whitman. He thought Walt dangerous ; although he
always did all in his power to help young writers (surely
he confounded the age of the author with the late publish-
ing of *Leaves of Grass*), he could not recommend him.
He seemed shocked at Mrs. Gilchrist's expression, that
he was carrying on Christ's work. Strange, this judgement ! " The virile Robert Browning could not give
recognition to the frank American—the Comrade ! "
I should never have thought it possible to shock the
" Old." Tennyson said of Walt, that he had not the
first requisite of a poet, he could not sing.

[Arthur Symons writes :] You have of course seen
the birthday letter of Browning to Tennyson, which has
recently been published. . . . Theodore Watts told me
how he had just been visiting Tennyson, and how
Tennyson had shown him the letter, and how he had

[1] Edith.

said, stroking it tenderly with his hand, " How kind, how good of such a great man to write to me like that." I, on my part, remember well, in what a deeply moved tone Browning spoke to me, four days before leaving England for the last time, of a birthday letter he had had from Tennyson, " It is too sacred to show to anyone— it was inexpressibly kind—no one would believe what a letter I have had from Tennyson."

[A visit to Miss Heaton.] [1] So much talk of the " Old," and how he longed to take Miss Barrett to Italy, reflecting he could only do so by marrying her. . . . He was slow in taking to society after her death, but the inevitable magnetism of the world of men drew him at last to his right place within it. Miss Heaton spoke of the " elastic ring " of Mr. Browning's wonderful voice. When Mrs. Browning saw Talfourd's portrait of herself (done for Miss Heaton), she exclaimed, " How beautiful ! " ; expressing thereby merely a contrast with all others, which were libels. The first time Miss Heaton saw Miss Barrett, talk fell on contemporary poets, and Miss Barrett spoke with reticent warmth of Robert Browning's poems. She kept him waiting a year, before she could bring herself to overcome her fears as to her health.

[Extract from a letter written by Miss Heaton to Katherine Bradley about Mrs. Browning.]

. . . It was said of her, that she had the intellect of an angel and the heart of a child. " The little name,"—

[1] Edith.

was—Ba—(a, long).   Mr. Browning usually calls her, I
think, " my wife."   If Miss Browning speaks of her to
me, it often is as " dear Ba."   It sounds as natural as
possible ; it recalls the time when many—most of whom
have left us—called her by that name.

[Miss Browning kept up a correspondence with
Michael Field after the Poet's death; the following are
extracts from these letters.]

. . . Which did he prefer of the *Asolando* poems ?   I
can hardly say—only I know, that on the very last Sunday
he was up, before the last, Fannie [1] and I were alone (she
had been unwell and was lying down), he came into the
bedroom and had afternoon tea with us, and Fannie
asked him to read to her—she wanted something from
the new volume just coming out, she said.   He fetched
the proof-sheets and read *Rephan*, the *Reverie*, and finally
the *Epilogue*—half ashamed that the latter might seem
boastful ; as he read it, a cold feeling crept over me,
though I said nothing, that those lines might be a real
farewell to life—as they were.

. . . When our Queen was telling Robert how much
she admired his wife, he said, " Those who only knew
her by her works, did not know the best part of her."
The Queen replied very earnestly, " Oh, how easily I
can believe that ! "

[May 30, 1893.]   . . . You ask me of Robert's experience of the stage.   He was fond of the drama . . . but

[1] His daughter-in-law.

his experience of the actual realities of the stage of his day was utterly distasteful and disenchanting. He was naturally very pleased at the production of *Strafford*— the play of a very young man, brought out by Macready at Drury Lane, was considered an exploit—but the *Blot* was nothing from first to last except a vexation of spirit —he would not allow me to be present at the first night. (I ought to exclude from the black list, Helen Faucit, of whom he could never speak too highly.) The incessant asking for alterations chafed him.

. . . Robert seldom went to the theatre in later years, except to see his friend Salvini, or a play by his well-beloved Tennyson. He had not much sympathy with the elaborate decoration and dressing of the Lyceum, but I can answer for his having gone with delight to see a drama of Michael Field's performed [1]—had he still been with us. Do not let either yourself or Edith be discouraged at partial eclipse. Remember the middle part of Robert's career, when none of his works were sold. He outlived it, so will you.

[January 3, 1896.] . . . Robert always said he would like to be offered the Laureateship, for the pleasure of refusing it. He thought poetry out of and beyond the judgement of politicians ; and said he would equally decline the verdict of Mr. Gladstone or Lord Salisbury, both of whom he admired in their own sphere, but neither of whom he thought capable of understanding poetry.

[1] This probably refers to *A Question of Memory*.

CHAPTER TWO

A JOURNEY TO DRESDEN

[The following extracts do not deal with their contacts with famous people, but reveal the amazing zest with which these ladies encountered experience. Extraordinary is the manner in which Edith's study of pictures mingled into her delirium, and not less so the tact and humanity with which she put aside, without wounding it, the violent passion she aroused in the poor heart-starved Sister who nursed her.

They had planned a tour of the Art Galleries of Germany, with many nights at theatre and opera during August, 1891. A severe illness held them up at the fever hospital in Dresden. On the way thither, they had carefully visited Charlemagne's Tomb at Aachen, with a view to a drama on a Merovingian theme to be called *Otho* : this however was never carried out.

Edith Cooper is Puss or Pussie or P., or Henry or Heinrich. The whole commencement of the narrative is in her hand, but she mentions copying passages out of an MS. book of her aunt's.]

The moment we reach our hotel we are persuaded to scurry to the station and catch a train that will bring us to Dresden by 11 in the morning. . . . O weak, to be caught by such a bait ! We have no evening meal—a bottle of Nierstein and six " petits pains " are tumbled

44

into our basket. At the station we ourselves are deposited in a 1st class ladies' carriage by a compassionate guard, who overlooks our 2nd class tickets. But the guard is too compassionate, and soon a 3rd class passenger enjoys his pity, and enters with bundles, short hair, pallor and a cough. We think she has had the " grippe."

Darkness falls . . .

. . . Charlemagne's Tomb-chair reappears. We stop at a nameless station—the two eldest of the Norns, out of breath and sisterly, struggle into the carriage—that guard's face is behind them. For a long time they recover ; we venture English, French—but the Norns understand only German. They smile sunken, misty smiles, then they bind up their heads from the air, and the shortest, mounting the seat, closes the vampire eyelids of the gas-lamp fatefully, as a rite.

Something that is not sleep falls.

Charlemagne's Tomb-chair reappears—not in memory but in actualising imagination—I go down those steps one by one into a vibrating abyss. . . . At this moment I start and find that I am in a train in the midst of the night. The Fates sleep—every now and then an anomalous sound, hardly voice, passes between them—they sleep—one has her chin bound up with a handkerchief —of course in Greece she would be Atropos. They stir and weakly drink from a little flask.

Something that is not sleep trembles over one's brain. Charlemagne's Tomb-chair glimmers furtively round the corners of obliviousness. . . .

One is blown awake—the door opens to a lanthorn

and a German face—tickets are torn off. There is a bang and then the sleepy whirr goes on under one. How far away are the horizons of that noiseless substance of merely varying gloom that a few hours ago was the inhabited earth!

There are steady lights outside—there is a sound of illegitimate business, against the laws of darkness, then moving lights and again the great dream journey and its functional movement.

Across exhaustion shoots the pang of famine. We have no bread—Nierstein is not a fortifying juice.

I watch the painful appearance of things visible—the world looks common and very black—poor little patch as it is! One is hungry—one feels that one's eyes are purple and swollen, as if one had fought with an adversary. Suddenly there is sweetness in the world—the Sun himself introduces isolated objects, and it is day. Then shame comes and one hastens to the sponge, the comb, the mirror. One begins the comedy of toilet in the space of a square yard—one re-seats oneself, curiously reconciled to the view and one's fellow-passengers.

But famine cries piteously in the currents of goodly morning air . . . and we have no bread.

The train draws up at a lank station. We rush—I in hat, as befits one who dislikes the ill-opinion of men —Sim in a " cloud " and the roughness of her hair. Cups of coffee are seized, no bread can be bespoken on account of the crowd, no bread is near at hand to be seized. Sim vanishes from my side ; I watch her rush down the room to a table appropriated by little German soldiers—she breaks in between two of them with cries through her teeth of " Brot, Brot ! " The little German soldiers wonder naturally of what kind this new Orlando comes, who darts on their feast and insists ragingly that necessity must be served. As she bears off their rolls— " I almost die for food, let me have it "—Teutonic amaze slackens into a disciplined smile and a few moments after develops into a titter. But the new Orlando, the despiser of smooth civility, brings the food like a doe to its fawn, unconscious of the regiment's laughter, or of the appearance made by unfastened hair, excited eyes, and the bread, borne along in triumph. . . .

The Fates, assisted by daylight, recollect words of French learnt at school—forty years ago. We guess that we are not on the line of our Cook's route. A guard rages in Pandemoniacal words. He vanishes. The Fates condole with us in German-Neo-French. . . . A great fellow with vast blond moustache and kindly northern eyes appears at the window and accepts our tickets—Leipzic ! We are in a known portion of the globe. . . . The Fates disappear with their bundles— their dead, straw-like hairs, and goggle eyes.

We taste meat at last in some rolls bought at a name-less station. Sim's excellent knowledge of German literature and grammar had availed nothing after twenty years' neglect. We were as dumb as sheep, carried on through places no map had ever shown to us, angry with ourselves, shamed, helpless, unrepentant and con-temptuous of all things German.

Dresden is nondescript, as all cities are, seen from a cab . . . the sight of one's pale, empurpled self in the mirror . . . then a Pension dinner, scrappy, of no strength . . . Fräulein Wolfel, demure, humble, self-depreciatory, firm, sensitive ; and her sister, a tiny, nervous invalid, who plays with her soup and chirps forth remarks no one even hears, still less accepts or answers.   My nerves are so acute, so fearfully conscious, that I almost scream when Sim touches me in walking and I feel the unemitted screams incubating.   The night is synonymous with illness, we are both intolerably, disgracefully ill. . . .

[They arrived on Saturday, August 9th and were too unwell to see *Lohengrin* on Sunday evening.   " On Monday to the Gallery in a cab. . . .   Giorgione's *Venus*, that ideal sympathy between woman and the land, which nations have divined when they made their countries feminine. . . .   Here I am called away to see the *Heilige Sebastian* of Antonello da Messina, the gracious Saint who is half a pagan and was a shepherd boy before he knew of Christ and martyrdom."   They buy Morelli's *Kunstkritische Studien über Italienische Malerei*, ". . . hugging this treasure we reach the gallery, with the powers of old women and the remnant enthusiasm of youth." There are forty pages of alert and careful description of pictures, written during the incubation of the malady, while both continued far from well, broken only by a vivid description of Herr Druck's *Hamlet*, at which they managed to be present on the 13th.   On the 16th the last entry is also about Giorgione's *Venus* : " No stranger from the sea, no apparition, no enchantress, but simple as our fields, as nobly lighted as our harvests, pure as things man needs for his life that use cannot violate.   No one watches her. . . .   Here Sim became too ill to stay longer in the Gallery.   It is painful with

noise and figures and straining faces. We find the
fountain playing outside and the sky quite grey. I have
a hot sense of regret in leaving the Zwinger, a kind of
' malaise ' and disappointment. My throat is fearfully
swollen and gives me continual pangs."]

I lie on my bed, I gargle with eau-de-Cologne that
increases the atrocious pain in my throat. We have an
early tea and start for *Tannhaüser*. . . . I sit before Sim
in a comfortable box—choking, suffering, full of gladness
and divine unease . . . we reach the flat [*sic*]. A
mustard plaster or the Doctor ? . . . The Doctor
comes. Herr Faust—a great, broad-cheeked Teuton,
who lisps English. *It is not diphtheria.* I instantly
acknowledge the relief I have in the denial. I must go
to bed and remain in bed. I have a bare, calm feeling
as I go to our room . . . I have a fearful night.

I feel almost the patient agony of dying while we wait
hour after hour for the Doctor. At last he comes and
thinks I am going to have some infectious ailment. We
ask what he means, " Oh, we call so many things infectious now," he replies evasively. Sim sits down and
writes home I have a slight attack of pneumonia.

[Next day.] Again a long waiting for the Doctor—
I lie almost voiceless. At last he comes, looks at my
feet, and says that I have got scarlet fever, and I feel that
a sentence is gathering against me. I know what it is.
"You must go to the Hospital." Dismay scatters our
fortitude. Sim goes out to speak to Fräulein. Doctor
Faust implores me to influence her to go to the Hospital,
he waits to hear me repeat his lesson. In weakness and

impotence, I hesitate and am judged by the sturdy medico
as if by a judgement-angel; a blast of condemnation
reaches me, though he says not a word, and stalks out
of the room with Sim. All is settled. I get up as if I
were dressing for a great event—with the exaltation of
a bride—I am dressing for the last time—but not as
maiden, as mortal. . . . No one comes near us, not
to the door. There is the silence, the sense of flight
to far corners, that one feels in a house before a coffin
is brought out . . . and yet our belongings and my
yellow gown and my Love are so familiar in the midst
of these tyrannous, appalling circumstances.

An officer enters—burly, black, prompt—two men
follow in deep-coloured blouses. I am borne through
deserted passages on a chair and descend, descend—till
I come to piercing grey light and free air. Then I am
shut with my beloved in a coach—very like a Mourning
Coach. We clasp each other with an awful weight of
anxiety on our hearts, for they may strive to part us
and we have no German with which to plead. We
make a vow, which neither speaks, that nothing but
death shall sever us. The black coach stops—we wait,
wait; I have almost lost consciousness. Everything
happens as in a dream and to someone I watch. A
carrying-chair is brought, I have a sense of an invalid
in a yellow gown passing along cold stone passages,
prison-like in aspect, and then being set down in a
room, an insolent, dark-bearded man at a desk. Then
I hear a loved voice repeat, " Hier will ich bleiben,"
and gruff rejoinders—appeals to be heard in French
—" Deutsch in Deutschland "—assurances that the

" Krankenhaus ist für die Kranken "—refusals to admit
anyone who is unstricken.   I have a feeling, that the
dying must have, of external powers taking possession
of me . . . yet I can do nothing but implore that we
may be allowed to try at another house, if we can remain
together.   At last a young Doctor—a blond, with kindly
blue eyes—appears.   Joy! He understands French.
Sim pours forth Gallic floods, with an eloquence that
besets youth, " O Monsieur, on ne craint pas quand on
aime," etc., etc.   He paces about—finally he approaches
Sim—" you said your own throat was bad—if it were
bad, ' ce sera magnifique.' "   Yes, the obliging throat is
red—I hear him say, " Zwei Scharlach-Kranke."   I am
borne out—my darling running after me and refusing
her ink-bottle and wine-bottle vainly rendered to her
by the heroic young Doctor. . . .

Then a tiny room, a tiny bed on which I am stretched.
We make the nurse understand we must have a larger
room. . . .   I close my eyes in the hot joy of repose
. . . my next remembrance is of a strong arm round me
and white flaps above me—difficult, slow marching . . .
a vast room with six beds, facing each other in couples,
a few children's beds. . . .   A very reasonable glance
round to escape draughts and I choose a bed at the far
end of the room . . . my Love is distracted and as
Nurse told us afterwards, " said many things."   Officialism has fed the sick at 12.30—so it is impossible for me
to have anything till 6.0—even tea and coffee can only
be ordered for the next day. Nurse brings a china
spoon of wine and gives a draught to each.   It is jacinth-
brown, sweet, powerful, warm.   It is the Mavro-daphne,

the Greek wine given to the fever patients in this favoured Krankenhaus. Sim's mind is knit to stay where I shall have such potent juice.

A great, fair official comes—asks questions about our grandparents and desires to know the exact meaning of "Durdans" [their Surrey home]—requires money— I know there is a vast deal of fuss; but I am lying at the very centre of heat, satisfied as Demophöon when Demeter laid him on the embers to become immortal.

Before tea, a dark little fellow with round head and round goldfinch eyes came to my bed—I thought him a medical student. No—he was Doctor Wagner, the house-doctor. He came later and bending his small, ridiculous, emphatic face over me, said, " Sie müssen Wein trinken "—it was the only thing he said I understood. I was quite kindled enough to follow this Bacchanalian counsel of health.

In early morning light I open my eyes. Where am I? In a cabin ! . . . I become aware that I am in hospital. . . . I feel a hunger that is a dreadful impotence . . . the nurse at last appears with a tray, I am raised to the coveted food and immediately, as if I were Tantalus himself, fail to eat a morsel and drop back in a fainting condition. My Love resolves I shall have nourishment in the night—she will fight with all the weapons of her determination and of her German for the grace. I am revived by Greek wine and Sister washes my face as one would wash coarse earthenware.

At eleven the doctors are to come. I dress my nails for the occasion and have a sense of panic at the thought

that students may surround me. Sister, interrogated by
Sim, reassures us. Dr. Wagner and the young doctor
to whom we owed our dual entrance yesterday—named
Schultz—appear, with a short, middle-aged man, bald,
bearded, with medical eyes set in spectacles and small
resolute mouth—a man whose pate shines with responsibility and across whose brow is care. This is the Herr
Geheimrath Fiedler, Physician to His Majesty the King
of Saxony. He speaks fluent French with the basest
German accent—and a kind voice. He says he will
do all in his power to restore Mademoiselle to health.
When he looks at Sim's throat he declares there is no
trace of Scharlach. Dr. Schultz casts down his eyes
in silence ; Dr. Wagner evidently primed, comes to the
rescue, " It was very red last night when I examined
it," and the matter is left. We owe much to that blond
young Schultz, who exposed himself in our service to
that glance of his Chief and to the shame of a wrong
diagnosis. I remember nothing of what passes. . . .

My Love opens the striped blinds that I may watch
the August full moon, making a poetic daylight throughout the sky, defining with stern blackness the roof of the
near station and touching the green of the embowered
plane-trees till they are magical as an enchantress' robe
in colour. I feel the outside beauty has an ominous
calm about it. I am fervidly hot ; the white beams lie
on my brain and provoke it—they enter it clear, quiet,
precise, they make it vague, distracted, visionary. They
evoke their contraries. I create phantasies that come so
fast that they form an element round me in which I
sink, sink—then float along under them and then sink

again. . . . My Love finding how it is with me lies on
her bed and in a grave, low voice recalls the lovely
things we enjoyed in Italy. . . . As she speaks her
words turn into fair, hurrying visions. The moonlight
through the blind becomes more powerful—delirium is
glorious, like being inspired continuously . . . forms of
art and poetry swim round and into me. Every moment
is plastic. . . .

A great dromedary comes along, with red trappings
and trophies, in the midst are set the words *Two weeks at
Dresden* ! ! The ironic beast passes. . . .

Vast Bacchanals rush by, Rubensesque, violent—
(Here *Tannhäuser* feeds the phantasy) I fall into an
attitude of sleep like an Antinous on the ground. I am
Greek, Roman, Barbarian, Catholic, and this multiform
life sweeps me toward unconsciousness—only the shine
through the blinds tortures me so that I cannot lose
myself. I beg my Love to keep a candle lighted to put
out the moon with all its terrible spectral frilliness and
to obliterate the white cavern-arch of the door—Death's
Door—that I keep approaching, that I cannot pass, for
as soon as I am near it, the brilliant swirl of images is
round me and I am caught back to life. Again and again
I am magnetically drawn to the grey portal and as often
rescued. Then I see our two straight beds—they are
coffins—we lie near one another in noble peace. . . .
At last I am carried away into unconsciousness . . . I
become aware of a figure in a short night-dress—a girl
almost at the other end of the ward, who has leapt to
embrace a hero, a dark, magical man in the corner (a
cloak-stand) who does not respond. In horror at his

coldness she struggles back and falls across the bed half-
fainting. I see that wan creature on the bed (an ocean
of gold pouring down).

> I could not tell to moonshine
> What I would tell to *light* or *dark*

—that is the dilemma. I am saved to consciousness.
Schwester drenches me—the gold-red wine runs down
my night-dress and the sheets . . . oblivion . . . I fling
myself down to the foot of the bed, half-uncovered . . .
I am covered up by Nurse, turned back on the pillows
and again drenched by Mavro-daphne . . . oblivion . . .
I have my Love close to me and I am telling her about
the tones of the light that is coming in by the window
—she says I was wonderful on it, but I do not recall a
word I said, nor does she.

The sun shines broad and yellow over the ward. I lie
half-slumbering with deep, blissful breaths and with the
sense that corn-fields, harvest meadows, the great
enlightened fruitful Earth, is all around me. And the
joy of life—*here*—in the world, enters my soul and body,
stays with me and re-consecrates me a mortal being. It
is beautiful to feel the ideally familiar claiming me with
delicious insistence; the sun as much sending down life
to me in his August ray, as the Angel sends it with his
voice down the Trumpet to the Skeleton in Blake's
drawing on the first page of Blair's *Grave*; it is like
being born again to light.

[Katherine writes :] It is 8.0 o'clock on Friday night.
The good Sister sits praying silently, I fancy, by P.,
waiting till " das Mädchen kommt." Good, sweet,

homely woman—as a bundle of sweet herbs is her presence in the room.

How I fought for my young, with how many tongues, with what agony. . . . So strange my part here ! For the division in Germany between the quick and the dead is not sharper than between the *Gesund* [sound] and the *Krank* [sick]. . . .

I walk about the State garden here, the sick ones from their pale hospital gowns look at my English clothes as the Shades at the shadow cast by Dante on the ground. One meets the baskets of bread being borne along. One sees the little band of delicate, healing children. . . . Long-coated men, like sick wasps, are seen in the further garden, through the trees. The breeze is carbolic. I have not shed a tear—scarcely—through all the biting trouble of this week. But my heart is as thickly inscribed as an Egyptian tomb. . . . A better night—the great experiences of the previous night not repeated.

[Edith continues :] On Saturday night a strange Mädchen, with an odd face, is introduced. She ruffles me, she distracts me with her ugliness—as I recollect her, no feature was in its place, her jaw was aside, she croaked. She is frightened at me and remarks with a finger on her forehead, " She is very wrong here."

Sister had read from the Bible before she left and my whole nature grew elfishly wicked as she read. I determine I will have as much pleasure as I can. I dance at balls, I go to Operas, I am Mars and, looking across at Sim's little bed, I realise that she is a goddess, hidden in her hair—Venus. Yet I cannot reach her (I had been writing on Botticelli's *Venus and Mars* (National Gallery) just before I left home).   I grew wilder for pleasure and madder against the ugly Mädchen.   Sim comes to quiet me and assure me she is " The Little Horse "—" You're not the Little Horse," I cry out.   " Take away your great, big head—it frightens me ! "   Poor Sim in heart-broken humility tries to squeeze and wring together her mane— then in a recoil of passion turns to the Mädchen, " You cough, you disturb the patient—Be off ! "   The astonished deformity makes away and is never heard of more.   And I drink my Love's soft-natured tea and behold no more the serviceable monster who had annoyed me.

[Katherine writes :]   Sunday.   Visitors' day.   To see the pale little hospital maiden with a youth at its side and an apple it ought not to eat in its hand !   Friends meet—the dear world for an hour mingles with this kingdom of the captive sick.   Even the poor men are visited by fair forms in their garden.   The pallors of the Shades are changed into a Watteau picture, or one might say, the ghastly group brighten into the half-gay, half-ascetic pictures of Fra Angelico.

[Edith writes :]   I remember Schwester sitting by the further window on this Sunday morning and saying that she had no tie on Earth—nothing but her sick and Christ. She had no relations, no friends.   She reproached Sim for too anxiously spending her whole love on me.

[On Monday afternoon Mrs. Costello and Mr. Berenson, with whom they had meant to visit the Gallery, call on them.   Katherine writes :]   The latter, rather pale and quivering :   " You will never know what plans I have been forming for your happiness, nor how I looked forward to being in the Gallery with you. . . .   I have been privately swearing at Jehovah ; if he had knocked up a pair of philistines it would not have mattered—but you who can enjoy so much ! He has no culture." (Little Blasphemer.)

P.'s vision. A little love comes to me and lays his little cheek against my heart. He shows me in a vessel his broken wings, his broken bow and arrows, his broken heart. And then he sings. . . . In the vessel it looked such a bright-feathered smash.

[Their friends called again on Tuesday, bearing roses. Katherine writes :] I asked Bernhard what business a Faun had to come and visit the sick in a Krankenhaus. He said it was just a Faun who should do this, with no " arrières pensées " of taking infection, etc., etc.

[Edith writes :] I shall never forget those roses—their beauty nearly stopped my heart. A bright wire basket was filled with moss and set with about twenty blossoms of a fresh, old-fashioned pink, such as one sees in 18th-century pictures—the colour was soft—a little sad as those fading pinks are, yet over it was the shine of youth, of water-drops, of silver bloom. In the midst of the flushing pyramid was one single rose of opaline white, the long leaves scarcely severed. I have never had a gift so beautiful, so generous—as a young man's gift should be. Nurse looked at the smooth and dazzling petals with disapproval—as if the world " were too much with them " . . . but oh ! I lay and gazed intoxicated with the glow, the colour of life itself swelling the buds, fading in the blossoms—with the perfume round me, within me. An insatiable rapture, almost delirium, haunted my eyes and brain. . . .

[Edith writes :]   On Friday I must have my locks cut off. Sim asked the H.G. if Nurse should do it or should I have " un Barbier." Little Waggie [Dr. Wagner] and his companion Dr. Millar broke out into laughter they could not hide. I was very grave and depressed at the thought of being clipped. While Sim was in the Garden, I got Sister to do it, while I held a glass and directed her scissors from tuft to tuft. The little white cotton jacket with black and red spots was chosen by The Youth and brought on Thursday.

[Katherine writes :]   At last this morning even the Herr Geheimrath says there is no danger from the fever. She looks very pretty in her short boy's hair and fresh cotton jacket. . . .

Yes, every day on which portions of the *Ring* were performed all the force left in me seemed to gather in my throat and the tears burnt worse than fever—This was the " *Wagner-weh*," a vast, imperishable regret that I was losing my chance for many a year, perhaps for ever, of hearing the *Operas* in their own land. During all my life till then I never knew what a passion of passions disappointment can be. I only got relief when I thought of Antonello da Messina's *St. Sebastian* in the Gallery—his virile, reproachful face reared against the blue heavens—his eyes asking, " Why am I denied what I was made for ? " That picture was constantly with me. . . .

Little Waggie brought a very tall, dark young man, with gentle lines of beauty and a thoughtful face. He was coldly—superciliously received. He was to take

Waggie's place while he enjoyed a holiday. His name was Henner and he spoke English.

[Katherine writes :]   This afternoon I find about the steps a small child with roses and violets, " A gentleman and lady have ordered that every second day flowers were to be brought." This indeed is sensitive kindness !

Uncertain sunlight, in the midst of which Herr Dr. Henner arrives, light-minded and inclined to flirt. P. is so minded. His eye falls on the German characters, with a flattered joy he exclaims, " Was können Sie ? " ["How much do you know?"]   P. replies, "A few little expressions like (with a vague gasp) ' Es thut mir leid,' [I am sorry, but she took it to mean, I am in pain] " " or," says the gallant young doctor, " ich habe keine Schmerzen." ["I have no pain."]   P. in a moment was transformed from the most ethereal flirt into a perfect gaby.

[Having little German, the ladies would seem to have discovered more point in these remarks than was there. Many more are reported in the diary.]

But when he came this morning and found P.—a wild, sweet play of life on her face—sitting up, he slipped away from her German greeting, felt her pulse and retired, saying to me she was to go to bed immediately after dinner. But after dinner Puss made the tour of the chamber like a veritable creature of her race—made for the tap, almost upsetting the Sanitas bowl, rubbed up round the furniture, peeped, pried and put out a paw till I was almost beside myself. Then it sprang back to bed and lay exhausted till revived by big draughts

of coffee. But before this happened, in came the Herr
Geheimrath and laid a great fatherly, approving hand on
the whole of its young hair. What is he thinking of
and why order the bath so soon? We have sharp
spasms of "Krankenhaus-weh," mixed with "Drang
nach die Gemälde" [a longing for the pictures].
Pussie sprang into his bath. Pussie's remarks thereon :
"It was delicious to be flexible in the pure flexibility of
the water and to see the record of disease on the body
obliterated by tender, limpid movements. And when
it came out the flesh seemed to remember its own self—
it was so wakeful ; it had been dreaming. "O freshness, as of the dews of many mornings ! " P. said to
Herr Dr. Henner, "Es war sehr schön im Wasser "—
"Nicht wahr ? " ["It was lovely in the water."
"Wasn't it ? "]
Schwester came and while we both rested on our beds,
talked to us long. Her children, as she calls the patients
whom she prefers, are Arthur, Paul, Bruno and Johannes,
not to mention "der sanfte Heinrich." [This probably
refers to Edith, the nurse frequently calls her "Heinrich" or "der sanfte Heinrich"! Obviously connected
with her boy-like appearance after having her hair cut,
and led to Michael's calling her Henry.] When we told
her about Otho, "Wofur besingen Sie solch' einen
Mann ? " she asked. When we told her he had
sinned and repented she was quite willing we should
continue to *besing* him. Yet she could not discover
the attraction, and when we gave her the date of our
hero, found it, "ein bisschen lange her." To-night
she has been talking of many things—the healthful-

ness of wearing four pairs of stockings, strong boots, etc.

While I am away P. drinks " Kaffee " with Sister for an hour. Sister kisses her with a kiss that plunges down among the wraps (Yes, as the wolf did when he sought the child—O Eros !—in Browning's *Ivan Ivanovitch*—a fatal kiss).

Then Puss goes into the garden—actually walks on earth again and feels how lovely is the height of trees when one is under them, although a rolled-up brown leaf falls every moment. P. walks on firm but slow limbs. It sits down as the " Kranken " troop up the alley from Church and, seized with panic at the diseased blue of their gowns, returns to its balcony ; there it sits with Schwester, who leans against it, pressing her old weight close, close—as if it were the first time her body had leant in love against another. She says, " Meine Edith, mine for so few more days ! " and there were little silver rills on her cheeks. P. weeps, then Sister calms her and withdraws. Poor old Schwester ! She has in her eyes a two-fold divineness when she looks at P.—that of the mother who has done everything for her babe, and that of a dog who watches for the love of a higher Power.

In the evening Waggie says, " At the end of the week —out of prison." " Ein Wunsch ? " [One wish ? = let me have my will.] asks Schwester, to which P. gives the classic answer, " Kein Wunsch, ich danke." Schwester comes in and in—never wearying of " der sanfte Heinrich."

Pussie wakes from its " bye " and rings for Schwester,

who comes straight to grasp and kiss. She is like one
who has been in a desert, who finds an oasis and simply
throws himself down and drinks. The kisses are almost
too rapid to have an aim. Suddenly she raises herself
and says, in answer to the forgotten ring of the bell,
" Ein Wunsch ? "

I go into the garden and watch the fish, leaving P.
with Schwester, who encloses her with passionate
embrace and plunges down on her cheeks with kisses,
" Ich bin so hungrig," she says in a stifled sob that
came out in a smile of anxious love. P. kissed her
cheeks, then, giving a little slap to the round, honest
cheek, kissed her lips. " Danke, danke," she said and
it was her heart that spoke. After this came Waggie.
P. proposed he should draw her evil tooth ; he left to
fetch his instruments . . . and Schwester confesses he
was very anxious lest P. should shriek. " Sie hat sich
sehr fest behalten," was his praise. The tooth that had
been degrading P. with mental fear for so many months
was wrenched out in one instant of courage. " Lord,
what fools we mortals be ! "

[Edith writes :] My experiences with Nurse are painful
—she is under the possession of terrible fleshly love,
[which] she does not conceive [of] as such, and as such
I will not receive it. Ah, why will Anteros make one
cynical by always peering over the beauty of every love
. . . why must his fatality haunt us ?

After " Abendessen " Schwester and Heinrich play so
pretty with the annuals bought by Sim as a present for
Station [ward] 44 and Heinrich laughs, laughs. (I am
always safe with Nurse when I am Heinrich.)

Schwester, while my Love is in the garden, embraces me bodily and from the outer precincts of language I catch the sound, " Eine mächtige Liebe." She makes me shiver, but I play with her passion like a child and she is utterly deceived in it herself—I am her child she has washed and dressed with her piteous clinging hands ; and her honest, stern eyes, altered to a mother-hen's, belie the welling-up of all her frustrate nature at the touch of first love for any mortal. . . . I must fight Nurse's unreasonableness. She comes while I am resting, throws herself about me and kisses me with the persistence of madness : I manage to make her understand she grieves and fatigues me—instantly with repentance she retires to the arm-chair and I pretend deep sleep with anxious ears. She strives with herself and scarcely ever breaks out after—but the strain makes me dull by the time my Love returns . . . [Michael adds] with fearful passion she threw P.'s hospital shirt away, saying, " Sie wollen das nicht mehr brauchen—fort ! " [" Shirt, thou art no more needed—be off " ! Edith continues :] This night Sister kissed me almost as we kiss the dying—gently, hopelessly, with dread—realising we shall never see a living face again greet us from their pillow.

The Herr Geheimrath and Waggie enter to make their adieux. I say to the H.G., as he holds my hand, " Je suis très reconnaissante de votre bonté envers moi pendant ma maladie." Sim speaks of her gratitude.

" Grâce à Dieu, qu'elle soit guérie," is his religious, deep-toned answer.

" Ein guter Mann."

I did not expect such fatherly kindness—the physician

put aside completely—nor that the " Mächtiger Geheimrath " would so humbly recognise that the sources of
health lay beyond his science. Waggie and I grasped
hands—" Adieu, Merci. . . ."

I give one look of concentrated meaning at my little
bed and the great, green, simple ward—then I kiss the
moist, powerful lips and look into the brown eyes that
bless me and weep for me—I fly, on Sim's arm, from
the stem-filled Alley, where I feel mysteriously a stranger
—I look back at the little Villa in the wood—to see a
big, round, grey shape wave a handkerchief, bend and
wave, wave, wave, till the dot of white becomes an
invisible mathematical point among the trees.

CHAPTER THREE

GEORGE MEREDITH

[Meredith is not discussed by the poetesses before 1890, though they had received during the preceding three or four years at least three letters from him, thanking them for copies of their books. The first of these letters has disappeared, the second would only interest close students of their *Canute*, but the third, written on the receipt of *Long Ago*, a volume of poems each inspired by a fragment or phrase of Sappho's, will, I hope, prove generally interesting.]

> Box Hill,
> *June 12th*, 1889.

Dear Madam,

I have been told that it is an addressing-of two when one writes to Michael Field. You are certainly in the book which you have done me the honour to send me, a voice of one heart—I have not recently or for years read verse that moved me so for the faultless flow in it and the classic concision. It could have come only of the deep love of your poetess [Sappho], combined with genius to express it, such as she would have smiled on. The hedonic philosophy, informed by realist passion, is

given in a manner to make it new, almost convincing, as if her blood were in your lines. I speak from remembered effects of some passages.
The volume will be treasured.

I am, most faithfully yours,
GEORGE MEREDITH.

[1] We got into the train for London at Redhill, as a gentleman was taking possession of a discarded foot-warmer. When he sat down, he addressed me, "I can easily push it further, that you may share the warmth." I bowed with thanks. Then he became absorbed in a paper. The scales fell from my vision, almost instantaneously—it was *George Meredith*: Sim had a suspicion, which she put by as nonsense. Perhaps he became aware of an interest in our looks (I had whispered to Sim, " G "), for every now and then the fulgent eyes swept us in survey. We were reading the *Contemporary Review* (containing *The Lumber Room*, just received from Percy Bunting), together. Sim says my eyes grew sharp as crystal points in their brief search for traits of the person fixed in his portrait by Hollyer. He drew out letters from Turkey and dropped an envelope under the seat. At Cannon Street he got out—our eyes flashed into one another as he passed—easily raising the window at the very moment of descent from the train. He made a step or two on the pavement and then doubled back a minute's space to throw an uncertain glance into our carriage. I was sure of our man—why ? I recognised him on the instant—the iron-grey hair and beard, the forward sweep

[1] Edith, 1890.

of the moustache, the large, beautifully modelled eyelids, the unusual shape of the ear's " porch." Only the eyes were new—for in the portrait they are covered—quick, much the colour of nuts at Christmastide ; yet, with all their rapidity, a certain profound languor emerges, and slow recluse smiles, that send their ripples no further than the orbs themselves. Must I confess ! I took the envelope—(all is fair in war)—but it gave me no clue, having been evidently enclosed : on it was a list—" a few packets of envelopes—a banjo case—a stick of sealing wax " (not in his writing). We still thought that imagination might be fooling us with a mere London man.

On our return, at Cannon Street, the same figure passed by our carriage, went to the next, and finally returned to ours. His appearance, thus sudden, was so like the portrait, I was certain, but the name on the document in his hand made assurance sure. At first this document absorbed all his attention and I could watch the grave profile. Finally, I took out my pocket *Othello*. He put up his document, and then seemed to wake to the fact that his travelling companions of the morning were again in the same carriage. He laid the paper on his knees, and his hands on it, and turned full round to watch and receive. I was obliged to read closely, for his eyes were well prepared for my least look in his direction. Sim, who could only see his hands, says they were folded, determinedly observant. Soon after, she came to sit by me, and we talked vividly each to each. Sometimes his lids covered his eyes as in the portrait ; but if we took the moment for a study of his features, the brave lights were upon us, like a tiger's through the jungle. We actually went on to Reigate to give him a clue to what he, I am sure, more than guessed : it had a strong effect on him. He knows Michael writes from Reigate, and that it is " an addressing-of two " [1] when anyone writes back. We read together, Sim and I, our close black bonnets were the same, our faces have a family resemblance.

Shortly, he is fascinating—O strange allure !—All that is Meredithian is in his wonderful glance and the compass of expression in his mustily hazel eyes : the rest of his face is full of studious wear and unobtrusive dignity.

" It could but have happened once, etc."—we'll hope for a more fortunate sequel than that of *Youth and Art*.[2]

Entry by Edith Cooper in " Works and Days "
Jan. 8th, 1890.

Reiterated wonder ! Sim travelled again with George. His horse-shoe pin identified the vision—and his eyes— dusk as bloom on purple grapes, yet generative of fire and at moments with the alert brilliancy of lighted wine at a festival. Why does heaven play with us like this ? It is trouble merely to see this being and not to know him as a friend.

. . . William Sharpe came to be introduced to us ; he is comely and ruddy as David in manhood—with neck-tie in a vermilion knot. We talked much of George Meredith whom he was going to visit. He told us of his ways of life. At the end of Flint Cottage garden is a Chalet, with two rooms—one, lined with books, is the study, the other, the sleeping-room. George rises early,

---

[1] See letter, p. 66.   [2] Browning's poem.

often waiting on the sunrise—he comes down to the cottage for 11 o'clock breakfast, then spends the rest of the afternoon in rambling or writing. At night he dines with his daughter, and listens to music, but returns to the Chalet for sleep. It is his habit to work at two novels together—writing one and re-writing the other. He has finished a story (short), *The Amazing Marriage*—and has a longer one, which will be published first, on hand, beside *The Journalist*, which has been announced to appear, but has tarried. He loves wind ; with special ardour he loves the South-wester, and will throw up an engagement in town when it blows, rather than miss it on his hills. He is a firm recluse, coming to London not more than once in three months. Sharpe is certain we were mistaken in our travelling companion. He describes George as very handsome and distinguished—endowed with strongest magnetism. He told us how George admired *Long Ago*—adding, " and Mr. Meredith is very hard to please." We expressed our wish to know him. He has been dismayed and resentful at the way *A Reading of Earth* was received.

BOX HILL.
October 4th, 1890.

DEAR LADIES,

Your letter from Italy came to me in Scotland—and when I had just been looking over Skelton's *Lethington* ! I have now read your *Tragic Mary*. I have also seen a Review of it, most unjust, to my thinking. Let me hope that such stuff has not wounded. I fancied I was the only one to receive that kind of measure from English Reviewers.—Your verse is abused. I should pronounce it a singularly dramatic, nervous line, credibly uttered to the ear by the speaker, as one reads. Your Mary, who feels " the hailstorm rushing through her blood," and who " never can grow holy among men," is the possible Mary, an arresting study. Bothwell has in his look and language the rocky brine of the Scottish pirates (toned by lunar brains of the woman) that he was. Maitland is excellent. The Darnley seems to me too closely sketched from the tapestry figure of him woven by recent historians. But the presentation accords with Lallant's for Mary's feelings.—Of course the book is bleak—and [a] final catastrophe is wanted to close it with reflective emotion following a tragic blow. But I read it with my proper thirst. I put it aside impressed, I retain the sense of poetical power in drama, rare at all times. Once more of the verse, it shows, to my judgement, a measured advance. You will believe that I thank you for the book.

Very truly yours,
George Meredith.

[Lewis Morris says:] . . . [1] Meredith " talks at such high intensity of epigram " that . . . the stout hand [L.M.'s] moved with meaning desperateness across his forehead.

Meeting two ladies on their way to church, Meredith said, " Well, Miss . . . well, Miss . . . are you going to partake of extreme unction ? "

[1] Edith, 1891.

By the by, Mrs. Sheldon Amos told us on Sunday that she had been staying next door to Meredith at Boxhill. She sought a runaway kitten with soft tread, and approaching the hedge she heard a high resonant masculine voice say, " My dear daughter, I have heard you declare several times of late—' My dear father, unless you dress better, I shall not be able to acknowledge you in society '—You seem to think you are a queen and we are only here to do you service."

[1] While at tea a small book-parcel is brought in to Sim, addressed " Blackberry Lodge." [They had left Blackberry Lodge a year before.] Feeling no good could come with that address she impatiently casts it down. I take it up, cut the string, open it and find it to be *Modern Love* and find in it an inscription to Sim herself from George Meredith.

We dance a Dionysic dance, we sit with our chins in our hands and our vision away in the misty possible.

Then Sim writes :

Dear Mr. Meredith,

When I read *Blackberry Lodge* on a certain small book-parcel that arrived by this evening's post, I flung it away angrily, saying that nothing of interest could bear that address. My companion, of more patient temper, quietly unfastened its strings and returned it to me. The rest of the conversation would, if reported, convince you of the profound pleasure your gift has laid in my life. *Modern Love* is known and honoured of us ; and we love to remember with what fervour of admiration Mr.

[1] 1892.

Browning spoke of it to us.—For I imagine even the greatest of English novelists must still care most for his poems.

While correcting your postal knowledge of us . . . may I ask whether it would be an intrusion on your leisure to call at Flint Cottage ?

We have often ourselves serious thoughts of dying— one of us nearly did last summer—and we would fain not leave this earth without seeing what, I doubt not, the prophets and Kings of the next century will desire to see —vainly.

And we are not far away. We can almost hear the bleating of the same lamb.

Sincerely yours,
Katherine H. Bradley.

The letter was posted deep in the shady evening and we were left to pleasure and conjecture.

Box Hill,
March 17th, 1892.

Dear Miss Bradley,

But for a streak of bad health that is equivalent to imbecility, I should have knocked at the unresponsive door of Blackberry Lodge, to pay my respects to you, before this. As it is, I question whether at the moment I am even ready to receive you ; for though I know you will be benevolent, I desire to be something more of a summer day to give you greeting—and I feel wintry, and with the knowledge of looking so, which pinches and contracts us, as when cocks are made conscious by their moulting.—It may pass in a couple of weeks. You would not find me spiritless. But it would be curtailed —and rather unhappy as to the impression produced— as is the case with even ordinary women afflicted with a cold in the head. I am like them or anything wizened at present. Perhaps in two weeks it will be over, and that being so, I shall beg permission, for my pleasure, to invite you and your sister Muse to lunch here one day in April.

Most faithfully yours,
GEORGE MEREDITH.

[1] At last George's reply—see the roll of his letters —full of comic dread that if we were to see him pinched with a cold, the impression would be unhappy. A modern, characteristically psychological, ironically humorous letter!—a very treasure—tortuously frank, a male confession from the satirist of men. . . . Come, April—and bring us no disappointment: one of the hopes of our lives is in bud, and will flower, all being well, in a couple of weeks—what a long time to one's impatience!

[At Dunthorne's Gallery.] . . . A pretty girl comes in. The word, Miss Meredith, goes round. Lane brings her up to us. She says, "We are expecting you to lunch." Meredith is better. We do not like the daughter—she is frank, cold, spoiled, shallow. Her complexion is very fair, her eyes steel-blue, blond hair in

[1] Edith, 1892.

masses, deep lips with lovely curves. Dress—plain
black, long fawn jacket, black lace turned over the neck,
a black hat with pure blue ribbons. She is elegant, she
bears herself haughtily—has no graciousness in the eyes.
She is anything but a Nesta. If his nature is like hers,
I shall hate him. Yet Lionel [Johnson] says he is like
her in face—with beautiful steel-grey eyes, fair complexion. I always imagined him dark.

Meredith suffers from temporary paralysis of nerves
and muscles. No wonder he cannot see us till better.
Worry brings it on—sometimes work. Miss Meredith
has to copy her father's novels for the press. The son
of that *Modern Love* marriage was a dwarf—a clever
fellow, brilliant in talk, who died a few years ago, and was
not beloved of his father.

[1] Smiling weather—in the afternoon my Love and I
stroll round the garden walks—suddenly we speak of
Meredith, and clenching our fists towards Boxhill set to
work to *will* with power that he be moved to ask us to
lunch—we *will* and WILL with increasing emphasis of
word and movement.

We wake in hope that has lost all liveliness that we
shall receive our cover [Cover to *Sight and Song*]. I hasten
down—it is there—under it I see a blue letter with the
Dorking postmark. I remember our rites of volition in
the garden and fly upstairs. It is from Miss Meredith:

[1] Edith, 1892.

" . . . Will you and your friend come over here to lunch
to-morrow ? . . ."

Sim is engaged to breakfast with Amy Bell at Bays-
water. A telegram rushes off to her—we have a prostrate sense of not being able to eat, or to do anything
all the morning. Cold, dark-grey rain begins to fall ;
worries tangle round us. The cover is provokingly
imperfect. . . . I go about, curl my hair, see Sim drying
her mane with a conviction of the futility of life—the
grim smallness of its occasions. . . . The uphill way
is very damp ; in the hedges is the cool hum of rain
—the lovely valley is at once fresh and sullen. The
" wild white cherry " is in flower, as in Meredith's *Reading of Earth*. I love the grey chalk-turf and the sudden
little yew trees. Our cab mounts above Burford Bridge :
on top of the grass fence lies a pool of violets—we turn
to the right between a silver down and the woods—we
pause at a red gate, enter a space sunk amid box-hedges
—grass and bare flower-beds in the centre, a drive round
the flat, red-mottled front ; a door with small pillared
porch, a company of Solomon's seals looping over the
steps. Through a window I have a glimpse of an
æsthetic head—a woman's : I wait on the threshold, suddenly a grey figure jerks out of the door—I see a knot of
vermilion under the throat, a grizzledness, brown skin
beaten by life—nothing definitely strikes me but the knot,
yet from the indistinct vision I am instantaneously conscious of disappointment, that is a sorrowing pain. " I
must come forth to bid you welcome," says a voice
highly artificial, measured in pronunciation and rather
rigid in timbre. In the hall he asks us if we know Mr.

Le Gallienne—" By sight," I answered—" By name,"
answers Michael. And the door opens. Miss Meredith
receives us and chats a little. In the right-hand corner
is the æsthetic woman and a young man—tall, gently
aquiline, with dark unshaven hair, and eyes that give one
the sweet smile as it rises in them.

We are introduced—Meredith excuses the delay in
asking us—" I thought you were delivered up to engagements, private views, exhibitions, opera and theatres,
like my daughter," and with this mounting series of
mistakes he disappears. It seems the Le Galliennes had
been four hours in getting from Hanwell to Boxhill
yesterday—owing to the stoppage of omnibuses due to
the Labour Procession ; we talk of the woes of distance,
of Surrey, of Whistler. The Le Galliennes must soon
start for the train—lunch is ready. . . .

Here I sketch the drawing-room—a cottage room with
tiny bluish paper, a floorcloth of greenish-blue covered
with iris heads—a heavy greenish-blue mantel-board and
curtains rudely embroidered with yellow and tawny tulip-
shapes. A door curtain of like colour and likewise
embroidered. A piano—two great arm-chairs by the
hearth—small, uninteresting furniture, few photographs
or pictures, many small portraits of women—several
paintings of the daughter. Dingy Syrian curtains tied
with pale blue bunches—a side window looking into a
case of geraniums and over it into a steep garden and
greenery of dark kinds : a front window containing a
table, on which is a glass of wild-cherry boughs. In the
window corner a chiffonnière, supporting a fiddle and
some more cherry blossoms. No special distinction in

the few ornaments—rather a quiet and pleasant simplicity in the look of the little room than any individual note of taste.

Miss Meredith wears a dark serge, tailor-cut, with gold edges and brass buttons, a white blouse and sky-blue bow. She is a nice maiden after all—a little spoiled, and only distant through awe, which soon melts away. Mrs. Le Gallienne is a boneless heap of green Liberty stuff and smocking—over her happy æstheticism she pokes her chin. Her hair is light and frizzled—her features common—queer and yet commonly so ; and her eyes seem to curve like blue bays—monstrous and convex. Those Sphinxian eyes have betrayed Richard into his premature marriage. She is much below him—of the type of the artist's wife. Richard Le G. is charming—young, modest, spontaneous, very handsome, with something of the sweet sacredness that used to be about a poet in his youth—a look of being delicately set apart. On the definite Roman features there is a sincere nobility of expression that takes from them any abruptness : the eyes are blue, the mouth slightly depressed, in spite of lips with a full curve—the brows are a dark line, the forehead white, the face hairless as a boy's, the hair " dark and dear." The carriage of the head a little reared ; the voice has a huskiness in its music. We are friends with the first smiling look.

Well—we go in to lunch in a tiny room—greenish in colour, I believe. The dishes arrive through the wall, there is no ceremony in hostess or guests. Richard Le Gallienne has been trying to get the promise of one of Meredith's neglected MSS. These have been lying at

Chapman's. Marie has claimed *Dianna*. We talk of MSS.—I say how much more alive they are than the printed page. We discuss the misfortunes—well-known to R. Le G.—of our Cover, the beauty of our two last covers : we tell how when we came to the episode of the mill-women in *The Book Bills* [by R. Le Gallienne], we forgave him the wicked deceitfulness of the title—as we praise the book (I say it has been one of the freshest pleasures of the Spring—Sim says it is a *book*, and therefore brings comfort)—a deep ingenuous flush mounts to his temples—a glow of such joy as we never know after twenty-five. Soup is finished, we are taking salad to the cold lamb, when the Novelist-Greyness bursts on us again—a presence that confounds. We had been chilled not to see our host at his table ; to see him interrupt the meal is disquieting. I turn, he asks me if I enjoy old Hock. Remembering Herbert Spencer's hock, I intrepidly say, " Yes." " Then one of the oldest bottles in my cellar shall be brought for you." There is a sense of fuss as host and housemaid disappear.

The hock reaches us before the master—and I drink the calm bitter-sweet ; its invincible heat touches my cheeks. Sim fails to drink—she with the real taste for wine—but no wonder !

" Will you sit down with us, Puppy ? "

" Yes, sweetie, I am going to sit down beside Miss Bradley, if she will permit me."

Then with slow enunciation he assures us that all the " Bacchus " in his house is *old*—this is a point from which he diverges into a Dionysic homily on the rich power in wine of improvement—the example to our senile years enclosed in it. The dark lash of Richard has a dip full of meaning in my direction, while the elaborate sentences develop and close perfectly. The portrait by Hollyer is discussed—the only portrait into which Meredith has been tricked. He has genuine hatred of being reproduced—nothing would make him allow his portrait to be painted and then exhibited " between a bishop and a demi-rep." There is something touching in the passionate affectionateness of Meredith's manner to Richard, and in the young poet's clear raised voice, frank discipleship and unrestricted amusement. He speaks again persistently, though with diffidence, of the MSS., " I should so value one. I hope you understand I am only asking for one MS.—for nothing large. I should be contented with only a Poem, like that you were reading to me this morning." " Only a poem ! Ah, you are like the rest of the world. If you cannot have prose—*only a poem* will do." Poor Richard Le G. struggles with brave innocence to get out of the bog and only gets deeper in ; but his shamefaced boyish laugh pleads for him. The husband and wife depart for the train—we gather round the door and wave to them as long as they are enclosed by the box-tree hedges.

" Not love you, you beautiful boy ! " one quotes from *The Book Bills* inwardly, as one watches Richard—why did he darken his fate with a wife ? But even this is original in a world of young men who do not marry— " Husband "—when used of such sweetness and beauty is not a word without charm.

We are invited to continue lunch, but protest we want no more, and settle in the drawing-room to conversation.

I seek to win Marie by talk about Private Views, about her life at Flint Cottage and our life at Reigate. Sim talks with Meredith—I have had time to get an impression of him. Lionel Johnson told a great lie when he said that Meredith's eyes were steel-blue—they are worn hazel—there is a little nervous difference in their focus—about them something of that piteous old-dog decrepitude one sees in portraits of Carlyle. The hair is in tint stone colour, what there is of it curls. The mouth is gaunt with suffering, the nose fierce and withered, the brow rather narrow, much lined, the laugh a brilliant contradiction to the features.—Tragic life written over them—a certain restricted distinction in his look and manner, that of county society : solitude looming above every other record on the face—solitude that has embittered.

He is dressed in dark-blue trousers, a white-grey buttoned overcoat and the vermilion knot. Lionel said his head was the handsomest in England—it is one of the most significant, but not physically illustrious as I had expected. He is somewhat deaf ; he is a wreck and yet his conversation is of value and of range beyond that of any man I have ever met—(except G[eorge] M[oore] at his very best). With humour his voice becomes more pliant, even imitative, so that he gives a reed-like key to a woman's words—his movements have Celtic suggestiveness. He is sensitive about his age and we do not lighten the burthen of the sensitiveness, through some unconscious betrayal of surprise. No one has said the truth : that bodily he is a ruin, that deafness shuts him from the *nuances* of repartee, of allusiveness in others, and that his own wise, witty, discourse, emblazoned with metaphor, crystallises into formal sentences that take the warmth out of speech.   Men have spoken to me of his magnetism—I felt none, neither as an atmosphere nor as a flash.

I overhear this story, told with waved hands and deliberate, ironic emphasis.   Tennyson is in society—a dame of the fashionable world offers him tea which he accepts.   She goes up to the table and proclaims aloud —" The great Creature will take a Cup of Tea."   She brings it with genuflexions.   " There ain't any sugar in it," says the Poet brutally.   " The great Creature takes sugar—bring some at once—and the tongs," she chaunts.   Tennyson grunts sullenly, " I never use those things."   " Oh !—then from this day forth, we will none of us use tongs—we will take our sugar with our fingers."   I hear him say that Renée in *Beauchamp's Career* is his best-loved woman-character.   There are such capabilities in her.   She is a Frenchwoman to her finger-tips.   He asks which of us " *does the Males ?* " (the highest compliment implied in any question asked of Michael).

" Who did Bothwell ? " comes next.

The Tragic Mary is a fine dramatic study—but the English hate a study.

Through my talk with the daughter I catch portions of the story of Ellen Terry's marriage with Watts—of how he, a grey-beard and valetudinarian, was cajoled by a fashionable woman into this pathetic marriage with the adoring young girl—who was his model before she was his bride—of how her abnormal need of caresses fatigued him, of how at Little Holland House she was suppressed, chidden till it came to pass a guest trod on her weeping body on the mat, as he entered the studio—of how she was at last got rid of and thrown on the world, a wife and no wife, with a nature ravenous for love. There was something deliciously Meredithian in the description of Watts as a bridegroom pining to be at work, brooding, sad, a white woman-snake creeping round him—the girlish head on his breast, just at the angle to catch a slant look from her God's eyelids.

"Your lunch is ready now, Puppy," suggests Marie. We second her intimation with entreaty that he will leave us at once. "Food is nothing to me—I shall be with you again in a few minutes." He stalks out.

Marie breakfasts at 8.30—her father at 10.0. She lunches at 1.0—he at 3.0. They join dinners at 6.30. He works and sleeps entirely at the Chalet. Marie and her brother, in their childhood, rejoiced when the Chalet was built, and they could bang the house doors without feeling that they "shattered something" with the noise.

We suggest that we should love a stroll in the garden, though drops still fall one by one through the wet air.

Meredith re-enters—puts a chocolate cap on his head and forth we fare. He and I are side by side—what an opportunity! This is how I use it: I look at his asparagus beds, I play with the cat, I speak of the ideal retreat he has in the Chalet and of the fret with which home life wears away the brain-force of women: then we come to a paddock, green and buzzing with rain, in

which are many cowslips—he speaks exquisitely of the
" lusty freshness of a cowslip in rain." The garden is
that of a cottage with wild bits of hillside amplifying it :
narrow paths, with little lines of boxwood running wild
along the edges, wend by the beds, the currant bushes,
the shrubs. Then we turn to ascend, at the side of a vast
espalier-apple, to the field and the Chalet. The Apple is
vaster than a boa constrictor, but is flecked with here and
there a ruby group of buds, moist and perhaps showing
one half-flower out among them.

The pathway winds higher through grass, cowslip-
buds and clusters, the accentuated blossoms of the
pheasant-eyed narcissus—till under a fledging beech, it
reaches the door of the Chalet. I enter—Sim enters.
We act like two she-asses. I find nothing better to note
than the basket of box-fuel and the cones that, added,
make the fire sparkle. The room is wooden—on the
floor some old and dusty Eastern mats—solid, old, inky
desk, covered with books and papers—*Revue des Deux
Mondes*, etc. Books on table and chairs. Book-case
not that of a library, but of a cultured reader. Fearing
lest I should seem to be seeking a sight of Michael Field
—his volumes, I give small heed to the shelves—I see a
large paper edition of *Carlyle*. The window is full of
scarlet geraniums—vivid colour pleases Meredith ; he
has the front beds filled with geraniums, red and pink,
yellow calceolarias in separate companies—this for his
own pleasure.

We ascend into the wood above the Chalet, where a
brown walk skirts the hill ; juniper, daphne, box grow
above, and below it a view impinges on the evergreens

—a view of thickets, knolls, pale downs, yews, spraying cherries and the distant roofs of Dorking.

Again in our arm-chairs we talk as before, only that I lend more undivided attention to the father, though the daughter is beside me.

He speaks of the hatred between men and women— he has known men who abhorred women, and women who abhorred men. The depth of this sex-enmity can be gauged by men's after-dinner talk. Separate education is answerable for much. He speaks bitterly of Frederic Harrison's sentimentality over women's position. To root out from man the sense of contempt toward woman is the great point to gain, and this can only be done by giving her knowledge of the world and an independent status. Therefore Meredith holds that the labour for the franchise is ill-advised—it exasperates the deep opposition of men; whereas woman's best course would be quietly to enter the trades and professions, win their independence and then enfranchisement would come as the ripe fruit of their still growth, for which their sex would be ready. Personally he is fonder of women than of men—he likes their rapid wit. To get men to understand him, he has " to drag them by a halter up Boxhill."

He believes that women have intelligence, distinct from, but equal to, men's, and that there is far deeper likeness in physical strength than appears, owing to the false education and debilitating conditions that mould women. " I do not believe that Nature would choose for breeding a strong and a weak—she wants a strong and a strong."

Tea is brought : then Pussy must show his one trick.
. . . Puss indulges in mere prancing, followed by fits
of irrelevant purring and chair-leg caressing.   The Novelist-Greyness looks into the matter as if it were of
psychological importance.   We give up Puss as a char-
latan, when suddenly he leaps like an acrobat, till he
hangs as if he were a china cat on some fancy piece of
ware.   Our deep interest rewards him—Long Live
Pussy ! While we drink tea, a girl and her youthful
knight call to arrange that Marie should go with them
to a ball in the evening : we are disappointed at the
interruption, but it becomes an advantage, for it is
delightful to hear Meredith's polished banter with the
girl, and his prosaic battery of questions when he turns
toward the boy. . . .

Each sentence springs out like an electric eel.

To the girl he speaks of the time, long past with him,
when a grey-beard is audacious beyond any youth—of the
erecting influence of her smile, etc., etc.

They go away—to us he is not courtly and teasing and
light-witted—he is confidential, anxious, intellectually
brilliant.   One almost envies the girl.

His nature is bitter with the neglect he has suffered—
he cares now but little for praise or blame ; he is out of
sympathy with his audience—he does not trust them, he
has no love for them—or rather this is his mental attitude,
his conscious attitude—practically, unconsciously, his
few disciples, his earnest readers are more to him than he
fathoms.

While we finish our cups of tea, our sluggish cab
darkens the drive and crawls toward us under the box-

hedges, as if it were a vehicle of Fate—the Fate that severs. At the door I turn suddenly to say good-bye— with nervous thrills he ejaculates, " How do you do ? " Painfully checked, I enter the cab, lower the window, meet his eyes, and with a bow lose sight of them.

The down is before us—Flint Cottage behind—and Sim is saying, " Speak—say something ! "

Once before, just as the cab was approaching I met his eyes, stayed with them intrepidly ; and then very quietly my gaze slipt away from them, without spoil, without assurance or interchange, from failure of courage, from want of resource.

We had been in contact with greatness, that astonishes, irritates, pursues—that has nothing of breadth, peace or geniality in it. Like his work, his character lacks ease —there is a deep spontaneity in each that is super- ficially belied, and cannot be recognised at once under fantastic disguises. In youth, I should say, he was vain, and the sufferings that vanity leaves haunt his age, as well as the sufferings that Tragic Life inflicts. His influence is cumulative—one wants to see him again— not when one is with him, but when one has left him for some time.

After-thoughts :

George asks Sim if we write continuously—she answers " Yes " for herself—less affirmatively for me. " Then probably she is not so strong—it is natural for the healthy to work always, those like you *whose blood spins round and round.*" It was so right for George, who has rarely written a letter to us without the word *blood* in it, to find out Sim's blood power (all my power is in the nerves), and emphasise it.

Box Hill,
October 6th, 1893.

My dear Miss Bradley,

I read your *Ferencz* [1] last night : and it is good : I think it should act well. But bear to hear this from me :—I do not find in your dramatic prose the complete ring that there is in the sound and volume of your blank verse lines. In the *Tragic Mary* and *Stephania*, for example. Only by having you beside me and reading to you, could I give the notion of the " translated " tone of some parts of the dialogue.—I would offer to come to you, but am pressed to work all through the day. Will Michael Field dine with me ? A fly shall meet the twin Muses and a fly take them back to the station, dropping them at Reigate. Doubtless there will be a friendly train. Or if not, I can get beds at the inn hard by. I have much to say of *Stephania*, which I greatly admire in the poetry, but yet have to criticise. For you do not mean that one should give one's heart to her case less than to Otho ? But so it is with me. Her case cannot be pleaded in the abstract. To win sympathy with her to the end, her situation has to be pictured. A scene is wanting.—I read it three times and meant daily to write of it. I was under agreement to finish a Novel for the *Pall Mall* magazine. Now I

---

[1] The hero of *A Question of Memory*.

am bound to do the same for *Scribner's*. And verse
will spout at times! And I am not robust. Think
how little time I have for letters.

Your most faithful
GEORGE MEREDITH.

[1] . . . Well, we go to the inn where Keats wrote
Endymion, put on evening clothes, and ascend to Flint
Cottage. George looks far more vigorous; he has left
off wine and sweets, and now can work from ten to
five. A novel comes out in December's *P.M.* magazine
and another in January's *Scribner's*. The small table
was fleckered with maidenhair round a sunshine strip of
satin, and George sat pressing his delicious wine with
pleasure in Bacchic appreciation. He loves *Stephania*,
but he thinks that to obtain sympathy with her, she
should have entered with the hoots and insults of the
people following the harlot, not with the calm retro-
spection of her disgrace that opens the play—a curious
point of view. Round the cottage fire he read and
commented on the first act of *A Question* [*of Memory*].
He, the Euphuist in language, rallied us on our tendency
not to use the vernacular—his laugh was delicious, with
no more offence in it than a brook's on stones, and as
much eloquence. He said a thing about *Ferencz* in
Act I, that I cannot write down yet . . . not till the
play is played—a thing! confound him! His talk
foamed before us and we had good draughts. There
is great magnetism in his eyes—brain lays hold of one

[1] Edith, 1893.

from them. His voice rolled out Sophocles. He called Lewis Morris the Harlequin Clown of the Muses.

George Meredith to " Michael Field "

Box Hill,
August 19*th*, 1895.

My dear Michael Field,

I rejoice to know of you as in good working order, and trust the Drama will not fall short of *Stephania*. Pray visit me when the noble mood is on you. . . . As to the periodical [*The Pageant*], I have refused to contribute in so many cases that I cannot make an exception.
With my homage,
I am your faithful
George Meredith.

Box Hill,
August 19*th*, 1895.

My dear Michael Field,

You are oddly affected by trifles, but I am reminded of the quivering reed after the breeze when I think of your valiant power to recover. Now bear with me, I have little praise for the line or the characters of your *Attila*. If you had irony in *aim* you should not have made drama. You could of course produce keenest irony through clashes of your personæ. But poor Honoria is hardly a subject for it. Perhaps you meant the reflecting of grim light on the sex-mania current. That would be satire, quite enough to kill your poetry.

Will you come and hear more? I have not time to write a criticism. It seems to me that your present failure comes of the design to do too much. Your naturally splendid dramatic line sinks broken under the burden of satire and stage constrictions.

Your most faithful

GEORGE MEREDITH.

[1] We travel beside the grey chalk downs—the train seeming slow and then quick—to Box Hill and drive up Mickleham Valley, under a flushed sky . . . not a flushed West, but from zenith to horizon, colour and gloaming in one.

The down opposite Flint Cottage bronzed with night and sunset ; the little yews blot ominously—we turn in at the gate, and as the carriage curves round the flower-beds, on the other curve I see George—a stick, a body clothed in more crimson-bronze than the down beyond the gate, more gaunt and antiquely distinguished than those chalk slopes . . . and from the midst of the glow and grimness a hat goes up, like an eagle from roost.

A maid takes our rugs at the cottage door and the master comes first to the further carriage window—" I am delighted to welcome you, ladies "—and then round the carriage to the steps. His courtesy is disconcerting —it is not a breath, but an emphasis—not an encourage-ment, but a declaration of itself . . . a race war-cry rather than the peace of gentle breeding.

[1] Edith, 1895.

I am a heap of tumbled snow inside, confused and chill at heart as I enter . . . the new dog is petted as " Dear " and " Sweetie," both words pronounced with a clinging slowness that is almost " mouthing "—an artificial habit of speech that is not a caress . . . the dog attacks my boa with all the gallantry of puppyhood and George makes some " la, la, la," notes of song deep in his throat, that somehow are an artificial offence against his aggressive courtesy.

Michael seats herself in an arm-chair, a table between her and me—George faces her, his eyes on her face nearly the whole two hours and a half. I have time to watch him and listen with a notebook open in my brain. His head is of Elgin marble perfection. I have never seen a cranium like his for strength and purity, for line and modelling; the hair floats out from the beautiful structure, silvery, with swirl and softness that is natural and grace that is obtained by the scissors. A same perfection haunts the eyelids as the head—form, with a life over it that spiritualises.

With these two features, nobility is at end—the nose is shrewish, lacking in generosity, breadth of inspiration, flutter of sensitiveness—a not ill-shaped, but poor nose. The mouth is sunk, grim—the words form in the brain and are emitted ; they do not rise fresh on the lips. There is no eloquence, no magic on those lips of almost parallel lines ; under the beard one has a prophetic sense that the chin is peaked like the nose. Those eyes have perhaps been worn out by age and sorrow . . . they have no lightnings, no prehensile power, no malice. They neither inherit the eyes of others, nor subdue them, nor bewitch them. I can never be sure they move together, but even this does not make them interesting—their colour is a mere vagueness between brown and indigo.

The intellect has devoured the humanity of the expression, that only asserts itself in the smile—not bright, but without cruelty, and with less artifice in it than in the voice and manner.

The whiskery space between beard and hair is a masterpiece—there is charming work there, in the slight suggestion of ripples of carving on the jaw and cheek.

The neck carries the head well out of the coat. The tie is scarlet-red, the coat mulberry-brown, the trousers a rough mouse-grey—the linen spotless.

He lays a French book in limp parchment beside us . . . memory refuses to give me back the name of book or author. The poems are short and, to a glance, cut into shape with real artistic knowledge. " I know now the French work—these little things are exquisite. Would you like to take them home ? You will not mind it . . . they are a little *warm*—but you read the classics, Sappho. We who write can afford to take a skiey survey of all life."

We have not been reading French lately—German.

" You will perhaps be surprised to hear that I find Schopenhauer most tonic reading, that braces me like an East wind. He has laid out the elements of life, exposed their nature and value as no other philosopher—he has sounded life—but he is not content with that ; he must give a personal judgment on his exposition, and the judgment is of no value, being the result of a nature vitiated by sour ancestry—his mother. He was not philosophic enough to abstract his personality from his inspiration. The one was deathly, the other vital; and as such, I reject his personal estimates, while accepting his doctrine of life. Yes, Schopenhauer gives us an exposition and a judgment—one true, the other false."

We murmur the name of Nietzsche as a man who accepts the exposition and reverses the judgment of Schopenhauer. "Nietzsche is a wrong-headed madman of morbid tendencies. I am not speaking of him; but of Schopenhauer's satisfying analysis of the elements by which we live."

George then goes on to speak of the folly of self-interest as opposed to absorption in the good of others, in the life of the race. When we live to others we are conjoined to Nature, who only cares for the race. (This conversation seemed to taste of mid-Victorian, Tennysonian views.) Old people should never die while they are alive, for the sake of the young: they should not cloud the expansive years of those around them. "When I was young, all the middle-aged people seemed to live only to spread disenchantment round them."

We ask him of his daughter and hear that he is again a grandfather, this time to his daughter's daughter. He points to his grandson, "A jolly little fellow—you see in that photograph. He is hesitating as to whether he shall be Hercules or Falstaff; Falstaff somewhat in the ascendant." His daughter he regrets, because she answered his letters. He has more than a dozen every morning, only one of which he often answers. Because he wrote of swimming in his last novel, he is asked to subscribe to Swimming Baths—we threaten him with Alpine Clubs after his Swiss chapters in *The Amazing Marriage*. Americans write that they want to come to Flint Cottage and give a cordial shake to his hand—" while I have the supreme satisfaction of knowing that they long to do the same with the hand of everyone whose name is on the lips of men."

He is glad to see his grandchildren, since they are healthy—there is no tragedy like a weak child.

We ask—has he forsaken the Chalet?—" At night— yes ; I sleep at my house now, and miss going out at all hours into the wood, as I did. I know all the darkest darknesses of night among the boughs and all the changes of the light for dawn.

" But this morning I saw a most beautiful sight. Venus was large and firm between moonset and sunrise, at half-past six. Day was pulsing up and the moon still shining, but Venus was unmitigated ; I shall never forget that undrowned lustre. It seemed as if a beautiful angel beat wings in mid-air . . . for the image expands the fact—an angel with streaming brightness secure from every earthly light."

We tell him he overpraises the Welsh in his book— we can scarcely forgive him—" They have one great quality—*fervency*, but they are wrong-headed, perverse . . . every village has at least a dozen poets ; they are not unnatural to the population, as in England. The English are wholly inartistic—the pig-body of the nations. Matter is all they understand. . . . They materialise every ceremony—the Guildhall gives the

tone—they could not even bury their Wellington
without dragging through the streets a golden calf that
had the staggers. They ruin all their poets, for they
only praise what they find easy to understand. Tennyson, who had poetic endowment, but no intellect, let
them have their way with him. He wrote *The Farmer*
—then to please them he must needs write a *Cobbler*;
he found they liked *Locksley Hall*; he wrote a second
one, and so on.

"Tennyson had unequalled power of vignetting landscapes in words." Then George quotes the opening
lines of *Oenone* :—

> "The swimming vapour slopes athwart the glen,
> Puts forth an arm, and creeps from pine to pine,
> And loiters, slowly down . . ." etc.

giving the planes of the landscape with a voice that
brings out the value of the position of each word in
the passage—his voice passed over the word-painting
like mastic, strengthening the impression.

He then quotes :—

> "On one side lay the ocean and on one
> Lay a great water, and the moon was full."

Simple but perfect—and the writer of these lines could
perpetrate the sloppy lines of the *Idylls*—emasculated,
untouched with the magic of the Middle Ages.

He praises Lucretius also.

Richard Le Gallienne he hoped would have made an
excellent light essayist—but he too had been ruined by
English stupidity and forced editions.

The English have no tradition of manners—even

Browning transgressed in the unpardonable lines on E. Fitzgerald. Michael says, " Not unpardonable, since he believed an attack had been made on his dead wife." " Yes, wholly indefensible. But then he was a Jew."

Why did we let it pass ? Miss Browning has assured us that the family knows nothing of any trace of Jewish blood.

He has heard that Alfred Austin will be Laureate—he thinks it will suit little Alfred to hymn the babies of the house of Hanover. Swinburne could not be Laureate because of his lines on the assassination of the Czar. . . . *Anactoria* and youthful sins could be got over, but not a political utterance, though it meant no more than the whistle of the Scotch express going out of Euston.

" You are not giving us what we came to hear—more about *Attila*."

" I am afraid you are abashed by what I have written."

" No, be sure."

" Not abashed ? "

" We are come to hear more."

" I have not much more to say, but it shall be said."

.   .   .   .

We say firmly that we know the play would act well, that the full animation would come with the players' voices—we calculated their part. Honoria was conceived with Sarah Bernhardt before us all the while.

He admits our plea—then talk drifts on the contrast between Sarah and Duse. Meredith hates Sarah as a Tragedienne—when the great breath of tragedy is needed one loses her argentine voice—she never suggests what is at the back of passion and therefore only presents rhetoric. Coquelin agrees with Meredith that she is the perfect comedienne of the world, lost to it—he once played with her when she took a light rôle after twenty-four hours' study. It was not acting with her—it was living with her. He fell on his knees after the performance and thanked her as a goddess.

" Duse is the great Tragedienne ; the passions disclose themselves in their depth and compass as she acts. She takes the harp and all the strings unfold their utmost of music—Sarah claws and strains them and they are reticent."

Meredith says he regrets the death of our friend Wharton—a friend from what his book brought to us, not a personal friend, I explain. " His *Sappho* is delightful—I got it the other day. But how filled with pallor, from the metrical versions of Sappho admitted !—One turns to the prose translations for healing. Even Swinburne fails—he is too full of the swoon . . . Sappho never approaches languor of the deathly kind . . . she has such sustaining passion."

Then Meredith hopes we are setting to work again—not allowing any paralysis from the world's breath to seize us—we must work to be encouraged. " You and I are outcasts. We are doing work that is not wanted. I am only alive because *I would live*."

We tell him of our ten guineas—" For a poem—you move me to envy." He then proposed it should be spent in giving ten poets (himself included) a holiday on Leith Hill—a guinea a head. There would be no difficulty in finding the poets, if we did not enquire too deeply beneath the title . . . but the peace of the hill-top !—and he sketches the diatribes of one poet against his fellows, and of them against him and each other, with grim copiousness of burlesque and humour which is his usual cross between wit and humour.

The cab rolls up and blinks a light in. We rise at once, for there is the pace of fatigue in the brilliant talk, that went on the first hour tirelessly. George takes my hand and says with quite inhuman polish of manner :

" I have been delighted to see you, my dear lady."

Michael thanks him for letting us come and for scold-ing us. " Oh, I don't scold *you*—I suggest and am honoured that you listen. You are among the few who are *workers*, who are working with me for the same things."

" Yes, we do work—we joy in that."

A smile makes the ruin of his face bland : we step into the darkness while his voice enquires anxiously if Peto, his dog, has slipped out and is in danger of the wheels. From the carriage we see him, a lank shadow against the hall-light, keeping the form of an arrested bow as we depart.

One goes away chill—one's being unexercised—the conversation one has heard is like marvellous conjuring ; one's mind is in a dazzle—but one's nature has not received virtue, nor been eased of the pressing of its own virtue.

In Browning an overplus of the Intellect was vitalised by the Heart.

In Meredith the living Heart rarely kindles the overplus of Intellect. He sits by one, a Stranger—almost belonging to another planet, where the laws of life are reversed, and the head generates. His great women, so completely of this earth, come from creative depths where *The Mothers* hide in caves—inaccessible to Welsh wrong-headedness and Keltic antipathies, modern self-consciousness and sententious sterility.

After-thoughts.

Michael speaks to him of our delight in his *ladies*— " Women untainted by religion and untainted by lust." His face gives thanks for the appreciation.

When we asked him about his health he replied— " The body !—ah, there is no fault with the mind. I hope to work on to the last spark, to do otherwise would be to own myself defeated."

(So Browning persisted and came at last to *Asolando* —where age through persistence had almost completed the circle and drew itself into youth again. *The Amazing Marriage*, coming after *Lord Ormont*, promises this hard-won beauty of renewed youthfulness in Meredith.)

When on our arrival we asked for assurance that two and a half hours would not fatigue him, he assured us, " No . . . Life is too short for me to tell lies." He repeated what he had said about sex-hatred. He knew men who detested women and women who detested men. This was due to severance of interest and education. Boys and girls should be brought up together— the black sheep—for there are female black sheep as well as male—being weeded out. He would have girls learn to take a cuff—a cuff on the cheek.

[1] With George Meredith for lunch—we asked for an afternoon call, and against our will are constrained to lunch. A cold east wind deadens sky and air and makes the distant coppices look distressing. We walk to Burford Bridge and pause at the Inn for coffee. On the table are bulbous chrysanthemums, rich in colour, old, vast—" Like entrées," Michael remarks. We wonder how we should feel if Keats entered. Michael would at once treat him to her method of the leading question. In the labyrinths of the Inn, we agree, he must have had great difficulty in finding his bedroom.

At the bottom of the hill a photographer challenges us to have our portraits taken, " The two together, this moment, for a shilling." We almost yield to the fun of catching our pilgrim expression as we ascend Hill Difficulty—but the wind!—it tames the heart out of such resolve. A red house is rising on George's hillside, with hammertaps and voices as accompaniment. The woodland sanctity is gone for ever. As we curve round to the cottage, we hear a clank and shuffle behind the box hedges that is ominous—yes, George himself comes into sight on his stick and in an old grey coat. He takes a hand of each—" I am very glad to see you," a formula, but said gently.

Then at once he tells us he is working at great pressure on three Odes. " It is an attempt to make History sing." The subjects—French Revolution, Napoleon, and Alsace-Lorraine. He acknowledges, " It is extremely difficult to be discriminating and yet songful."

[1] Edith, 1896.

At command, we leave the ode-subject and enter the cottage. Cloaks removed, we find him in the drawing-room, deep in a chair, and beg him not to rise from the deep, seating ourselves where we can ask questions and reply, yet be heard. He speaks more of the odes— Napoleon is " heavy artillery " to manage.

Then he demands our news and Michael tells the story of Raoul and Anna. He takes in the *Débats*— for its writing, but missed the article that struck us. . . .

Michael. What do you think of the morals of the story ?

George. All depends on the character of the repudiated wife.

Michael. She is corrupt and faithless.

George. Then Raoul was quite right—there is no law I acknowledge that can make a man live with a vile woman or a woman with a vile man. (The voice is sword-like.) . . . (He muses.) The story is most interesting and possesses dramatic merit.

Then he looks at his watch—a lady is expected from town, a Mrs. . . . , who makes three hundred a year " in picking over *our* work." The hearing of her is an influence that turns the East wind heavenly by com-parison. . . . He says *she writes* to come, or we should be angered through every bristle at such an unhonoured guest being asked to share our few hours at Flint Cottage. How infelicitous those who should feel happily are !—and the gallant Celt is capable of the outrage infelicitous in a high degree.

However, the lunch bell rings and the female

picker and stealer does not arrive. We sit down joyously.

Then Meredith questions, "Do you know Mrs. Meynell?" He admires her essays. They are full of "justesse";—"they have a remarkable measure; they are critical in the best sense." "You wrote of them!" "Yes, I said what I felt ought to be said." He describes her as having a very lovely temperament, humble and retiring in all truth. She hero-worships Patmore, and when she writes poems he welcomes them with "strains of the double flute," that do them harm.

Pete is rebuked with Gargantuan phrasing: "Pete, my darling Pete, now don't you set yourself in this sweetly seductive attitude before that lady—Pete, Pete." The dog barks as if he had dynamite in him—a voice passes over the threshold. . . . The picker and stealer arrives, whilst her host closes his eyes in dismay and opens his lips with semi-imprecations against people who do not keep their appointments. She has a fleshy face—all the features flesh, as an uncooked pie is paste— eyes that are points in the unmeaning knobbiness, a laugh that sibilantly flatters, stiff body and chestnut clothes. I begin to look at the clock—one hour and three-quarters before our cab comes!

She mentions a certain child as precocious—this launches George on a delightful sketch of Wycliffe, Tom Taylor's precocious offspring.

"Tom and his wife made themselves ridiculous at London dinners by reciting the marvellous cleverness of Wycliffe—That morning, he had put a spoon in his mouth exclaiming, ' Pa ' . . . and as he withdrew it, had uttered . . . ' Ah ! '

" Some eight years after, Tom was lamenting that Wycliffe was incapable of learning anything. Tutor after tutor gave him up in despair—what was to be done with him ? Eight years more went by and Tom and his wife announced in Society that Wycliffe was going to be an artist ; they grew eloquent on his studio, his industry. One day I was in the New Gallery and met Tom, his wife and Wycliffe. I rashly asked if Wycliffe had anything on the walls. The six eye-balls went up in one direction, earnest, solemn, whitened eye-balls, and there, in a dusty far-away corner, I could just see a lion. It looked as though it were sewn up round saw-dust, as if a roar would have split it to pieces. Nothing was ever so funny as those six whitened eye-balls and that lion ! "

The talk goes on to the portraits of George—praise of the Hollyer photos—. . . George gives a wondrous account of his portrait in the new issue of his works and the effect of the original.

" Sir Trevor Laurence asked me to sit for only three hours to the artist—I hate it, but he said it would please his wife. But the three hours gave no satisfaction, and next day the young man begged so prettily for grace that I had to yield, and the result was pronounced satisfactory. I beheld a face of gruel in which floated balls like the eyes of a cod-fish kept for three days in ice. (There were also brown concaves in the gruel.) The nose was a reed shaken in the wind ; the grim mouth was packed full of savage teeth—and this

was an Impressionist's impression of me. One eye
was completely dead. Sargent made me an amiable
Shade."

In the drawing-room ill-luck reigns for us. The
picker and stealer gets hold of the chair that is George's
ear and the goal of his talk. I have a corner and the dog
and enjoy after my kind. Every now and then George
asks us about R. . . . ! as if we had any concern
with him, a correspondent of years ago, self-consti-
tuted and unknown to us! We are riled by such
nonsense. George's proudest achievement is a parody
of R . . .'s sonnets. Coffee comes and cigarettes
are proposed—Michael says she is somewhat surprised
that he proposes smoking to ladies : does he really
approve ?

His face clouds with some memory that is as a Gorgon
to it—out of a frightful pause floats, " Ah well ! "—
In a moment or two he is speaking as if it were the most
natural thing in the world, and laughing at a boy who
said it was funny to see Mrs. Meynell smoking with
evident dislike and a very evident amateur—when in
truth she had smoked with her father since girlhood.
George himself looks remarkably fine with the delicate
gyration of the smoke-circles round his sinuous face
and perfect head—not a prophet but a god of snarls and
irony in Pythian comradeship.

He would rather have half a dinner than lose his
whole cigar—but man has to be raised to enjoy
tobacco, as is always the case with perfectly celestial
things—one must be in a blessed mood to engage
its blessings.

Sudermann is mentioned—George knows him but little : Hauptmann, not at all—though he makes the remark that the latter has a *Tendenz*, and to have that is like having a hammer behind a pointed thing.

It was Mrs. Meynell who, while staying at the Inn, persuaded George, with those feminine wiles that are so charming even when one sees through them, to undertake the *Odes*. . . . He is reading hundreds of French Memoirs. He no longer works in the Chalet, but in his drawing-room arm-chair.

A break in the conversation—

The Picker gets up and draws out of her string-bag a parcel she begins to unwrap—" Not a gift, I trust," groans George. " We won't call it a gift—only a little thing to amuse you," she warbles. . . . " You see, dear friend, it is only a toy,"—it is a model of the Dresden bridal-cup—with a hollow of good size for the bride-groom to empty, and one of a thimble-size for the lips of the bride. " You must forgive me, but this is for a young couple ! Give it to Will [his son] and his wife. They would say ' I have drunk my share—I mine— and it is quite too delicious a gift.' But I am a wild-boar in a wood ; I rush out with my tusks (his hands curve the form), and then, when I have frightened people, I rush back with my tusks." " Oh, do take it."—" No, no—give it to Will. You see, I have not an ornament on my person. You must forgive a hermit curmudgeon like me. Give it to Will." " Oh, if you wish it, you shall give it to him." " No, no—you ! "— " Then it shall be *our* gift."—" You are tremendously tenacious ; no, it must come from you ; you must take

it to them." "Well, if you wish."—and she shudders
with humiliation and turns the subject, leaving the
cup on the table. It is a cruel scene to witness, but
deserved—the gift is indelicate from a widow to a
widower, presumptuous to a great writer, not to be
accepted.

George keeps up an undercurrent of bitterness against
English literary life. Authors will be the shoeblacks of
the next century. . . . Michael asks what he would
have done if he had had a fortune left to him—" Having
felt the pulse of my public already, I should not have
cared if my works were burnt—except that I should have
liked to be read in France."

He describes the style of Lemaître as rash, full of
after-communings, rich in welcome, the blame reason-
ably disposed on the suppositions of the moment. He
gives some French stories, dramatically. One is delicious—the saying that marriage after a liaison is a decent
way of separating.

Sarah Grand came to see him with Mrs. Meynell and
laughed till she declared her sides ached in bed—" She
seemed *satisfied*," he remarks with comic emphasis. He
thinks she will improve, for she has said she has begun
to care for nothing but literature—" And you think
that a good sign ? " says Michael—" I should think a
writer who was worth reading would care most of all
for life."

" Ah, well ! " he hums.

Our cab is late—we leave the room to fetch our wraps,
intending to start on foot for the next train, if the cab
proves faithless.

I hear George say as we go, " I hope you are not vexed with me, Hortense."—When we return, the cab is at the door, George deep in his seat with the new edition of *Richard Feverel* on his knees, feverishly inscribing it. With the absorption of age he hardly notices Michael's hand with a touch—he says to me carelessly, " You will excuse my rising,"—I am silent and bow like a snow-laden tree, while Michael's voice rings out as if a challenge were thrown down, " Goodbye, Mr. Meredith,"—an alarmed, hurrying " God bless you "—and we are in the cab with seething hearts.

Box Hill,
July 26th, 1898.

Dear Michael Field,

Let me hope that your mood may have softened since you wrote to me : and also that you did not write in such a tone to another. The article was harsh, but we who publish books of verse must put on a mantle of philosophy when we do so. I speak from my own practice. Be sure that readers appreciative of animated lines will be keenly sensible of the fact of an existence of hostility to Michael Field. It happens that present literary tastes are feverish—and your themes are drawn from history, and remote. Your work is hastily read, hastily summarised. Refuse to be wounded by the comments : refer your mind to the public which values you, and continue to produce what you can issue with the knowledge that it is good.   If not many, yet a worthy minority may be counted upon to support you.   If you are in the temper for taking advice, my simple words may be of service.

Yours very truly,

G. M.

Box Hill,
November 16th, 1899.

Dear Michael Field,

Your noble stand for pure poetic literature will have its reward, but evidently you have to wait.   If only for the beauty of the verse, dramatic and lyric, it should meet with cordial greeting, and even that, as far as I see, is unrecognised.   Nevertheless, though you are sensitive, you have courage ; sustainment as well in the perpetual springs of verse within you.   I have had it in mind to write my appreciation of *Aura* and *The Noontide Branches* for some time and would do so if the penning of letters were not, in my present state of health, so great a burden. I hope you find indemnification for the loss of country scenes in your town suburb,[1] and can work cheerfully there.

Your most faithful
George Meredith.

[Possibly on both sides disillusionment had been felt ? If, as seems evident, the Picker was the person addressed as Hortense on page 108, jealousy may partly explain their

[1] They had moved to The Paragon.

show of temper and ensuing coldness.   The preservation
of his last two letters without comment may indicate
that the estrangement was rather regretted on his side
than on theirs.]

CHAPTER FOUR

VICTORIANS GREAT AND SMALL

[In Paris. Sunday, June 8th, 1890.] [1] To the morgue
this morning, quite early in the glowing sunshine. It
has been our worship ; that temple of death, to us the
temple of the living God. Liberté, Egalité, Fraternité,—
true *there*—realised—the grey marred faces within laid
brother-like—freed from the mesh of life, and equal at
last in their destiny—bound, all these voyagers for God.
I saw first an old man lying very calm—the whites of
his eyes giving the appearance of spectacles, so that he
looked like Time lying dead in glasses ; then a deeply
bronzed face, full one would say of sin and of experience ;
finally a rather kindly, common-place fellow, gentle
enough in his fixity. It is Michael's church, that little
morgue—and he found it quite impossible to remain
afterwards in Notre Dame, amid the mumbling and the
lights. God has provided for worship in the facts of
life. If we will but look deep into birth and death—
unflinchingly—accepting all the physical repulsion, and
read on through the letter to the indwelling mystery, we
shall learn how to conduct ourselves between—under
the tri-colour, and with the divine gospel written on our
hearts.

[At Miss Swanwick's.] A good story of Tennyson :

[1] Edith.

III

at a certain house he was asked to read from his works :
in a memorable monotone he gave the *Ode on the Death
of the Duke of Wellington*. He ended—there was a
silence, a pause I suppose of English sheepishness : at
last a voice was heard—his own—in strong commenda-
tion, "It's a fine rolling anthem." Last summer Miss
Swanwick went to see him, when staying near Hasle-
mere. He saluted her in Greek, and as Lady T. was
frail, made tea and "honoured" his guest with the
dropping of sugar in her cup. After, in his study,
exacting a promise that the titles should remain un-
revealed, he read to her *Merlin's Gleam* and the *Leper* of
the new volume. When she spoke her thankful praise,
he grimly remarked, "You would not have cared for
them so much if I had not read them."

In the evening Mr. Gray told us of the genesis of
Tennyson's *Crossing the Bar*. One morning (we have
heard it was that of his 80th birthday), his housekeeper
remarked that he had never written a hymn. The old
Poet was tickled with the housewifely comment and that
evening worked out in hymn metre the last poem in his
volume and the highest reach of his lyrical genius. May
we all set about hymn-writing, if Polyhymnia endows
us with such result—with such eternal praise !

Lunch at Miss Swanwick's. A big man rolls in. . . .
I wonder from whence she can have constrained such an
one to her feast. His eyes are ' ternes '—the French
word alone expresses their heavy, unintelligent surface ;
his face with no cutting about the features is mottled—
his hair greyish, his form unwieldy—the strained coat

over his chest, a little flecked with grease. He is the
poet of the middle-class in his middle-age—Lewis
Morris . . . yet the man is unaffected, good-hearted,
depressed with his fatal popularity, almost rebellious at
the power Tennyson has had over his mind. He envies
those who are not dominated by his gifts. He loves
Keats (ah, poor Keats, nauseous in his disciples!),
Milton and Tennyson. I think he has some consideration for Michael. He often visits Tennyson, and one
day suffered agonies of anxiety, when the old poet,
bothering about a disobedient dog, was almost caught
between two thunder-clouds. I am sure L. Morris felt
that the solid frame of this great earth would have dis-
solved if T. had been struck. . . . L.M. introduced
himself to me by showing that supreme achievement of
nineteenth-century verse—the line in Edwin Arnold's
Light of the World.

In red palludamentum lacticlave.

Poor L.M.—he finds popularity bitter—the disgust of
it has taken hold of his finer self.

Then to Miss Swanwick—We met her in the hall—her
smiling wrinkles as sweet to see as ever.
A dull lunch—part of the unmarried crush at the
bottom of the table. No talk, no surprise in the
dishes.
After, a talk with Lewis Morris. Sim calls him " Contemned Salvator." One is patient with his egregious
face, his ' bêtise,' his bad art, out of pity, because he
is dimly conscious he belongs to darkness. There is

something of deplorable tragi-comedy in the way he quotes his own lines.

Later I have a very long chat with old Dr. Martineau. When he is introduced, I feel a struggle of tears and breath round my heart to think what it would have been to my mother—once—could I have returned to tell her about her favourite preacher, of the only sermons she could read.

He is a whited sepulchre—taking all condemnation out of the phrase : deadly white and cavernous—his humour, sympathy, great intelligence are buried in him, and only rise like ghosts. When he speaks of Dean Stanley tears come to his eyes—he says if the Dean had only lived ten years longer the unity of all creeds (in England) would have been fostered beyond expression. Also he deplored that Jowett has gone off to his Plato and Aristotle : many can translate, but Jowett's theological work no one else could do. I venture to say that few could give to a translation of Plato that subtility of style, that genial Attic humour that J.'s translation so happily suggests. Dr. M. loves Scotland for Art purposes—I hate it and tell him that in painting I have lowland tastes.

[1] Yesterday Edith and I lunched with Miss Swanwick. Mr. and Mrs. Holman Hunt were there. She has large, clear blue eyes through which, as through a window, blue light strikes out. Her manner is direct and firm—proceeding by unwavering outlines. There is nothing undulating about her—the simple straightness of a

[1] Katherine.

Roman road.   Canon Bell spoke of Matthew Arnold.
His wife in a letter speaks of his face after death as
" nobly beautiful, with a smile about the mouth, the
peace of which deepened as days went on."

Canon Bell quoted these lines from Obermann :

> " Oh, had I lived in that great day," etc.[1]

—and told us how he had said to Matthew Arnold, he
trusted these lines expressed the conviction of his highest
moments.   He answered with a smile . . . sadly, " I
was always sincere in what I wrote."

Miss Swanwick told us how the Dean of Westminster
(Stanley), sitting by her one day at dinner, said that the
only thing he had against her Justin [MacCarthy] (*Life of
the Century*) was that he was not quite just to Matthew.
Holman Hunt was heard to speak of the impossibility of
sculpture nowadays—the face, and not the body, was
now the glory of man.

[2] Miss Heaton also knew and knows the Rossettis.
To Dante Gabriel she gave five or six commissions.
The first picture he painted for her was *Paolo and Francesca*.   Ruskin said, " It was not suitable for a lady,"
and Miss Heaton weakly made an exchange with him.
There is to me a speckled silliness in Ruskin's dealings
with women—spite of his chivalry and exaggerated
estimate of our sex as Queens.   Rossetti had a con-
straining fascination.   His sister is striving to work out
his redemption by prayer and denial.   She is bent on

[1] *Obermann Once More,* Stanzas 35–38.   [2] Edith.

being Love's Martyr for his sake. There is a small chance we may be able to call on her. I should like to see her once. Rossetti had a most spontaneous manner. Miss Heaton only saw his wife once—metallic lustre came from her hair—her face was that of Beata Beatrix, but a little smaller in moulding.

Sim left *Effigies* with Percy Bunting : he told her how Dr. Hatch, a delightful man, knew Swinburne when he was an innocent young fellow at Oxford, and afterwards introduced him to Rossetti—an act which has always been heavy on the introducer's conscience. " O, contemned Rossetti ! "—one thinks, the more one hears of him. " Yet the pity of it, the pity of it," with that mystic, pictorial, operative genius and that initial vision of the *Blessed Damozel.*

Introduced to William Michael Rossetti at an At Home at Percy Bunting's—our dull god-papa ! So handsome and blank, with fine lidded Roman eyes—a wax-work of his brother, his cast in mortality. He talks of the " uncomfortable " days when he, Dante, Swinburne and Meredith lived together.
[At Miss Swanwick's]. . . . At this point callers entered—Mrs. M. Drummond, Burne-Jones' famous sitter and model, with her mother. The daughter sat like an " Angel of Creation." Every wonder of the type was there—blue eyes, inclined toward infinity in which sits no subtle spirit ; the uplifted growth of hair, the colourless blur about the mouth, the pure lines of brow and cheek. She wore a cloak of dark peacock

green and fawn boa; round her bonnet, like the cloak in shade, little peacock feathers of softest hue and shimmer mingled with the hair. She spoke in a reed-like voice, which was to the ear what pallor is to the eye. Delicious story: a child was heard to ask another— "What has become of Papa's leg they cut off?"— "Hush," was the answer, "it's in heaven." This was told to Burne-Jones—"I can see it standing by the Throne!" he laughed—and his laughter was immoderate. S. was full of humour over Watts-Dunton's introduction of the Romany tove (smoke) and pove (turnip) into the English language, as rhymes to love and dove.

By Underground we reached Portland Road and soon found Fitzroy Street and a white door with dull brass ornaments and fittings—no number on its lintel. Here lives Herbert Horne, editor of *The Century Guild Hobby Horse*, here Selwyn Image has his studio [Image was to design the cover for their *Tragic Mary*, hence this visit] and other Artists and Art-men dwell in unity. The various storeys represent the arts from Architecture to Design—hence Selwyn Image has his place at the top of all the stairs and his walls are inhabitated by the great figure designs he makes for stained-glass windows— spaced into thick irregular lines for the inevitable leading . . . Selwyn Image himself is very "likeable," with firm lips, indicative of that self-control essential for the art of design—yellow eyes illuminated with genius— giving the element of brightness and freedom, without which no combination of lines will live and combine into symbolism or beauty. His complexion is parchment, his hair cropped, his grasp of hand assured and frank—his age about 38 I should fancy. As we gave him the clue to our conception of Queen Mary, the flame in his eyes grew intent. . . . As we were parting he suggested (by pre-arrangement, we divine) that we should look in on Herbert Horne and see his fine collection of contemporary woodcuts, from Mantegna and Raphael. We consented, feeling somewhat shy from previous correspondence with the editor of the *Hobby Horse*,—he looked as if he would fly up the chimney and mow like Lucy Ashton. He has squeezed features, eyes that are drawn like a single thickened line repeated, spent complexion and a grin. His effect on mere acquaintance is perhaps given by saying he is not a milk-sop, but a tea-sop—mild, effeminate, with an art aroma, a choiceness. Among his treasures he has the unique drawing of Walter Pater, taken by Solomon about the time of the publication of the *Renaissance*. Sim exclaimed, "What a pity he ever grew a moment older," which made the Horne and Image laugh. But the face is almost beautiful, with the large, clear eyes, that have the reticence of all true limpidity—the fine moulding about the mouth and cheeks, now lost, and the sober, pendant brow. . . . [Later] We fetched our design from Selwyn Image. "O Golden eyes " was out—we stole his little portfolio. . . . afterwards to the Pater's! Walter was not at home, which was unfortunate, as we wished to ask his permission to use his phrase " *The Tragic Mary* " as our title. The sisters could not help us to track this phrase to its article or essay in their brother's works. They were both soberly kind in their friendship. I was never with such slow minds, that crept over a subject as snails over leaves, and yet with a certain comeliness in the unhurried direction they take. Sims says well that Hester and Clara are like Walter in a third or fourth state—borrowing her simile from Rembrandt and his fellow etchers. [Sim evidently did not understand her simile.]

We went to call on the Hobby Horse community. . . . Horne came in and told us that Pater is going to foreswear holiday and finish *Gaston de la Tour*—a longer book than *Marius*. He has struck out the *Essay on Æsthetic Poetry* in *Appreciations* because it gave offence to some pious person—he is getting hopelessly prudish in literature and defers to the moral weaknesses of everybody. Deplorable !

In heavy mist Sim and I stepped into a cab and reached the station, two bundles of shawls—but a great pleasure drew us through the weather to town— Pater's lecture at the London Institution on Prospér Mérimée. Till the appointed time we took refuge in the National Gallery, simply guessing at the outlines of the new pictures and divining the old ones by memory. Yet so perversely human were we, that we started to Finsbury Circus a little after four, though we had come to town early and knew the doors opened at 4.30. To gain time we drove for some distance by the Embankment—the merest block of building, the commonest trailing barge, were soft wonders in the mist. After all we had good seats—at first beside Mrs. Barrington. Selwyn Image came up and told us there was a great opportunity we must not miss—*Orfeo* at the Italian Opera—he had spent all his money on it—Horne sat by Lionel Johnson—a learned snowdrop (his friends say he is so old he has become a child again). He is quite young, quite pale, drooping under book-lore, with curved lids, nearly as fine as Keats' *Hyperion*. Oscar Wilde on our left gave to the tiers of faces his lambent eyes. Arthur Symons was the last to enter. He was charming to watch, with the crossness of isolation on his brows and mouth. His colour dazzles even from a far distance . . . " but I love his beauty passing well " ! !

Pater came forward without looking anywhere, and immediately read his " slips," with no preface, and into the midst of movements and coughs. He never gave his pleasant blue eyes to his audience—there was a weight of shyness athwart them. Above his eyebrows the light so fell as to throw up two ridges over them with strange effect. What determination—almost brutality (in the French sense) there is about the lower part of his face ; yet it is under complete, urbane control. His voice is low and has a singular sensitive resonance in it, an audible capacity for suffering. I always feel that, like every Epicurean, his courteous exterior hides a strong nature, not innocent of barbarism. There is something of Prospér Mérimée in him and a strain of Denys l'Auxerrois, which he expressed in the creation of that northern Zagreus. Wouldn't one give much to surprise the Bacchant in Walter Pater ! The even flow of his reading went on—save when the same voice asked if all could hear. Oscar was visibly delighted to find that Mérimée regretted the decay of assassination. The lecture ended abruptly as it began, abruptly through disregard of any popular customariness.

[It was on this occasion when, after the lecture, Pater said, " I hope you all heard me," Oscar Wilde, because he had seemed to be reading to himself, replied, " We overheard you ; " and Pater, " You have a phrase for everything."]

At half-past three, Fitzroy Street. Horne taught us the meaning of his design for our settee. It is to be in dark mahogany, cushioned and canopied in the fore-ordained lavender. Horne, who always simplifies elements in his decoration, insists on lavender velvet curtains for our book-case.

There is defect in every inch of Horne's face, and yet what pleasant defect—it is used by sensitiveness so well that it becomes interesting and has a kindly appeal.

Tennyson writes much in bed, and as he composes, his nailed fingers destroy the sheets. A whole sheet end has been known to be demolished thread by thread.

Pater advises Horne to write for two hours in bed before rising. Coventry Patmore remarked of the Over-ture to *Tannhäuser*, " It is not intense, it is tense."

Horne said, when we admired his sprays of dry Butcher's Broom, " It has an early Florentine look." We rise to go. " Can you wait a little longer ? Mr. Johnson wants so much to meet you. He wrote about your *Tragic Mary*. He has all your books except one— the *Sappho*, which he cannot get." Mr. Johnson is sum-moned. " He is engaged," says the man-servant. " Oh, . . . say Miss Bradley is here." We talk on—after a while a little figure is seen rooted a yard from the door; he is introduced and flies like a dove to Horne's protective side. The silence is so fearfully ponderous—we feel it will fell us all to the earth—I gasp out nonsense about the settee—the nonsense has the effect of salts, we revive, and discourse on *Hedda Gabler* and *One of Our Conquerors*. Lionel is reviewing the last, and says it is Meredith at his very best. I mentioned the obscurity of the first chapters. Meredith told Lionel that he always wrote his first chapters last—which explains the complex thought of all the distracting first chapters to his novels. Alas, this is false Art, for art, like nature, should draw the issues of her river from the source where the currents are at one. Lionel contrasted Ibsen's women in *Ghosts* with Nesta and Natalie. Charm has been denied to Ibsen and therefore woman does not really live in his plays.

Lionel has a minute being—his face is small with round white features and eyes like the brown shadows in a wood—shy, reticent, yet straying dreamily. The brows are square; a little pursed-up smile, very gentle, comes into view now and then. Sim says he looks like the foal of the Pale Horse. The night before Pater gave his essay on Mérimée, he read Wordsworth at Toynbee Hall. On his way Underground he met Lionel, but would not walk with him to the Hall, on account of his need of " recueillement." He went to a dark city church and remained half an hour steadying nerve and mind.

We looked down at Lionel's feet ; they were fabulous : tiny in girlish shoes and blue silk stockings.

George Moore's *Opinions* were liked—not his *Impressions*. A man's impressions are valueless—nothing unleavened by thought is permanent.

Sim and I strolled into MacLean's gallery. We are fixing our eyes on the Madonna and Child painted by Millet—when I feel the flash of other eyes enter mine— I look quickly for the intruding glance, and see a form turned from me in cape and top hat, that reminds me of the Selwyn Image—the peccant Selwyn. And beside him is a form like the exiled Horne's. The couple seem determined not to have the discomfort of a meeting— we are determined they shall meet us and make the moment inevitable. Then with frank greeting I shake Selwyn's hand—with slow cordiality Horne shakes Sim's, and we go off like the couples in Watteau—only not to talk of love, but the safer subject of Art. . . . Sim comes up and I leave her to forgive Selwyn. She says, " I know what you thought when you saw me :— ' There's that Miss Bradley, and I have never sent her drawing for Queen Mary back.' "—" That's just what I've been thinking all the time. I'll send it to-morrow," was the quick, relieved answer. I found my knight so sick and clayey, that I persuaded Sim to part as soon as the big Bohemian, who lives to his big desires, was soothed and forgiven.

[At Mrs. Chandler Moulton's.] . . . Then Edmund Gosse was introduced—fluent, friendly—a citron man, with the eyes of a wag or a scold under glasses. They were waggish as he mentioned Arthur's [Symons] name.

The little villain had told him we should meet at Dresden. " I said, ' You must be gallant and take them to Saxon Switzerland,' " remarked Gosse. We talked of that " rococo place Dresden "—of how one could hardly go to a wrong place in France and scarcely to a right one in Germany ; we heard that the great charm of Aachen is that it is so near England. Then the roguish littérateur brought the converse again round to Arthur— the genuine love he has for literature, the taint of journalism and interviewing, of which " we must cure him," his poetry still uncertain in quality, his poet's face. Gosse is interested in his nonconformist parentage and education,—" such virginal soil.'' Then we heard of the strong joy of " the Old " when our white book [*Callirhoë and Fair Rosamund*] came out, before he left Warwick Crescent and before he had any personal know- ledge of us. I always feel to grow shallow listening to these sort of things in society—the great sea in my heart goes away.

Gosse has had a tablet put up over the Home, which the Old's friends cherish, while they grudge a thought to De Vere Gardens.

We parted. " You must keep Arthur Symons out of trouble," came as the parting words from above the short cleft chin and beneath the glances of the myopic eyes alive with fun. Once he spoke of us as M.F. Where did he learn those familiar letters ?

Immediately after he left, Sim introduced me to Theodore Watts [Dunton]—he shook hands with the whole Michael and we formed a trio on the sofa. When he heard we were aunt and niece, he exclaimed, " It is more like a fairy tale than ever." He told us at once he was deeply interested in our work, but there was one of our plays with which he quarrelled—*The Cup* [*of Water*]. One day when he and Rossetti were striking out stories, he sketched the Cup story, and Rossetti wrote it down. Watts had evidently felt the pain of one whose ideal possessions are tampered with, and very rightly he objected that we had taken a lyric subject and forced it into drama. He had felt so much about the subject that he would not review the *Canute* volume. He added, "Not that there is not beautiful writing in *The Cup*, as there is in all you write." *Michael Scott's Wooing* was a story told (not of Michael Scott) by Watts' mother. Rossetti had eagerly begun the subject when Watts found it had been treated by the Ettrick Shepherd, and killed Rossetti's muse by saying, "This is not original." I inwardly execrated the good little soul for his honesty, that robbed the *Ballads and Sonnets* of a masterpiece.

He said that he knew Rossetti so intimately that they could sit silent in a room for hours with no discomfort.

He said he should "take it kindly" if we would read his article on *Rossetti* in the New Edition of the *Encyclopædia Britannica*, and the Essay on *English Literature* in the same edition—which he regards as all he has done of value.

He spoke much of Swinburne—who has not had an illness for the last fifteen years, and who "will die when he ceases to write"—of Swinburne's wonderful old mother and equally wonderful old aunt—of Swinburne's fast walking like "that of a tuppenny postman," which pace he, Watts, has been obliged to give up. "Swinburne sees nothing when he walks." Watts spoke of his own early stroll every morning on the common when the rabbits have it to themselves and the birds. He told us how the nightingale keeps to the tracks of the old forests that have disappeared, and sings where it knows the trees have been—with fidelity to an instinctive vision. That voice is among the branches of old days. We told Watts of how, in our country homes, for many years, he was to us "the Man" who writes in the *Athenæum*, and has such a quiet, sure influence on us. He was pleased.

He is a man to deal with poets—a noble nature, full of allowances but true to principle—his intelligence warm, deliberate, sure ; there is affectionate response in his temperament. He is a little creature, he has a gnarled face and deep in it a pair of grave kindly eyes, that see and do not look, rather dark, and somewhat hidden from the light.

Since I first met Mr. Browning I have not met anyone to whom I felt more able to give confidence, who more kindled one's latent gratitude for sympathy.

CHAPTER FIVE

REVISITING CAMBRIDGE

[1] A sudden invitation from Miss Clough on Friday, Feb. 13th. I start.

The green scum of the ditches affects me as I drive to Newnham. Beholding it, I feel how vain it is to try to belong to Oxford. The stones of my heart grow moist with tears and yonder is the Cam and King's ; but it is not these things that draw me, it is the dear, green scum.

I pass a long range of rosy buildings—I pass and am almost thankful. It would be too formidable to go under that gate of honour. But lo, the cabman in his stupidity has passed. He turns the horse's head. We are in Newnham.

And that night I lie in my straight College bed, and, watching the fire-light flicker on the walls, muse on many things. Sixteen years ago I came to Newnham empty-headed, with vague ambition, vague sentiment, the pulpy lyrics of the N.M. [2] in my brain. I return a poet and possessing a Poet. I look forth on the stars and kneel down and give God thanks. . . .

[Next Day.] King's, then a divine walk with Mary Paley Marshall. . . . We speak of George Meredith and his retirement to his Chalet : she says Mr. Marshall can

---

[1] Katherine.   [2] *The New Minnesinger.*

see but little society : *but to live with genius*.   Ah, so the old fires burn.   And so the face with its quaint aspiration and transfiguring smile still holds her.   And she, the inarticulate creature, with her sensitive, excitable temperament and strong, accomplishing brain, is the happy handmaiden of the broken-winged idealist.   Ah well !

In the afternoon Professor Sidgwick calls.   I had been brought before him sixteen years ago—a shivering student—for him to hear how far I had got in declensions, and give me my place in the Latin classes—now he calls to pay homage.   We speak of the *Shorter Poems* of Robert Bridges.   No. 16 he likes—he liked it even though a friend brutally forced him to read it on the spot. For some time he could think of nothing else.   He was indifferent to things about him.   For the *Dramas* he entertains sincere but cold respect.   He would have been proud to be able to write them ;   but he does not care so much about reading them.   He laughed at Edith's expression that Bridges had already secured for himself " a nasty little immortality."   " Yes," he said, " before he has won fame his works are almost curiosities." When we passed on to the consideration of Austin Dobson, he recited with great emphasis, introducing his stammer with malicious emphasis.   He had never himself been guilty of " log-rolling."   Once, after he had expressed pleasure in some book, an editor asked him to review it.   He fell to reconsidering and the review came out rather " mi, mi, mi, mim-mi-xed."   Then the editor felt himself betrayed and was furious.   But the mild Sidgwick bade him look at the middle of the review.   " It does not matter a straw what is in the middle of a review. The beginning and the end are of importance." " So after that, although my words always expressed my convictions, I sometimes varied their order."

Meredith, he agreed, did not speak the truth of his imagination in making Diana deliberately betray her lover, or in the end of *Richard Feverel*. He said he was like Shakespeare—his imagination did not fail. When he went wrong, his imagination went wrong. Sometimes he gave one an idea what really intellectual conversation was.

To tea that night certain students were summoned to meet me. They asked would I make selection. I appointed Miss Stopford Brooke for her beauty. The mischievous Athena strove to match her with fair compeers. We discussed human selfishness, the harm done to one's nature if one forced oneself to take the small nuts [biscuits]—the impossibility of voluntarily choosing such—how " we needs must love the biggest when we see it " ; we " laugh free." I felt it Eastern and magnificent to say unto beauty, " Appear," and it appeared. The damsels themselves were slightly self-conscious.

A nice student conducts me to Mrs. Marshall for lunch. I sit next to Alfred, who talks nobly, struggling with two fat fowls. He again instances Goethe's lyrics as the highest things in art. Simplicity he must have. He is a " worn-out hack." He likes his amusements neat ; he does not like comic elements in a tragic picture. If he dared, he would like to say he thought the Greeks wrong in introducing a farce after the great trilogy. Harper, when the talk is not too big, gives him great delight.

General Booth's scheme he thinks is sound : it is not his scheme, but he himself who is mad. Though he subscribes, he does not advise others to, because he is always afraid by some gross blunder the man should spoil the whole. . . . I said, " I know there must be some great good in the Salvation Army by the faces of the Captains —the men one meets up and down in the world." The divine look came into his face as he assented. He said no really worthless people would stay with Booth under the conditions of no drink, no smoke, no pay—only rations. After lunch more talk.

An Egyptian stool—he takes it up, he does not like queer things, he does not like logical things.

" What does he like ? "—

" Activity, freedom."

A brief call on Mrs. Sidgwick. She is plain and bare as the white of a fresh-cut loaf, nor are her features more interesting than the dull currants up and down the dough. But in the brave plain face there is much to reverence, much in the still presence, with its suggestion of spiritual sweetness, to admire. Oh yes, and her appearing will be most delicate in its divineness hereafter. One feels she is a stronghold of goodness, and her pale wisdom sheds stealthy beams. . . . Packing, bed.

CHAPTER SIX

HERBERT SPENCER

[1] We went to meet Herbert Spencer at lunch, invited by our sweet Miss Bakers. He is a character—with a sharp, kindly, positive face. Hazel eyes of extreme intelligence, tarnished hair just over the ears and under-growing whiskers. But of all faces I find it most difficult to present his in words, even to myself. I cannot fix the characteristic of mouth and nose and look—yet they are not subtle. The brow wholly without artistic or imaginative qualities ; but he wore a black silk skull-cap which hid what in his portrait is magnificent—his domed, philosophic head. He speaks like a man whose every sentence is connected with a general principle—yet there is humour and interest in his talk. It is delicious to hear him making disarmed fun at May's perfect frankness of most sweet folly in conversation. He laughs till the tears flow. I am certain our friends are reforming him, for there is the possibility of disagreeable things in his features. He is very faddy about the small-nesses of eating and drinking and comfort. It was sad to find the great Altruist so self-concerned. For all his giant powers of thought, Robert Browning far surpassed him in moral dignity. At the end of lunch, he said childishly,—" My feet are cold. I must warm them."

[1] Edith, 1890.

131

" We will all turn to the fire and warm our feet," suggested gracious Miss Rosa ; but no !—off he went to his own room and, unless reminded, would have left us without salute, in the oblivion his creature need occasioned. I was shy, for he put on his spectacles to examine a creature so strangely and hopelessly poetic. Sim was mighty audacious. We were talking of picturesque old houses and how beauty endeared a home for us. He said he was devoted to the useful and what tended to life. " We live by admiration, hope and love," rang out Sim's voice. " But if you get a fever and die ? " " Then I shall go on admiring, hoping and loving more and more," was the intrepid answer. " You comfort yourself like that," he said, but his glance appreciated the independence of the stranger. He conversed on slang, under which he includes no misuses of words, only invented expressions which are an end in themselves, with no relation to the history of language and no place in logic. He said the general principle underlying landscape gardening is the emphasis of natural diversities. He was full of the death of the late Japanese Ambassador. It seems he helped the worthy to draw up the new Constitution. On the day when it came in force, the ambassador was assassinated in revenge for his having lifted a curtain with his stick in a temple of the old religion—which curtain he had been warned to respect, as none but the emperor could go beyond it. After Herbert had started to his club, we saw his drawing-room —by permission. It is bare and false in colour : muddy terra-cotta walls ; muddled carpet with suspicion of blue ; fawn curtains looped like the hangings round a hearse, with edges of impure purple and yellow cords; olive-green couch trimmed with violet velvet; chairs of various deadened puces and pinks; Japanese screen with yellow birds; a nymph Egeria on the mantelshelf in front of a pier glass of convolved gilt, also two red glass vases and two Worcester pots with red and purple artificial roses and tart green leaves in them. The same I saw in his bedroom as I passed. His marble bust and a large picture of him are the most interesting objects— also the table given to him by his Japanese Ambassador. On a table in front of the window was a desk and two book-holders. I saw in them Burns' poems, Congreve, a novel by Buchanan, George Eliot's *Life and Letters*— *Middlemarch*. On each side of the mantelshelf hang two landscapes, for one of which he gave the highest price he has ever paid for a picture—£20. It has not the least merit, mon père Spencer! We hear he has a habit of frequently stopping his carriage to feel his pulse; also he raves at the sight of curly parsley about his dishes. When he is wondering what the millions of the suns in the universe can mean, with a religious thrill in his voice, he says in the same breath and tone, "There is fluff coming out of that cushion." Once he was expounding his nebular theory to Miss Rosa, who is rather deaf. She replied about his abstruse subject, while he was saying, "I don't think those sausages were sufficiently done this morning—I will have fish to-morrow."

CHAPTER SEVEN

OSCAR WILDE

[1] Yesterday, Monday, July 21st [1890], we were suddenly summoned to Mrs. Chandler Moulton's last " at home " in Weymouth Street. The first moments were misery and humiliation. Mrs. Moulton introduced us as a poet, as Michael Field, and we stood, our wings vibrating in revolt : fashionable women lisped their enchantment at meeting with us. A moment came when this could be borne no longer. I laid a master-hand on the hostess, and told her to introduce us by our Christian names. After that, George Moore was brought to us. He had heard our names across the room ; but he is a brother—one of the guild of letters. His admiration for *William Rufus* is unbounded. . . . " By Jove, it's fine. . . . Ma foi, it's good. That old fellow with one eye and the passion of the hunting. The scenes in the forest —I have only read the play five or six years ago—the moment it came out—and once—I never read a book twice—yet I see it before me now." He has even proposed it to the Théâtre Libre as one of the English plays to be acted. *Long Ago* has disappointed him. We were engaged on an impossible task. It had not the versification of Keats, still there were some fine things in it. Edith continued the conversation, for I, from far,

[1] Katherine.

recognised Oscar Wilde, and desiring to make his better
acquaintance, found him by my side, talking easily.

He has a brown skin of coarse texture, insensitive surface and no volcanic blood fructifying it from within—
powerful features, a firm jaw and fine head—with hair
that one feels was much more beautiful some years ago.
It is pathetic when bright hair simply grows dull, instead
of turning grey. The whole face wears an aspect of
stubborn sense, and the æsthete is discovered simply by
the look of well-being in the body (soul, take thine ease!),
the soft comfort of the mouth and a lurking, kindly
laziness in the eye. But the dominant trait of that face
is the humour—humour that ridicules and gently restrains
the wilfulness, the hobby-horse passion, the tendency to
individualism, of the rest of the man. There is an Oscar
Wilde smiling ironically at his namesake, the æsthete,
with almost Socratic doubt.

" There is only one man in this century who can write
prose." " You mean Mr. Pater." " Yes—take *Marius
the Epicurean*—any page." We spoke of the difficulties
of writing prose—no good tradition—he had almost
quarrelled with [Theodore ?] Watts because he wanted
to write the language of the Gods [poetry] and Watts
sought to win him to prose. . . .

" French is wonderfully rich in colour-words." We
agreed English was poor in such—I instanced *bluish-grey*
as a miserable effort, and he dwelt on the full pleasantness
and charm of the French colour-words ending in âtre,—
bleauâtre, etc. But we should grapple with this colour
difficulty. It should be our faith that everything in this
world could be expressed in words. I spoke of *L'Embar-*

quement pour Cythère,[1] of the impossibility of expressing what was happening on that fairy water. . . . By the by, he told me a whole story of the Infanta of Velasquez in the Louvre, with a pink rose in her hand. He was bent on learning the history of that rose, and found it in a portrait near at hand, of a dwarf. Now the princess—let history go off with her rags—had given the dwarf that rose—the dwarf was dancing before the court, and she took it from her hair and flung it to him. He went away in rapture at the consciousness of her love . . . then the doctrine of doubles, and inattention on my part—ultimately the dwarf discovers from a mirror his own hideousness and when they come in and try to rouse him to dance, lies stretched responseless. He is dead—dead, they tell the princess, of a broken heart. She replies, going away—" Let those who love me have no hearts."
. . . " Fiction—not truth—I could never have any dealings with truth—if truth were to come unto me, to my room, he would say to me, ' You are too wilful.' And I should say to him, ' you are too obvious.' And I should throw him out of the window." Michael : "You would say to *him*. Is not truth a woman ? " " Then I could not throw her out of the window ; I should bow her to the door."

We agreed—the whole problem of life turns on pleasure—Pater shows that the hedonist—the perfected hedonist—is the saint. " One is not always happy when one is good ; but one is always good when one is happy." He is writing two articles at present in the *Nineteenth Century* on the *Art of Doing Nothing*. He is

[1] *Sight and Song.*

at his best when he is lying on a sofa thinking. He does not want to do anything ; overcome by the " maladie du style "—the effort to bring in delicate cadences to express exactly what he wants to express—he is prostrate. But to think, to contemplate. . . . Henceforth he is determined to write in language that will only be understood by minds artistically trained. The writing shall not be obscure—quite clear, but its meaning will be seized only by artists. He once wrote a story of Spain—a story in black and silver—in which he endeavoured to give something of the dignity and gloom of Spanish life— like heavy black velvet cushions—and this story, when translated into French, came out pink and blue. It taught him that after all there were certain colour-forces in English—a power of rendering gloom—not in French.

He has a theory it is often genius that spoils a work of art—a work of art that should be intensely self-conscious. He classed the Brontës, Jane Austen, George Sand, under the head " genius." This was when I said to him that there was one sentence of Mr. Pater's which I would not say I could never forgive, because I recognised its justice ; but from which I suffered, and which was hard to bear— that in which he speaks of the scholarly conscience as male—adding I did not remember where the passage occurred. " Yes," he said, " it is in *Appreciations*, in the essay on *Style*, page 7—left-hand side,—at the bottom " —and in all this memory the one tiny error was that the page is page 8. . . . Genius, he continued, killed the Brontës. Consider the difference between *Jane Eyre* and *Esmond*. Owing to their imperfect education, the only works we have had from women were works of genius.

" What's that pretty book you have in your hand ? "
" A book from our hostess." He opened it—and must
have seen the inscription to " Michael Field." Later on
he said he would send me his fairy tales—I gave simply
the address, Blackberry Lodge, Reigate. . . . I think
he understood.[1]

Plato's idea of heaven is simply one of beautiful
moments that enter into immortality, of their nature. . . .

He, when he gets to heaven, would like to find a number of volumes in vellum that he would be told were his.

What I like about him is the sense of bien-être, of
comfort, he conveys to the brain. All that a woman does
to a man by her presence on the hearth, or by the tea-
table, he does to the brain—neither lulling it nor stimulat-
ing it—introducing about it a climate of happiness, so
that it is twice itself, freed from the depression of fragility
or chill. . . . We mourned that the English people do
not live to art—have indeed no direct contact with it.

His voice, Edith says, is a bony one, and this is true.
His body is too well tended and looks like a well-kept
garden ; his spirit, one would say, was only used to
irrigate it. Blustersome torrent passing down its craggy
human bed—with him it is conveyed by skilled labour in
conduits for the ornamentation of his pleasure ground.

[2] We visit Oscar Wilde—being received by Mrs. Wilde
in turquoise blue, white frills and amber stockings. The
afternoon goes on in a dull fashion till Oscar enters. He

[1] This must mean that he had hitherto not known who Miss
Bradley was.
[2] Edith.

wears a lilac shirt and heliotrope tie, a great primrose pink
—very Celtic combination, ma foi ! His large presence
beams with the " Heiterkeit " of a Greek God that has
descended on a fat man of literary habits.

He sat down and told us that in his belief our *Tragic
Mary* and Rossetti's Poems were the two beautiful books
(in appearance) of the century—but he was going to
surpass us, and would send us an early copy of his *Tales*,[1]
to make us " very unhappy." He was delicious on the
illustrations, that are not taken from anything in the book,
only suggested by it—for he holds that literature is more
graphic than art, and should therefore never be illustrated
in itself, only by what it evokes.

He was full of the success of his *Duchess of Parma* in
America, and was beginning to feel that he must make
something and go to Paris ! He met Forbes [Robertson]
with much love, and introduced him to us at once—a
man of bony intelligence, with sensitive, thin features,
using as little flesh as possible for their expression. A
gay, charming time ! Bien-être expands from Oscar's
irradiated corpulence—from his mossy voice, the way his
hands fall and move, and from his courteous eyes, where
vivacity springs up round heaviness.

Wed. May 25th, 1892.

[At Mr. Benson's]

As we are looking at this Costa, Oscar comes up. He
shakes hands with Mrs. Costelloe, and therefore I put

[1] *A House of Pomegranates.* Designed and decorated C. Ricketts
and C. H. Shanon, 1891.

out my hand, which he takes (afar off) and never addresses a single word to me after. I have not often seen such rudeness—he is not of the men who can be rude offensively and yet escape. There is no charm in his elephantine body, tightly stuffed into his clothes—with a grass-gorged effect—no charm in his great face and head of unselect Bohemian cast—save the urbanity he can adopt or the intelligence with which he can vitalise his ponderousness. When he shows himself as a *snob* he is disgustingly repulsive. We were not well dressed, as the day had begun with rain—we do not belong to the fashionable world—so Oscar rolls his shoulders toward us. When next I meet him in my choicest French hat, I will turn my back on him, and that decisively. The artist strain in him is crossed with the vulgar respectable—Gods and women cannot endure such a cross. His conduct hurts Mrs. C. indirectly ; she conveys her reprehension to us.

Entry by Edith.
" The Duchess of Malfi " at the Opera Comique !
Fitzgerald gloats over executions behind us ; Le Gallienne wanders about like a young Dante in the shades ; Oscar sits as if blowing bubbles of enjoyment, so pervasive are his smiles—they float through the milieu. . . .

At the Master Builder. Entry by Edith.
Oscar is in a box, allowing the people to see him and the silver knob of his cane. He is with his wife. My

Love remarks he has a "well-nourished head." Yes, and that is not only a criticism of his appearance but of his work. It is well-nourished—its force comes from outside. Flaubert and Maeterlinck have fed *Salomé*.

Oscar seems to exhale Paris and this atmosphere makes one feel easy and gay to look at him. He watches the stage impassively but with intentness. Our claps help his and those of a few others to bring the curtain up at the end of Act 4.

[1893]   THE COTTAGE,
                                    GORING ON THAMES.
DEAR MICHAEL FIELD,

In the case of the Independent Theatre you have to rely chiefly on actors who are out of an engagement—those who have engagements being occupied or away. Tell Grein to select only young actors—there are possibilities of poetry and passion in the young—and picturesqueness also, a quality so valuable on the stage. Shun the experienced actor—in poetic drama he is impossible. Choose graceful personalities—young actors and actresses who have charming voices—that is enough. The rest is in the hands of God and the poet.

I look forward to listening to your lovely play recited on a rush-strewn platform, before a tapestry, by gracious things in antique robes, and, if you can manage it, in gilded masks.

So, you see I have nothing to tell you, except that I am your sincere admirer,

                                    OSCAR WILDE.

[1894]
DEAR MICHAEL FIELD,
              write to Miss Elizabeth Marbury,
                  c/o Low's Exchange,
                      New York City, U.S.A.
She manages all my plays. I have written to her. I
am a wretch not to have answered sooner—but I have no
excuse ; so you will forgive me.

Your third act [1] was quite admirable—a really fine
piece of work—with the touch of terror that our stage
lacks so much—I think the theatre should belong to the
furies—Caliban and Silenus, one educated and the other
sober, seem now to dominate, in their fallen condition,
our wretched English drama.

                                          OSCAR WILDE.

       [1] *A Question of Memory.*

CHAPTER EIGHT

JOHN RUSKIN

[The next extract is best introduced by the following letters from Ruskin to Katherine Bradley fifteen to twenty years earlier. They will recall Edith's exclamation in Chapter IV, on learning that he had made Miss Heaton exchange the triptych of Paolo and Francesca, as an unfit possession for a woman, against one of his own Rossettis : " 'There was a speckled silliness in Ruskin's dealings with women. . . .' "]

BRANTWOOD,
7th Jan. 1875.

MY DEAR MADAM,

I am grateful for your subscription [1]—more for your letter, which is every way helpful to me. I am quite sure that in a little while, you will trust me as much as I trust myself, or more—and though I like to be trusted, I like better to be thanked for work done, provided I am of the same mind as the thankful person, as to the thing that pleased them, being really good.

[1] As a member of the Guild of St. George.

Now *you* thank me for what indeed I am glad to know I have done for you. . . . .

Ever truly yours,

J. RUSKIN.

[Six months later Katherine sent him a copy of *The New Minnesinger.*]

OXFORD,
10*th June* 1875.

MY DEAR MADAM,

I was very grateful for your letter and book : and would fain have answered—many a time I have tried to answer such questions for myself.

But I may say at once—let children read the story of Christ—as any other history. Tell them—you do not know if it is true—that some parts are without doubt misrepresented. But let them know what is said—and find out, by their own personal effort—what is *for them* true,—that the character of Christ is lovely—and his words infinitely kind and wise and that the Bible if they read it *candidly*, will guide them into all accepting truth.

Ever faithfully yours,

J. RUSKIN.

LONDON,
13*th January* 1876.

DEAR MISS BRADLEY,

I entirely like your letter and shall be heartily glad to have you in our Companionship. But I do not, from your letter, clearly understand your position. You do not speak of parents—only of ' home '. That home only apparently three years old in Solihull. Supposing your parents approve—and that you are independent—or used to acting according to your own judgement—you may be one of the usefullest of Companions. My best but one or two are women; but nearly all poor. The poorest may come—but of all who can afford it, the tenth of their income is required; this is my primal test of earnestness. And you may forward St. George's work earnestly, without this sacrifice, by merely understanding it and explaining it, if you have other channels of charity which you think have better claims on you. Of your personal work I will tell you more when you have told me your exact position.

Most truly yours,
J. RUSKIN.

LONDON,
17th Jan. 1876.

MY DEAR MISS BRADLEY,

I am most happy to have your kind answer, enclosing your sister's letter; and I shall be very proud of you for a Companion; being especially pleased by what you say of the sorrow of independence and the comfort of obedience : but both your letters are quietly strong and right throughout. You shall do exactly what you feel easily able to do or happily desirous to do; and as to contribution—your present gifts and charities must of course not be interfered with, nor need you in any wise be anxious about the more or less—only pardon me if I take notice of the expression used twice in your letters, of possible interruption of your income by accident. Women should always make their income *entirely* safe, however narrow. Let me strongly recommend ' Consols ' to you—as the only right security. Sound sleep and three per cent are far better than the most brilliant dreams and six and seven.

I see from your sister's letter that you amuse—or exert —yourself in verse writing. Some of the best poetry of the modern times is by women (Mrs. Browning, Miss Ingelow and Miss Proctor). But (this is only a request not an order) might I know a little what you write *about* ?

Here is a tiny order however. You nearly write a beautiful hand—a little effort will make it quite so—and the difference between ' nearly ' and ' quite ' is in art— *all* the difference.

Forgive me for cutting out a piece of your pretty letter and see notes on the last page, remembering always that my writing is only to show you how not to write.

. . . always faithfully your servant,

JOHN RUSKIN.

[Katherine sent him a copy of a piece of a creed supplied by him.]

LONDON,
20th Jan. 1876.

DEAR MISS CATHERINE,

. . . to believe that much will help you to understand and reverence all human souls that are kind and sincere

—Turks, Jews, Infidels [1] or heretics—and to have better peace in your own. You would not laugh at my not having read your book if you knew—as I hope you will soon know—how much too serious my life is to be spent in reading poetry (unless prophetic). But I did accidentally open the *Minnesinger* and liked a bit or two of it —and I don't think I threw it into the waste-paper basket —generally the receptacle without so much as opening, of all books of poetry sent me by the authors.

You know German, I suppose then? and probably music—How much of the last? I want a great deal of help in that.

Ever faithfully yours,

J. RUSKIN.

[1] In the sense meant by our church.

[He thanks her from London, Jan. 22nd, 1876, for a cheque for " five pounds—very pretty to see in its writing and purpose."]

. . . Yes. You have misunderstood me concerning poetry—more than I should have thought it likely if you have ever read much of me. Nevertheless, I believe life will become serious to you soon, in another sense. To me it is the work of the helmsman on the lips of Charybdis —and the grief of one bound, by the isle of the Sirens. And besides do you not know that in the word ' prophetic ' I included more than is needful for *all* our lives.

Ever faithfully and gratefully yours,

J. RUSKIN.

Have you read much of Carlyle?

BRANTWOOD,
8*th June* 1876.
MY DEAR MISS BRADLEY,
    You are certainly an accepted Companion—and your
name is 28th on the roll at Corpus [Christi College].
Your letter told me I need not answer, if it was only by
mistake the star was omitted.
    —I should have hesitated in accepting you, had I
thought you had so little understanding of me, or trust
in me, as to imagine I would speak of any woman without
cause, publicly, as I have spoken of Miss Cobbe—I have
no time—nor much will to explain to you why I do so
—but be assured no word is ever uttered by me, far less
written, without some knowledge and stern purpose in
such matters.
                                    Ever truly yours,
                                        J. RUSKIN.

BRANTWOOD,
11*th June* 1876.
DEAR MISS BRADLEY,
    In utter haste, I can only give you peace of mind about
' orders '.   None are *positively* such, unless given directly
under my own hand—or marked as such distinctly in
Fors.¹   Even the dress order might be relaxed on
occasion—unless confirmed by private word.   I will
write again about it, and tell you more of Miss Cobbe.
It is not the wrongness of her views, but her insolence
in proclaiming them—contrary to St. Paul's order.   " I
    ¹ *Fors Clavigera*, the magazine of the Guild of St. George.

suffer not a woman to teach "—which is deadly in her
character and so harmful in its effects.

Ever most truly yours,
J. RUSKIN.

VENICE,
12th September 1876.

DEAR MISS BRADLEY,

I have kept your nice letter by me, wishing to answer
it—but always too tired.   I only wanted to say one thing
—that I don't expect my Companions to look nice : but
to bear the pain of looking not nice, so far as it is necessary, as the form of ' sackcloth '—and a very gentle one
surely, not expressive of monastic privation.   But in a
little while you will be able to teach your dressmaker to
cut neatly—or, all I shall say is—more shame for you
and more need for this law of St. George.

You were quite right in much of the feeling you had
towards Miss Cobbe ; she is a very worthy and conscientious person, but has the unfortunate modern habit
of talking violently of things she knows nothing whatever
about.   I only called her a clattering saucepan—a saucepan is a very good thing in its place ; but not when it
clatters.   That is very sweet of you to tell me of your
little nieces.   I long for time to write more of the
educational part of *Fors*, but am still dragged into con-
troversy on leading principles.   Have patience with me
and believe me ever faithfully yours,

J. RUSKIN.

VENICE,
16*th* Jan. 1877.

MY DEAR KATHERINE,

. . . I am delighted at what you tell me of the effect of your Companionship upon you. No matter how little you can do—if only you see clearly for whom you do it and are daily more earnest in doing what you can.

But how *can* you see clearly for whom you do it if —with the loss of your friend—all Christmas delight in the old sense is gone ?

Is not the entire meaning of Christmas to assure you that your friend is with you always ? Christmas *means* —the News of Eternal Life ; and of the First Born of Every Creature. If you have not the joy of it still— you never had it rightly. Make new friends—be the friend of the friendless. You may have angels to dine with you, and eat apples without paring—any Christmas Eve you choose.

I have two letters of yours to answer—to both I can but answer : Be not afraid, only believe and *do*.

I could tell you much that would be profoundly interesting to you that has lately happened to me : but you will see the consequent change in the tone of *Fors* and I hope the greater comfort in it. Send your sub-scription to Wm. Walker. . . .

Always faithfully yours,
J. RUSKIN.

VENICE,
8th Feb. 1877.

MY DEAR KATHERINE,

In a spell of technical business I can only answer your beautiful letter with questions. Chiefly is that lovely sonnet really your own—if so—it's not all about an old friend—surely? tell me more of your life.

—You might have made more of that *Fors*. Is St. Ursula's sending me her love, nothing? But another love was sent with it in the private message.

—Yes, the *De Officiis* is entirely admirable—but I respect it as a work rather of moral study than of true heart : it *ought* to be known to every teaméd schoolboy. I should have insisted on it more, but thought they would despise it in familiarity.

There is no need for your putting the devil into your creed. All I say is, you'll find there *is* such a person, as you find there are wild beasts, when you fairly set forth in pilgrimage. To disbelieve in him, in the dangerous sense, is to disbelieve in Evil—to say there is no Wrong! Therefore not to fight it. But there is no occasion to think of him—till you feel him : remember only to be *vigilant*, you may think of pleasanter things.

Ever your affectionate friend,
J. RUSKIN.

Yes—the lines are Blake's. You should have his poetry as a dear book-friend.

VENICE,

21st Feb., 1877.

MY DEAR KATHERINE,

It is very wonderful to me being cared for so much. Different it seems to me, from what I have read of other men—when they became in any wise esteemed by their writings—they don't seem to have been so much loved as I am—by friends I know not. And I am thankful—but yet—my life has been like your own—only it has been longer in the ' forest shadows,' and can now take—for itself, no pleasure in spring, in this world. The private message St. Ursula sent me was from someone who is with her—among her maidens—one who used to send me flowers sometimes. *Sesame and Lilies* was written for her—the vignette in *Fors*, July 1875, is in memory of her death :—I think she was very happy on Christmas Day, and coaxed St. Ursula to be good to me, and make *me* happy too.

But it is difficult, inconceivably, to live for that world, and I know not how far it is meant that we should— only, my real pleasure as far as any is left me now in this, is not in being loved, though of course it pleases me in a kind of melancholy way—but in being useful, above all in teaching or comforting people who can be easily taught—or greatly comforted. And though it is very sweet to me that you and your little Amy (you see how rightly she was taught to give me the sallows and violets) love me—still, it really gives me more delight that you believe in what I am teaching—and ask " what is to be done with the old clothes." This is just one of the principles which we cannot and should not wholly carry

out till the society is a practically united and acting body.
If you see good, you may always at present break this
rule, because, it is better to give old clothes than none.
But when all are rightly and simply dressed, then—
everybody's old clothes should be done with whatever
the final rags are now done with—parts of the material
would be of various use—the rest—burned.

. . . The verses are very good—better in idea than
rhythm. But the sonnet is the loveliest. I really had no
idea it was for me and am very proud of it.

As ever, affectionately yours,

J. RUSKIN.

VENICE,
4th April, 1877.

MY DEAR KATHERINE,

I was very grateful for your letter and would fain
have written some true answer to its sympathy. But I
must not think of what I have lost or may regain : my
only duty at present is to keep myself in active work and
thought for the present needs of people round me. Nor
must *you* allow yourself to wish for the quiet yonder ;
but make a quiet here, in patience and the gathering-in
of good harvest fruit.

I am very much pleased with your writing and want to
know if you can tell me how best to teach children such
plain round hand. Also, when you like to be in your
own little attic, without trying to do good to anybody,
what *do* you like to try to do ?

Ever affectionately yours,

J. R.

VENICE,
15*th April*, 1877.

MY DEAR KATHERINE,

. . . I am anxious and surprised at your having " given up music sorrowfully "—What for ? I don't understand what you say of your hands either—how are they " almost messengers of Satan " ? And I *should* like you to give up dreaming, and writing verses as far as you possibly can. By way of soft fall from such a Paradise, could you not take up any poet whom you really delighted in, and consider what he has said for or against St. George's principles—and what other sound advice he has given touching human life. . . .

Ever affectionately and gratefully yours,

J. RUSKIN.

BRANTWOOD,
23*rd Aug.* 1877.

MY DEAR KATHERINE,

I promised you a letter " to-morrow "—but on the morrow I found I had nothing to say—nor has anything to say occurred to me yet. For the truth is that no cheap art of any kind is of the least use. All modern stuff for children being worse than nothing. The prints of the Arundel Society would be of use, and the illustrations of the Lord's Prayer by Ludwig Richter ; and in general any books on natural history published fifty years ago, contain plates of examplary honesty and care. Donovan's *British Insects*, for instance, cut up, would furnish a hundred schools with models of exquisite engraving and colouring. But of figure subjects, it is almost impossible to find anything that would not vitiate the taste. Some of the chromo-lithographs from Birket Foster are however pretty and harmless.

But your friend may rest assured that *nothing* of any importance can be done in England in this direction. Does he suppose that what the child sees for an hour or two in school can neutralise the deadly poison of every sight it sees in the streets and in its home? There is nothing to be thought of at present but wholesome and honest life—and out of that—taste will come—never that out of taste.

Ever your affectionate Master,
J. RUSKIN.

OXFORD,
Christmas, 1877.

DEAR KATHERINE,

Your letter telling me you have lost your God and found a Skye Terrier is a great grief and amazement to me. I thought so much better of you. What do you mean? That you are resolved to receive only good at God's hands, and not evil? Send me word clearly what has happened to you—then perhaps I'll let you talk of your dogs and books.

Ever faithfully yours,
J. R.

OXFORD,
28th Dec. 1877.

MY DEAR KATHERINE,

I will be perfectly gentle with you—but you must be called a goose—because you are one ; and you must be called a false disciple—because you are one. When you called me master—I understood that if in *any* thing you would obey me it would be in the choice of books— and you had your books indicated for you in *Fors,* enough to serve—*Bible—Dante—Scott—Shakespeare—Goldsmith* —you chose instead—without telling me a word—to read these miserable modern wretches—I call them wretches for their bad English—their impudence, and their ignorance—not their impiety. I REVERENCE Voltaire ! but Voltaire is a grand and thoughtful Man—Harrison and Clifford—paltry puppies whom I simply don't chastise as they deserve in pity to them—Knowles (of the 19th Century) begged off Clifford, because he was in a consumption—or he would have had it hot, before now.

For yourself. I scarcely know how to deal with you. You are *too* stupid—saying I don't care for your grief— You double-feathered little goose ! ! Suppose a child whom I had sent on a perfectly safe road, deliberately jumped off into a ditch—wallowed there with the pigs without telling me—got torn by their tusks—and then came to me all over dung and blood—saying, " I didn't care "—what could I do—or say ?

I have no time to-day to write more—and am really too scornful of you—and of the egotism and shallowness which can be consoled by the love of a dog and by an entirely lying jingle of a song about fairies, for the loss of a God !—to write what could be of use to you.

Yet I love dogs fifty times better than you do—that's another of your stupid misunderstandings.

I don't believe you have *read* your *Fors* at all, only dipped into it—or you could not—dared not—have thought—or said—that to your disappointed and disobeyed Master.

OXFORD,
30th Dec. 1877.

MY DEAR MISS BRADLEY,

The first sentence of your letter, that my " words are wild and whirling " [1]—is as true—as it was of the person to whom it is first spoken.

You simply do not understand any of my words or ways—nor can I explain them to you. I see, however, that you could not but misread " I do not care how bitter it is "—which was spoken precisely in the sense of a surgeon, who—looking suddenly at the wounds of a soldier moaning in pain—would say to him—" Yes— yes—I don't care how much the wounds hurt you—but is there any place where they *don't* hurt you—it is THERE where Death is."

Now—exactly in the same way—I say to you, I don't care how much pain you are in—but that you should be such a fool as coolly to write to me that you had ceased to believe in God—and had found some comfort in a dog—*this* is *deadly*. And of course I have at once

[1] Horatio of Hamlet, Act I, Scene V.

to put you out of the St. George's Guild—which *primarily*
refuses atheists—not because they are wicked but because
they are fools. " The Fool hath said in his heart," etc.
   You go on from folly to folly—in your present letter
—chiefly in thinking that when I talk of " chastising " a
man I mean only to abuse him—when did you know
me abuse *any* one ? You think YOURSELF abused indeed
just now—but that is simply because you thought yourself very clever—and are astonished that I think nothing
of your poetry—and less than nothing of your power of
thought. Re-read every word of my letter. Read also
the story of St. Theodore in *Fors*—and tell me if you
ever read it before. As for answering Harrison—I know
Harrison—and challenged him in *Fors*. He declined the
challenge—as you could have seen in *Fors*—had you
read it. I tell you to read it now not expecting you to
obey me—but most assuredly—I cease—if you do not
—to consider you even my friend—Companion you can
of course be no more, but I am always faithfully yours,

J. R.

   [Enclosed in the same envelope as the foregoing letter.]

MY DEAR MISS BRADLEY,
   Read the enclosed with the best patience you can.
And—for postscript—this.
   I know the arguments of Atheists from the seventh
century before Christ down to this hour.
   I know many men of splendid faculty among Atheists.
Not one of perfect health of brain. All are deficient in
some essential quality of human intellect.

This I could show—to persons who do not need it to be shown—to persons who have the faculties which Atheists have not. But I never would condescend to argue with an Atheist himself. If I did—it would be with choice of a strong-facultied Atheist like Lucretius, for examination—Harrison and Clifford are mere school-boys—and I only noticed Harrison at all because he was a personal friend, for whom I had much affection. When he declined the contest in the terms I offered him—I for some time let him pass in peace—but of late his writings and Clifford's have become so pestiferous that I *should* have taken the pains to chastise both—had not Mr. Knowles told me Clifford was ill.

WINDSOR CASTLE,
2nd Jan. 1878.

MY DEAR KATHERINE,

I have not been able to open my letters till this morning—nor can I yet read yours—but I have glanced at it and see its earnestness and tenderness—and will be all I can to you. But you must not be grieved at ceasing to be a Companion of mine—poor child—when you were not grieved at ceasing to be a companion of the God and Father of all—and of the angels—and of the multitude of the saints made perfect—! Think, my dear—why it is you are grieved so much for this wretched nothingness of *farther* loss—having lost immortality and Deity—you lament—WHAT—after that?

You lose a kingdom and cry for breaking a tea-cup?

—I can't write more—only, my dear, understand that

the life of everything for St. George's Company is based
on the full sincerity of Faith in its whole creed.   No one
can join it on other terms or remain in it.   Keep this
letter—I may want a sentence or two copied—for others
to read.

Ever faithfully yours,

J. Ruskin.

I will write again when I have read your letter.

LONDON,
4th Jan. 1878.

MY DEAR KATHERINE,

I am so very glad—yes—you will find flowers and
children different creatures now.   Can't say a word more
to-day.

Ever affectionately yours,

J. R.

OXFORD,
10th Jan. 1878.

MY DEAR KATHERINE,

You shall have no trouble caused you by any use of
my letter.   I will not ask for any part of it, still less
refer to any part of yours—nor shall I have occasion to
touch on any subject connected with it in this next *Fors*.

Do not be discouraged at the difficulty of getting back
—when you have been two or three days wandering, you
don't return in two or three minutes.   That you are *on
your way* is all that God cares for.

You cannot read too much Mallock—all he says is admirable and logical as Clifford is otherwise. But I should like you to give up all metaphysical reading at present, be content with history—poetry (suppose you try to understand the Wars of the Roses? as relating to the religion of England—and indicating its corruption.) —Have you read George Herbert's works—Miss Edgeworth's? or Goldsmith's?

Ever affectionately yours,

J. R.

BRANTWOOD,

9th Feb. 1878.

DEAR KATHERINE,

I am so very glad to have your letter—and to know that you are happier—and that you see what you have to guard against in the future. You must certainly read no modern metaphysics. As much Plato as you like—and as much Emerson as you like—and almost any books you like from Mudie's that give you real knowledge of either persons or things—but none that profess to account for or explain things.

You must be greatly on your guard against dreaming. It is worse than the most profitless idleness—greatly dangerous to persons of your form of head (prominent forehead) and leads sometimes to the entire destruction of their health.

You have so much perception of natural beauty that I do not see why the conquest of this morbid intellectual tendency should be difficult to you.

But to give up absolutely the wish to know more than any child knows about God—and to be resolved whatever woods you get lost in, never to doubt He knows where you are and will keep you safe—and to think only what He has bid, by the mouths of all his servants —will lead your thoughts into healthy current, whatsoever you study. You know, you can't expect to get rid of all the effects of being left independent (that is unhelped) by human teachers at once—and must still say for a little while " Seek thy Servant."

Ever affectionately yours,
J. R.

BRANTWOOD,
St. Valentine 1878.

MY DEAR KATHERINE,

I am greatly pleased with your letter . . . and you shall have a special answer to most of it, but that is impossible to-day.

To the disappointment in my neglect of your poetry time will bring more balm than you at present fancy. . . .

Thursday afternoon.

MY DEAR MASTER,

I have heard from your secretary this afternoon that you are ill. I must not, dare not, tell you what this news is to me. Only—may God bless you, and if it may be, let you stay with us. I do not feel as if I could be left alone now. I hope my need of you is making

me over-fearful. But I will try to be quiet and faithful.
I have asked Mr. Hilliard to give you this, and to let me
know how you are. And I am *always*,
My dear Master,
Your own devoted servant,
KATHERINE.

P.S. I cannot write save brokenly and am far too sad
really to write at all :—but, if some of the failures of life
deepen now its long shadows, do let it comfort you to
think of what you have been, and must always be to
the few human creatures who have loved and trusted
you. What was the work of the Great Master Himself
but to gather together " a little flock " and they, though
one denied, and some doubted, and all greatly misunderstood, did not forget.

BRANTWOOD,
9th Sep. 1878.

MY DEAR KATHERINE,

" To-morrow week " will be here, before I know where
I am—not that people should expect—ever to know
that !—nor where my wits are—either. But I really *am*
—here, again—I believe—or—there—as people say—
pretty nearly myself—and I shall be able to write you a
word or two again, sometimes, but must not, very
positively—write for many a day—of any grave things.
Though always as truly as ever and as affectionately yours,

J. RUSKIN.

Sincere thanks for your letter. I am better than this
idle note would perhaps permit you to think.

BRANTWOOD,
15th Sep. 1878.

MY DEAR KATHERINE,

I fear my short note might rather frighten you than comfort you. I must send you a word or two more, both of thanks for your affectionate letter, and to ask you, very gravely, to set yourself to find out how little of a Wilderness, and how much of a Paradise, this world may be, whoever is taken from it, or whoever left.— Unless indeed they have been part of our home and hope —for then, to us, of course they are irreplaceable. But whatever I have been to you—in books, both I, and wiser and better men, may always be, whether we live or die ; and what the imagination of me, as your friend, is to you, you may far more easily and happily make reality in the friendship of myriads of kind and dear persons, who never write books, but are none the less worthy of love—nor the less able to return it. I think I told you however I was not going to leave England— and I don't think there is any more fear of my being taken from it, than there was before my illness, or must be—for anybody on the point of 60.

Ever affectionately yours,
J. RUSKIN.

BRANTWOOD,
19th Dec. 1878.

MY DEAR KATHERINE,

I am very grateful for your sweet letter—but I can't answer its questions, for Heaven knows what I may or

may not do ; the illness having taken away both confidence in myself, and power of resolution. I'll try to
be as useful to my friends as I can ; it will be little
enough at best, but I can still write a letter quietly. I
am very glad, on the whole, to see the tone of your
mind in your note and to hear of your good work on
worthy books. But I shall not be satisfied till I hear
of your being more cheerful. I hold cheerfulness, every
day, more and more a duty—for people who *have grace*
to be sorrowful. Then they must be, " as sorrowful, yet
always rejoicing." I'm very sulky myself, always—but
never without self-reproach.

Ever affectionately yours,

J. RUSKIN.

BRANTWOOD,

22nd April 1879.

My DEAR KATHERINE,

I don't write because I must be in the open air all day,
after my bit of book or drawing is done—you are all
ENTIRELY wrong in wanting comradeship—nothing will
come of that but German nonsense. Love, Justice and
Mercy—not each other, unless you necessarily come into
the joint work. Do you suppose I meant St. George's
Guild to be a little Bethel or Agapemone ? The next
beggar or babe is your " comrade "—and comrade
enough. But all the same I'm always faithfully
yours,

J. RUSKIN.

BRANTWOOD,
7th Feb. 1880.

MY DEAR KATHERINE,

. . . Mr. Girdlestone will help you much about usury. The proper thing is that a Government Officer, a true Chancellor of the Exchequer, should receive all monies the people can spare—be answerable for them—as for the Queen's Crown—to the last farthing—be ready to repay them in full—at any instant—and use them meanwhile in all good ways (paying *no* interest but answerable for the whole principal). But the deepest devil of existing usury is that only rascals borrow—and you can never be sure of your money on loan! In the meanwhile put your money in the funds and take all the interest the government will give you. I'll be answerable for your conscience to it. Trust me—in matters of conscience, as you have in matters of faith.

Ever affectionately yours,

J. RUSKIN.

LONDON,
22nd Mar. 1880.

MY DEAR KATHERINE,

That your desire to do right would " die out " if I did not think this that or the other—of you, is precisely what makes me so careless of you—I hope some day you will be blessed with a will of your own. For " love " as you call it—I have girl friends who would die for me at a word—and who don't care what *I* think of them—when they have a duty to do.

Ever affectionately yours,

J. R.

[Katherine was staying with cousins in London.]

BRANTWOOD,
23rd Mar. 1880.

MY DEAR KATHERINE,

I cannot in any brief words express to you the annoyance and sorrow given me by your utter folly in supposing that—after living forty years in London—I have so few friends there caring for me as to have the home of a ten days' visit at my own disposal—or that if they were so—I should think any of them well spent in talking to a sentimental disciple, who supposes herself—for all her sentiment—qualified to judge by my obedience to her ORDERS whether I am like my books or not.

Repent and be quiet.

Faithfully yours,

J. R.

BRANTWOOD,
24th June, 1880.

MY DEAR KATHERINE,

I came just now in sorting letters on one of yours dated " Thursday night "—it talks very prettily about my birthday—and asks if it will be right for you to lay by £100 for old age. Certainly—the rightest thing you can do with it. And it will, I should think, be safer in stocks than elsewhere—you may give the interest to charity—or use it in any way—so only you know what it *is*, the taxation of the people.

Ever affectionately yours,

J. RUSKIN.

BRANTWOOD (undated).

MY DEAR KATHERINE,

Your fate seems to be to know at present nothing but the rough side of me. Do not meddle in any drawing business—you can only do mischief, knowing nothing about it. These flower drawings, are, alas—utterly valueless—they were not even good practice—the poor artist never having had elementary teaching to enable him to direct his work and going on therefore for ever at the same level. Please also observe that you are still as wrong as ever in talking about finding me " gracious." You might as well talk about finding flint gracious. It will strike fire for good or evil to you—as you use it and understand it. I am always the same—always busy —always rough—if bothered *uselessly*—always kind—if kindness be possible.

Had I read your last page first—I should probably not have answered thus much—

Are you indeed so mad and so vile as to allow yourself to " hate " people merely because they won't let you plague them ?—and because they care more for worthier persons ? Few whom I have ever cared for at all— have been so little worthy.

[This is the last letter in the pile arranged by Katherine ; it is marked, apparently at a later_date, FALSE.]

[In 1893 they were staying at Neum Crag, near Amble-side, the home of Albert Fleming, a disciple of Ruskin's, who had started a village handicrafts school there.]

[1] We were to have gone a mountain expedition, but Frank is not well. So Albert confides the Brantwood tragedy. Foolish old Ruskin is a modern King Lear : some years ago he made over Brantwood, the furniture and pictures, by deed of gift to Joan Severn. Then came quarrels—not over the Fool, but over the pretty village girls " the Master " had up to pet and instruct in mineralogy and botany. They grinned at him and made dirt with their boots on the carpet. Then their presence was called scandalous—Joan would not have them, the Master would. He wanted to have hay from a paddock, she wanted to graze it with her pony. Quarrels grew furious—Albert was summoned by Joan, whom he found locked up at the top of the house. She declared " the Master " was raving mad and yet allowed he was visiting. Albert discovered him drinking tea at a cottage on the roadside. He walked with him and found him in great distress and great irritation, but quite sane. A short time after, the Master fled to an Inn in the neighbourhood, and called Albert to him. He said, " You must choose between the Severns and me." There could be no hesitation in the faithful Albert's mind. He got Joan to leave Brantwood for a while, telegraphed to Mrs. Firth, who was abroad, and immediately returned, and settled her with the Master at Brantwood for a fortnight. But Mrs. Firth

[1] Edith.

was too staid to cheer the old man, and he began to
grow ill. The illness increased till he took to his bed,
and Joan returned with nurses, and has ruled absolutely
ever since. Albert never entered the house after and
most of the old friends are met with ice and with hin-
drances. When they are able, they tell him of Albert's
unchanged love. " The Master " is now leading a
peaceful animal life ; his cold hands lie on his knees,
his eyes are vague, he does not read, only walks—his
memory is but for a moment at a time, his smile is
gentle, his only pleasure is in the sight of young people.
The days of conflict, of Lear-like storm and suffering
are over, and the poor old wizard is no longer on the
rack but in the arm-chair. As Albert reads his letters
the old attraction moves in us and we forgive his false
reading of life and of Art, in a pleased pitifulness, as the
sentences fall.

The truth of Albert's story is shown by what we hold
in our hands—a letter from Joan refusing to receive us,
with curt formality, and ending, " We were rather
startled by receiving your names on Mr. Albert Fleming's
card, as our friendship with him ceased some years ago."

NEUM CRAG,
Sep. 28, 1893.

. . . Dearest [Amy], yesterday was so tragic that I
really cannot write about it. We rowed over the lake,
and, as usual, when we got to Brantwood, Mrs. Severn
was out, and we were told that Mr. Ruskin was never
seen except with a special arrangement with Mrs. Severn

—but the kind and incautious little maid told us that Mr. Ruskin was gone on his walk and indicated the direction. Mr. Fawnthorpe had no hope that we should attain—from the first I felt we should, and as we quickly turned a sharp corner, I breathed in a terrified voice, " There he is ! ", and then felt I must fly to the ends of the earth. I saw a tall [*sic*] figure in long frock-coat and grey felt hat. The back curled on to the middle of the head as in Blake's old man going in at Death's Door ; the beard dripped white as a long waterfall thin with drought. Behind him was a small, sandy, brutal man, reading a newspaper. We approached. Mr. Fawnthorpe spoke and the old wizard face recognised. He never asked a question—he always answered. One seemed to be speaking into water and the answer came up through water—low and yet clear. *We* could not speak to him at first—he walked on with tiny steps, his hands behind him—the beak of the nose is strong and firm as ever, the eyebrows frosty, the head shrunk so that the cap rests on the cushions of the eyebrows, the cheeks are still comely red and in the long beard there are tones of bracken red. But the eyes ! They have a sort of shy tantalising pause, and then spring on you with a supple sweet rapidity, and they are blue as lakes to the rim of the lids—one sees no whites, the impression is all of blue. Michael spoke to him of Mr. Fleming ; with a beautiful smile he asked—the only question he put —" Albert Fleming ? " He did not remember Katherine Bradley, he thought, " at least not distinctly." When he fixed me, Sim brought me up to him and in the softest voice I spoke of the green road and how glad he must be to hear the lake plashing on the shore. "Yes, one hears it," he said with such a grateful smile. But, Oh, child,—one feels that he has no heart to raise his voice, any more than the dying, who are hopeless, will trouble to speak—he looks as if freedom had been murdered in him, and as if despair were all he knew of life. Every day he goes this treadmill walk ; no young people charm him with soft voice ; he is never taken a drive or row ; he is relegated to his study—no friend is allowed near him, lest he should be persuaded to revoke the deed of gift that has given him bound to hell.

It was anguish to be close to King Lear and to feel he was beyond the reach of even a Cordelia. If it had not been for the little maid we should never have seen him. Even at the hotel they told lies—probably paid lies—about the time when he walks. One of the things I shall always see is that long, humped form, with a look of timelessness about it, against the hazel-bushes of the road, with little coarse Baxter, a horrible Sancho, beside it. . . .

CHAPTER NINE

A QUESTION OF MEMORY

[Their prose play, *A Question of Memory*, was accepted and produced by J. T. Grein at his Independent Theatre 1893. The plot is based on an incident of the Hungarian rising of 1848. Ferencz Renyi, a schoolmaster, is captured by the Austrians, near his native village, and brought before General Haynau, who threatens to shoot his mother, sister and sweetheart unless he betrays the whereabouts of his regiment. Ferencz at first refuses, but under the strain he is at last ready to tell, but he cannot; his memory is gone. His dear ones are shot and he goes mad. Their friend Albert Fleming lent them his rooms in Gray's Inn, that they might follow the rehearsals more comfortably.]

III Verulam Buildings, Gray's Inn.

October 13th, 1893.

[1] At last we can write the blessed, the already highly prized address, Verulam Buildings.

This afternoon I dare not go to the theatre—I have such a chill. It is difficult for me to stay away, I so love rehearsal. It is wonderful to see one's words graving pictures, movements, persons—to watch a play being secretly fashioned down in the earth. I descend the

[1] Edith.

173

stairs and triumph in the bald dirt, the hangman ropes, the gape of the stage. I triumph; and in the dim obscure is a small table, a few chairs, the extinct foot-lights, and a few puppets—men and women in whom I take an interest—second only to that I take in the creations of my brain.

De Lange, the stage manager, is one of the most intelligent men I ever met; he has that foreign charm—his brain is always in direct relation to what he is doing. This is so rare in Englishmen—their characters are in direct relation with the matter in hand, but their intellects are scarcely ever practical in this bare, essential way. De Lange has a body and head like Napoleon's, if he had been conscious he was playing a farce; the eyes are brilliant chestnut brown—they pierce, decide, comment and mock discreetly; the voice is mobile, an organ full of attitudes, emotions, in perfect accord with the intellect —beautiful in timbre. The short form can also suggest, in a dashing sketch, all the conceptions of the mind and the sympathies of the voices. I learn an infinite amount of stage technique from him—his foreign reasonableness appealing to me as an artist who wishes to work with comprehension of my means.

He can be a bully when it suits his aim, he can be pleasant, can encourage, can leave things to come right, can speak calmly with a thunder-knot in his brow. [Acton] Bond, our Ferencz, is slight, with an earnest face; the difficulty of slow thinking gives a look like that on some of the imperial heads in Roman galleries, to his forehead. The eyes are small, slate-coloured, with every now and then a lizard-like incline of one lid to the other, which movement, like the mannered expression of the shaved lips, sometimes irritates. Yet he can smile elfishly and becomes almost handsome as he realises passion.

His convinced way of acting after real, thoughtful struggle to obtain his conviction will be valuable in the shooting scene. He has a quiet manner and small sensitive head. I shall never forget my joy when I saw him acting with Revelle last Monday, instead of Worthing, who read the part on the preceding Thursday, a man whose attitude suggested a bread poultice on the chest, whose face had the forms of perpetual toothache. No one could touch him, he was so repelling to emotion, and he mumbled his part. I was in despair, I felt like a gambler whose gold is being made useless to him by ill-luck. How I suffered! How all my nervous energy rose against the obstacle till I was nearly mad. Telegrams, letters of appeal (Tree would not let us have Holman Clarke), a meeting with Beatty, a meeting with Grein . . . and as a result Bond on the stage with Revelle!

Revelle, our Stanislas, is as sappy as spring grass—about 22, with Indian eyes, a large handsome mouth free enough to fall back, round diamond-white teeth, a little moustache and short hair, repressed but abundant. He knows that he finds favour with women, but his youth is too strong to rest in the knowledge—hence a boyish naïveté, self-forgetfulness, fire and devotion to his art that carry foolish conceit away with them. Would he were a gentleman! It is not birth, it is not breeding that gives this lush beauty! Oscar Wilde has welcomed it, bursting straight from nature as it does, like that of a young vine or a young colt.

Monday 16th. Oh, my goodness, we have got a Haynau—Beauchamp—the very man incarnate. And Acton is a heart-breaking Ferencz in the shooting scene. I can hardly bear to be present and see the torturer and tortured so life-like. And De Lange realises the emotions of the crisis unerringly. The curtain is tremendous. . . .

. . . At Tuesday's rehearsal De Lange, during the shooting scene, took the stage of a sudden and declared majestically, " There is nothing for it—Fina [the fiancée] goes slap out of this scene." We all froze, Miss Keegan went white as a corpse. There was a terrible pause in the scene. Beauchamp, who is supposed to know as much about situation as De Lange, came forward to say that the scene was " remarkably solid " and that we hopelessly damaged it by the Fina episode ; Doone agreed, Bond confessed that her part made it impossible to keep up the tragic relation with his mother ; De Lange kept thundering low in my ear execration of Miss Keegan —" These jabbering women never think of anything but themselves ; they have no sense of art—I will never be threatened by any member of my company—I would rather rehearse till midnight. If she won't submit, she goes—that fool of a woman, I won't have her in a cast of mine again." " Mr. De Lange, shall you want me for rehearsal to-morrow ? " asked Miss Keegan, white and with eyes that reminded me of Gerome's *Athena Glaucopis*. " No, not to-morrow," was the curt rejoinder, and after much struggling sympathy given her by Michael she disappeared and the act went on lifelessly —the quarrel had thrown the actors out.   That night we cut the scene.

On Wednesday morning, Miss Keegan came in grief that was pitiable, for she has realised Fina so well, that she felt as if a life had been sacrificed. . . .   De Lange ordered a scene for Fina *after* the mother's exit.   Next rehearsal, De Lange refused to weaken the mother's part by bringing Fina on afterwards—she must come first. In the evening at eleven o'clock Miss Keegan broke on our sleep and brain-struggles to say she liked the scene, rejected by De Lange at the previous rehearsal she had not attended, and she would not have it changed.   She was more like Glaucopis Athena than ever.   We fenced, entreated, and almost fell to the ground with weariness. On Friday De Lange rejected our new effort and wrote a scrap of dialogue, as he thought, to clear things up. But when we got home we found he had given away the situation too soon. . . .   Saturday's rehearsal was delightful.   De Lange, the cat, was away at a matinée, actors and authors had the stage to themselves. Beauchamp and Bond recognised De Lange's mistake, and the scene was taken with our final emendation. Poor Miss Keegan still wept, was cheered by Revelle, and finally read her small part very badly—still she read it, though she refused to learn it till next Tuesday.

. . . On Thursday I went to Dr. Russell Reynolds, ill, the colour of uncooked pastry, my inside like an angry wasps' nest. . . .   For the first time we judged from the

Dress Circle, and this seemed to break the magnetic connection between the authors and actors.   De Lange has
taken one of his hatreds to Bond—he says he is so much
a pedagogue, he wants to teach others what he does not
know.   De Lange has never forgiven him his early
insubordination.   " He wanted to stage-manage this
play."   It is true Bond is a distressingly English actor,
with every fault of the insular stage, but he is a most
conscientious study and he loves his part through and
through. . . .   De Lange called him a Marginal-note
Actor. . . .

. . . De Lange was trying with his animus against
Bond, his self-conceit and mechanical wit.   He defines
Art as " the algebraical x in use among poets, painters
and musicians." . . .   Oscar has taken a box.

Wednesday, Dress Rehearsal Day.   A dramatic critic,
a friend of De Lange, saw the shooting scene yesterday.
He said, " My word, that is a scene ! "   Act III is getting
hackneyed before it is produced. . . .   We shall soon go
mad !   No one comes—no letters—no telegrams—it is
the interim Brutus found so trying. . . .   Ellis is going
to Cornwall on Thursday, and finds—I know not how—
that he cannot alter his arrangement ; wretched little Gray
[Curator, The Museum, Edinburgh] has an influenza
and had asked the doctor if it were safe to travel !   Mr.
Fleming stays at the Crag because Susie is dying—a piece
of pure sentimentalism, for he is not nursing Susie, and
only sees her now and then, and she is old, old, old !
What friends we have !   Friendship in my experience is
usually a golden casket with nothing in it.

. . . [1] P. and I lunch together, P. ill with " crise," getting black under the eyes.

[2] At rehearsal we had to bear, for a little, the friction of Coppée's play [the curtain-raiser to theirs], which was not finished when we came in.   I must go back to Wednesday's dress rehearsal—all went well, except that the battery self-willed De Lange insisted on using refused to work at the right moment, and Ferencz' speech ante-dated the muskets.   Louie [Ellis] was present—passive, critically contented, devitalising ; and, Little Cat [Amy] did not strike her real enthusiasm out boldly enough for us to feel it through the worry.

Great triumph.   Abingdon, who refused the part, told Hoppé [business manager] he repented the refusal bitterly.   Holman Clarke was enthusiastic and said he thought we had good reason to be glad that he was not allowed to interpret *such* a character. . . .   De Lange was a trial—his temper on his tongue and brow.   After the show was over, he actually said across the stalls, " It went very well indeed, considering one of the actors did all he was told not to do and nothing he was told to do." I saw what he was aiming at—he does not think Bond will be a success, and publicly and ungenerously wishes to clear himself of the responsibility.   The insult struck, but Bond was very quiet in his anger.   I said, " I under-stand what you suffer, I am a poet," and we cordially shook hands.   He will yet do well.   De Mathos [secre-tary] urged us to stay for Coppée, and a terrible blow

[1] Katherine.   [2] Edith.

fell on us, for we had not read it, and found that it contained an hysterical heroine, soldiers and two volleys. Grein must have been a " congenital idiot "—to use De Lange's epithet, hurled at prompter York—when he chose to put Michael and Coppée together. The evening will be called shooting night—comedy will be let loose— so exquisitely laughable it is. Foreigners have keen wits, but no humour. I raged with the blackest rage— a passion against invited ridicule, and we sent to Grein a letter that expressed our wrath at his blunder—blunder inartistic as it is ludicrous. Mild Sydney Cockerell cooled us down toward midnight.

. . . De Lange defined cynicism as the outer semblance of disappointment. . . . To Sim he sketched a letter to Bond—a savage letter. Sim said, " You would not send it ? "—" Oh no," he replied with foreign blandness. . . . I found De Lange insulting him [Bond] as I have never seen a man insulted before. " You have disobeyed me. You have done nothing I ordered. I throw you over. Do just as you like and make a fool of yourself. I have nothing more to do with you." Bond took no notice of the injuries, but merely repeated through his teeth, " I shall stand where I am till the curtain falls." With perfect composure I took the middle of the stage, and said, " Mr. Prompter, you will see that the curtain falls as Mr. Bond wishes it, and as I wish it." I did not see De Lange afterwards, but as he continued pleasant with Michael, probably he rather admired my firmness. The man will ruin the play— Bond cannot act before him—they hate each other. De

Lange is a man who can only be won by feigned defeat, which turns out to be but one's victory. Bond with the narrow earnestness of his temperament cannot see this.

[After the performance.]   It seems more natural to be dead than alive.   We wake to the surprise of finding every morning paper against us.

Little Fleming falls before the crisis—he is too small a soul—but my Love is strong, pours him out his tea, cracks jokes with him, and is able to convey our gratitude for this Gray's Inn refuge.   I am in helpless pain like a dumb animal at first.   *The Times* and *Telegraph* are worthy of respect in their blame ; they have some good words for us and our actors, the rest howl !

. . . there are caves in my brain, through which cruel tides swing and rave—my stomach feels as it does when anyone you love is dead ;   my throat is dry and quakes from time to time.   I rise up from lunch and walk to the British Museum—the grim Egyptian Deities and the Branchidae Priests support me more than the Elgin Marbles—I long to lie in one of those sarcophagi, covered with hieroglyphics, and to know that the weight of ages would hold the lid down.   I find, in the Metopes and Frieze of the Parthenon, a want of contagious life among the figures . . . gradually the stoniness of the sculpture strikes me with intolerable anguish, and I walk home for the first time to cry a few moments.   My Love comforts me with tea, with a strong face and with tenderness. . . .   Then my Love quails, she who has been so strong.   The evening papers are worse than the morning. They are like a lot of unchained tigers.   We are hated,

as Shelley was hated, by our countrymen, blindly,
ravenously.

. . . We mark with a hall-mark, the people who have
courage to stand by us. . . . Not a soul has been near
us—our rooms are full of the sound of a winter-wind,
on our desk are the Daily Journals . . . but though
everything is against us, we are strong, thank Heaven
and our race.

Yesterday evening! Well . . . the first curtain fell
with success. Young Michaelians came to our box to
say the house was with us. . . . The second act was
received excellently, Miss Caine and Miss Keegan
charming the people at once. Again the box filled.

Act III was received silently, tensely . . . the curtain
after all was too long in dropping, then applause boomed
and the whole house gabbled. But no one came. At
last old Miss Scott swelled over one of our front chairs,
and she gave us compliments, and talked about her new
house, and must have made the effect of a Turkey-hen
from the theatre. . . . Grein, who had been estranged
in manner, did not come, and I felt suddenly as if I stood
in a clearing where there was no humanity—where I
was a mortal alone.

Act IV was lost from the beginning. The people
resented Mrs. Creswick's old-fashioned method, and her
costume (which we had never seen) was enough to kill
any scene in which she took part. Bond was really fine,
and Revelle crudely so ; but toward the end the Beattys
hissed, and there was a laugh and a shout of " no ! "
Revelle lost his head and left out the core of Stanislas'
last speech. . . . The applause must have been good,

for the actors seemed warm. I cannot say I heard it, and not once did I catch the word " author," although Doone, with rather Austrian manners, tried to force us toward the stage. . . . Then we greeted Fina . . . then Mrs. Wright, triumphant in pose, and behind them grasped Bond's hand and gave him our full thanks. . . . He looked very handsome in his own intellectual way— the chiselling of his face is distinctive and most refined. . . . Revelle joined us, amazed at the laugh and cry of " no " that had interrupted him—it was the amaze of a child stung by a wasp. His great eyes flashed disconsolately and he showed the prettiest penitence when he learnt of his omission. Then the crimson trunks disappeared round dingy stone walls, and Hoppé passed us, glum, with the cool words on his lips, " Well, I think it went very satisfactorily." As he spoke, a dampness quenched me within—I knew the play had failed with the critics. And little Fleming was a cold compress to any elation. With scarcely a word I bore his remarks, and went to bed as one does after a funeral. I woke feeling incomplete—I had lost my hope—any anticipation, and there was no triumph in its place.

. . . Our cast stands by us unfalteringly. Bond says, " Cut off Act IV—let me have the play in three acts, and I'll always hold to it, for it is one of the grandest things that has ever been done."

. . . to spend the evening with Dr. Todhunter. " Toddy " is glad to see us because he had feared we resented his criticism—we resent criticism ! Why, it is as familiar to us as the fiery wind to Francesca. We meet Stepniak and his wife—he an ugly, she a comely Tartar—and converse on Russian literature. Elkin [Matthews] is there, with a procession of virgin sisters with eyes that shine like tin plates. Young Addleshaw drinks to the success of *A Question of Memory* at Manchester. The guests find it difficult to get round the play to us—most of them manage it on hands and knees : but they all admire the pluck with which we have set to work. When I said to Addleshaw that I would go through the whole experience again, now I knew how it would end,—he replied, " A man would not."— " But then, you see, I am a woman, and to bring out a play is experience of life—just what women feel so crushingly that they need. You men get it like breathing."

CHAPTER TEN

THE NINETIES

[1] The borrowed studio in Tite Street, Chelsea, of little Rothenstein. Two candles, a great luminous twilight and the curly cub of an artist, chattering incessantly as a bird sings. He is blessed in his poverty, lunching on an egg and some marmalade and then taking a box for *The Second Mrs. Tanqueray*. He tells one incomparable story of Arthur Symons. He and Symons are at the Empire together. S. confides that he is just getting to know a certain distinguished artiste—a dancer, I think. Rothenstein knows her familiarly, and after the performance the two young men mingle in conversation with the ballet girls. Rothenstein addresses Mlle. X with careless, Bohemian freedom. S. draws him back, "You must not speak to them in *that* way." The man of *that* world laughs good-naturedly.

[2] Well, on New Year's Day I join Mary Costello at the New Gallery, where we are joined by Logan (Pearsall Smith), Rothenstein, Daniel MacColl, Walter Sickert and Steer. Will Rothenstein is a firm-footed materialist with a frenzy for art—just as naïve and "upish" as a kid, when he turns his little nose in the air and shows his pranks—for Will's convictions are but

[1] Edith. [2] Katherine.

pranks, though his obstinacy is solid. He has done a portrait of Le Gallienne—not liked, and rejected by Richard and The Bodley Head. He claims the right to judge of its likeness and actually got the money, though the portrait has been destroyed, and has established his claim to judge of the worth of his interpretation of faces —anyhow he will be paid on his own recommendation of himself, even if the portraits he produces go to the fire. Daniel MacColl—with a melancholy, hawk-featured, stale-complexioned face—is evidently as prejudiced against us as the *Spectator* itself. Conversation turned on George Egerton, "Women writers are indecent now-a-days—of course present company excepted," Daniel remarked, glancing cynically at me.

Steer is like a contained prize-fighter; Sickert is barley-coloured, gritty with an uncouth sensitiveness in his features, and humour he keeps in a strong box. We found him gazing at a Flemish picture, and the grim impressionist confessed he loved to have unprofessional enjoyment of sharp clean detail, when no one was looking. We all had tea together and chose out the most creamy confectionery, except Sickert, who had a bun— "Buns for bears," as Will Rothenstein commented.

Some stories.

Verlaine to Havelock Ellis and Arthur Symons. "I —have—got—mon-ay. I—will—have—pleasure. I— will—have—some—rhum !—rhum ! !—rhum ! ! !" [1]

---

[1] Mr. Havelock Ellis writes: "This will certainly be supposed to illustrate V.'s love of drink. In reality (even as regards the use of English and the choice of rum) it was a gesture of courteous hospitality."

Mallarmé : " What man desires is la rage, la colère—to create, to be a solitude. Woman requires l'amour—there may be—it is conceivable—an union of two solitudes. To become part of God—of God who opposes all that is and creates all that is not."

Edmond de Goncourt : " J'aime les fleurs supérieures, l'art supérieur, les livres supérieurs, la cuisine supérieure, le beurre supérieur."

An American artist sent Emerson a framed picture of his own. Shortly after, Emerson returned the frame, saying that he could not think of keeping anything so valuable.

[1] We went to see a small collection of lithographs by Shannon and portraits by Rothenstein. Both artists were there—Rothenstein looks as sure of himself as a bantam cock—yet there is something pathetic in his eyes that have seen so much of life—Bohemian life—and yet are so blank, with a kind of avarice in them after fuller vision—that gives lustre to their moral opaqueness and has come to them since he settled in England. His work is strong and careless. He seizes the salient characteristics of men far better than the more indefinite expressions of women. He has made a sketch of Ricketts and Shannon, that well contrasts the ivory and madder of the one with the carmine and brown of the other. It is a hasty sketch and only just to Ricketts.

The Shannon of real life came up to us and charmed us again with his calm gaiety and ruddiness, like that of a fine stored apple. He has made studies of dead mice, that, in their delicate handling, suggest the very dainti-

[1] Edith.

ness of the little wall-ghosts and nibblers of pansies.
He can give the drift of skirts, he can make black and
white shine into colour. His best work is modern in
its effort after light and classic in its attainment of composed movement. He has done a delightful rout of
children passing along as in bas-reliefs of the Renaissance.

A very delightful half-hour with work that is generally
sincere in line, sun-bathed, poetic.

November 22nd, 1893. Verlaine reads his own poems
at Barnard's Inn—a most " seizing " occasion (in the
French sense). The picturesque hall—eighty to an
hundred intellectual listeners, many of them women—
the personality of the reader, that can be summarised
by Strafford's " thorough " (for Verlaine is as extreme
a devotee as he is extreme a sinner) ; the June-rose
beauty of his young neophyte Symons ; the low melodies
of that cracked instrument his voice, and the congruity
between the poems and the poet—all these things made
the time from a quarter to nine until ten most singularly
new.

When Verlaine and Symons came in, the obvious
simile was that of a rose bush beside a blasted thorn ;
Symons almost supported his lame companion to the
chair and then retired to the second side row. Of course,
quite apart from the glimpses of the real man I had in
Paris, the many portraits of Verlaine had prepared me
for his face ; but no portraits can give the intent sadness
of the expression of each condemned feature. Yes, the
face of the man is his necessity—one cannot forget it, as
one looks at Verlaine's bare skull-line, beautiful in its

decisiveness, horrible in its confession ; at the tilted eyebrows, the eyes like those of a Chinese Mephistopheles—
only so sad, with the sadness of Northern Europe ; at
the nose stolen from an Attic grotesque, at the violent
mouth, curved vaguely with blonde hairs. The skin
has the appearance of parchment drawn by fire, and
every now and then a smile rises that is full of the
innocence of hell, I mean the " naïveté " of habitual
wrong-doing. It is quite delicious. Indeed Verlaine
is so necessarily criminal that it has done him little harm
to fulfil himself, and the religious fervour that is the
accompanying ecstasy of his sin, grows out of it almost
as a reward. He is sincere—I am sure of that ; no
psychologist could doubt it, and his voice, in reading
Sagesse, convinced one emotionally. He sat, his legs
stretched out—his vagabondism covered by clean and
middle-class garments ; he looked like the giant of
Bohemia brought out to be seen by Philistia, and he was
very, *very* judicious in the choice of his poems, and there
was not a trace of " vine-leaves in his hair "—I was going
to write, but I must rather say round his beautiful, bald
skull. It was such an English scene—Satan in a frock-
coat, reading religious poetry and darting pitch-spark
glances at a company incapable of understanding the
tragedies of hell (even the devils believe and tremble),
still less its bouts of free revel.

We start for town with our M.F. valise [a new conceit
of theirs to have their luggage labelled Michael Field].
Then to Fitzroy Street [Horne's invitation to a Dolmetsch
concert]. The men achieve a ladies' cloakroom, but no

adequate reception, the guests wander. We join Tottie [Pater] and at last find the room where the harpsichord stands—the studio. A man with large hair and panther eyes moves about—we agree with Tottie it must be Dolmetsch. The discord, the untidy business of tuning up, distresses the ear peculiarly and seems to take longer than usual. At last the six viols make the ancient, novel music. How strange the tone of these old instruments —what a far-off tinkling of youthfulness. They cannot express the subtility nor the volume of our modern emotion, the acuteness in what we feel. They have a sunny gala thinness, or a quaint sorrow that scarcely swells into passion. Men must have been half crickets when this music satisfied them.

The lute is a beautiful thing—one side convex, dull black, striped with inlaid yellow lines ; on the other, flat, unstained wood over which the strings pass to the black neck. The sight of it takes one to Watteau's shimmering groups under the mellow branches. It has the voice for light love and is in fantastic mourning for the transient pleasure its notes accompany. The viols, for all their strings, do not equal the violin, viola and violoncello—their notes flit and do not pierce—they have a lack of fullness of tone and of spiritual suffering. The piece for the viol da gamba alone, I described to Sim as " Tooth-ache calling unto tooth-ache "—physical torture, nothing divine in it.

How the harpsichord brought such an expression into the face of the middle musician in the Pitti *Concert* passes my understanding. It chatters steadfastly, while a brook chatters gaily—it pleases for a little, then it wearies. Of course one thinks of Milton sitting at it and one forgives it all its faults for the vision's sake ; or else, fair, remote girls, clad in great snowy skirts and a womanliness that no longer is the fashion with woman, rise up before one, sitting at the keyboard, in some remote corner of a farmhouse.

. . . But I turn to the present. Lionel Johnson's little form, weary little face, and brow domed like the British Museum Reading Room (and as full of literature) is seen at the top of the steps leading down to the studio.   Horne by him, with a fanatical smile of nervous ill-health, but genuinely kind, and Image red, shiny, urbane.   One woman is beautifully dressed, in pale heliotrope velvet with ample brown fur collar . . . all of a sudden I see a head that is quite unmistakable, a grey, foaming mass of hair like Beethoven's, a benignant inspired face—Henry Holmes.   I have not seen him for years.   Such a face ought to have done something for art and the character goes with the face as words to an air—yet he is a musical raté.

We leave before the last movement of the Bach is over, but delay in getting a cab keeps us in the hall till the sonata is over.   Lionel brings a gentleman to the door —then wavers on the toes of his little feet, looks shyly at the letters on the hall table and finally comes to me, a sweetness and concern on his mouth and pale under face.

L. I am sorry, Miss Cooper, to hear that you have been ill.

P. Yes, I had the fever at Dresden and since then I have had influenza.   Altogether I must say I am an unfortunate party !

Good Heavens! What demon made me say such a thing to Lionel Johnson " who is a scholar "—I read in the paper to-day. The little wren heart must have fluttered with disgust. He had watched me during the music—perhaps thought of the lines he loves in *The Tragic Mary*—I spoil all. I shake from my person all poetry, I demonstrate that woman cannot have the scholarly conscience. I am an occasion for cynicism —a stumbling-block to youth, the sensibility of male youth: a dream turned into a nightmare, perchance!

I dreamt myself last night in the company of Havelock Ellis. He remarked, " We have at last reached a stage when we are able to tell a lie." Immediately there was a burst of religious music from the next room and we became quiet, thinking of the days gone by, before we were artists in falsehood.

He also asked me for a cigarette, " to warm the man." I could only find some steeped in water—so I put them before the fire to smoke and so dry; when at last I presented them half-charred, I was rewarded by the assurance, " Now the man is warmed."

This was the tale of the [Havelock Ellis] wedding told by Louie.

He rose, breakfasted, dressed himself in his velvet coat and was dressed by her in tie, etc. He sat by the fire and read *Nature*. He remarked, " There are not many bridegrooms who would sit by the fire and read *Nature*." Louie was cold. He said, " Sit by the fire, child, I will warm your hands." Then they went forth in the slush. The bride was waiting outside the regis-

trar's and shook her umbrella ! ! The party was shut
in a waiting-room for a quarter of an hour. H. was not
nervous and talked . . . there must have been something fearsomely unnatural in that easy talk. Then the
civil marriage took place, the sun shining full on the
couple through the registrar's window. H. looked handsome in the light—he was calm ; his umbrella-shaking
bride, pale and disquieted ! Bride, bridegroom and
sister walked home arm-in-arm. Soon after the bride
departed to her rooms in town, travelling by herself in
the Underground. She gave an At Home, that afternoon, to which her husband came. They parted and
only met again next day when they started for Paris.
The bride was married in an ulster. This is a true
account of the modern sacrament of Matrimony. It is
revolting. "Free love, free field," is sacreder.

[1] In the evening Louie Ellis comes. We have a
Sunday in the garden. She tells us of Olive Schreiner,
Olive Schreiner home from the Cape, after years of
brute, wild life in Africa. The ambassador pays his
respects to her, Watts asks to paint her (he is refused),
she goes the round of the great. Lovers from Africa
come after her—to sink on their knees as soon as they
land—one simply asks for the beloved, demanding of
Louie, her friend. Meditating on all this I am filled
with jealousy ; this woman has been worshipped—she
has known solitude—she has walked naked in the open
air, she has handled politics, she has set up one and put
down another.

[1] Katherine.

I have lived at Durdans, neither breathing nor being breathed upon.

[1] Michael goes to the old Bodley [Head]. Why has Elkin Matthews not answered about the poems ?

Elkin. May I give you a personal explanation ?

Michael. (Wondering if she is to hear a confession of love or the bailiff.)   Certainly.

Elkin. Well—then, I've been wool-gathering. (With anguish of breath and obstruction of brain.)   I've got engaged.

Michael. (Anxious that this event should take its right place in the universe.)   Indeed ?   I congratulate you.   So you mean that under the circumstances you have had no time to read my MSS., etc. ?

I wonder if Miss Calvert will be a greater success than John Lane !   But the " wool-gathering " is delicious.

[The first of the following letters from George Moore was written after the meeting mentioned on page 134.]

8 King's Bench Walk,
Temple.

Dear Michael Field,

I write so that you may not forget your promise.   If I like the new play I shall be glad to write an article about it in *The Hawk*, and an article in that paper will be of use to you because it goes among theatrical folk.   I am not a quick reader and shall not be able to read your

[1] Edith,

play in a day—perhaps you'd rather I did not read it in a day. I will send you the number of *The Hawk* in which I spoke about you and *William Rufus* in connection with my project for a Théatre Libre. It was curious that I should have written about you only a week or two before I met you, and that was the first time I wrote your name.

I daresay you saw that I was much interested in you—my face is most indiscreet, it tells all my feelings far better than my pen. I was sorry that Mrs. Moulton took me away (the observation is only addressed to one side of Michael Field) just as you had kindly asked me to stay. I tried to get back, but Oscar Wilde was on one side and some one else on the other side of Michael Field and—Forgive me my very obvious joking and this long letter which ought to have been a note.

If you can arrange it I shall be very glad to come down and see you. I am afraid you will think me a very gushing person. In truth I am not at all, but I did like *William Rufus* and the first plays whose names I have never been able to pronounce, much less to spell.

Sincerely yours,
GEORGE MOORE.

DEAR MICHAEL FIELD,

I am glad you liked my article in the *St. James' Gazette*. It was *exactly* what I thought and exactly what one thinks is not usually pleasing. . . . I was particularly glad to hear that you liked what I said about your blank verse being vocal and that the idea was new to you.

Symons told me there was nothing particularly new in the statement and disappointed me much. I often stumble across wrong ideas, but I do not so often stumble across other people's ideas, and I do think that my criticism of the difference between your verse and Swinburne's was a novel one.

I have been working on my strike play. Tree has been writing to me about it and I think he will do it—my Hamlet of the East End, des bas fonds. But what amuses me most is the novel I am writing. All the characters are servants—servants devoured by horse-racing—le petit côté des courses. The human drama will be the servant-girl's fight for her child's life among baby-farmers. Of course all this must seem very vulgar to you—but no, I am paying you a very bad compliment—nothing is vulgar except the conventional. However ça grouille et mon petit monde m'amuse démesurément. You know the sensation of holding a little handful of characters that are all your own, their strutting and their fuming is so amusing to behold. But this morning I am garrulous beyond measure. I shall have a lot to do this week and but slight inclination to do it. But when may I come and see you? Saturday would suit me. Would it suit you?

Most sincerely yours,
GEORGE MOORE.

DEAR MICHAEL FIELD,

Very well, on Saturday. If I cannot get away I will send a telegraph, but I think I shall be able to manage

it. I have a lot to do—journalism is a curse. Many
thanks for your letter. I shall have a lot to say about
play-writing, and my criticism though often incorrect is
never vague. I take that to be a merit. I have received
Rufus. I do not think it would be possible to arrange
it for the stage. You must write something for the
stage. If you like we'll go through an act of *Rufus* and
I'll tell you why I think it could not be arranged for
acting. Stage composition is something quite different.
The intention is different. But there is no use in my
trying to explain on a sheet of notepaper. Perhaps
I shall not be able to explain by word of mouth, perhaps I do not understand the subject and there are
numberless other perhaps—still we shall æstheticise
agreeably.

Most sincerely yours,

GEORGE MOORE.

DEAR MICHAEL FIELD,

I cannot help writing to ask you to overlook the
many irregularities scattered through the articles I sent
you. I get up on Friday not knowing what I am going
to write—I devote the day to the article and put it out
of my head. The number of little blunders in this
week's article *Notes and Sensations* excites me to write
this letter. To let such unfinished work go out of one's
hands is unpardonable, but I only regard it as a task to
be got through as quickly as possible.

Sincerely yours,

GEORGE MOORE.

[1] George Moore came in the afternoon. I like the sincerity of his light eyes and the candour of his speech. I am sure that he is a man of good original instincts, however much his ways of life may have deflected them. We talked much of the construction of plays for the stage : he made me realise the leading fault of our work —its want of rhythmical progression—the haphazard development of plot which has contented us. The firm yet pliant structure of a work is one of the requirements of style. And preparation for events and entrances is the true forethought that gives dramatic art integrity and musical movement. He vociferated against the inhumanity of the Clelia motive suggested by Meredith's *Vittoria*. The heroine would likewise be weak—and even Shakespeare did not tell the story of Desdemona, but of Othello. Meredith fails in creating conviction. In *Measure for Measure* Shakespeare fails in the same way ; while, with Shakespeare's theme, Balzac, in *La Cousine Bette*, succeeds completely in obtaining conviction. We spoke of primitive motives—he asked if we had ever thought of laying a drama in the prehistoric ages, when men were first gathering into tribes and when a man was first in love. He sketched for us his new novel ; it will have to surmount some " unpleasant " things in its course as a work of art. G.M. whips out many " By George's " in right Celtic fashion—and in weary Celtic fashion he returned the type-written copy of *William Rufus*, no longer in favour because it has troubled him. His enthusiasm for Michael's vocal lines will probably be over in a month, if his long rail-

[1] Edith.

way journey into the country has not ended it already. He loves the English, just because he is so Irish and French.

His hue is unhealthy, his hair honey-coloured, his nose the " strong-man " among his features. He gets up at eleven and wears red stockings and shapely boots. He is likeable, spite of oaths and confessions. He is in the world, and yet no liar. Art he loves and he loves *The Mummer's Wife* (suggested by *Madame Bovary*). If he had made out he wrote the book for the good of the classses— as certain articles in the *Pall Mall* purported to have been written—he could have sold several thousand more copies than were sold. But he could not tell a lie. He is disinterested in his love of art—no salesman or trafficker. There is " blood " in his dealings with litera- ture. His tongue, not his manners, could give offence —he has the obstinate tactlessness of speech that comes of his race.

In the evening we go to Will Rothenstein's studio- warming at Chelsea. They dance like savages and the music thumps each little brain-crease separately. George Moore comes up. His smile is like sunshine on putty, his talk sticks to one with the intimate adhesiveness of the same material—it approaches the surface of one's personality softly and there it is, on one. I talked to him for more than half an hour as we sat along the end of a sofa. He told me about his novel and his experi- ences as a playwright, " The situation was quite per- fect, but when I wanted words they would not come." He said that it was said everywhere that we made no use of our first act [*Question of Memory*], that our third act was splendid and our fourth the worst anti-climax ever known.

[Paris, May 1897.]   At Durand-Ruel's we go from padded room to room, enjoying Monets, Manets, Sisleys, and pause before a magnificent Monet of *October Flood*—the beggary and rags that furious waters leave behind them, a rayless sun sinking over the ruin and lapse.   Michael says secretly, "I believe that is George Moore."   Yes, it is.   There is his innocent, white-mouse complexion, his impressionist eyeballs and thin blondness over lip and head.   He is dressed in " chic " Paris style and yet with delicious Irish perversity he carries a gamp by the side of his elegant trousers.   For an instant he does not know us ;   then breaks out, " Who would ever have thought of seeing you in Paris ! "   Evidently he has the " two shy ladies " idea of us.   We rally him lightly and thoroughly, he glances at our Pile-Cann-Verena toilets and says, we are looking very well.   Then he sits down to talk and tell the tale of his new book—the study of a woman living a life of free love against a religious bias in her nature and ending in a convent.   George is an earnest and clever workman—with no inspiration.   I always measure a man's creative force by his powers of silence, and George talks of his subject while it is weaving to everybody.   An artist who does this, is in the society of art a bourgeois—he shocks from the very sources of himself.   George remarks he has given up trying to see us—living at that place—Reigate.   His tone makes Reigate sound like Kamchatka : so he thinks he will seize a civilised opportunity and invite us to tea at Rue Cambon. Then he goes, and we delight in a *Woman Ironing* by Degas. Millet gives us the attitudes of labour (French peasant labour), Degas appears to me greater—he gives in this design the attitudes of a special labour—life is not arrested and given in mere static value.

Rue Cambon is a success. George is essentially human —I believe he lives as most men, but makes the relations he forms human and so disinfects them. He is harmless and courteous in manner—his voice is like a lime-tree hum, suggestive of white honey. He pours out tea while at Michael's request I give him the bare scenario of *Anna Ruina*. He holds that, as usual, with all our talent, we go irritatingly wrong at the end of Act Two. But we have to ask if the Creator Spiritus thinks with him. George tells us in confidence that he likes all we write—even when it is bad. He asks, " Who does the love scenes ? —they are so good. You get such words in them."

Dr. Garnett comes to lunch with us. He tells us a story of Swinburne's fame. Swinburne had fallen in a fit, one day, at the British Museum. A few days after, Dr. Garnett, at an eating-house, heard a waiter telling a petted but illiterate charge that if he looked in a certain direction he would see Mr. Swinburne.
" And who is Mr. Swinburne ? "
" The man that fell down at the British Museum and 'urt 'is 'ead." O Apollo !
He also told us the delicious saying of Henry James describing Meredith and Hardy—Meredith the Obscure and the Amazing Hardy.

The perfect "mot" of Pater, heard by Sim last Saturday, when she visited him. He had been inveighing against Greek drama performances, as boring. "Nevertheless I am coming to see one—*The Frogs*," says Mabel Robinson. "Oh, then you must come and see me and look on me as one of the Frogs," is the reply. Perfect! One expects him to come into the room with solemn leaps; his countenance and weight are so resembling and yet he is so classic a frog—one of Aristophanes'.

At the Vegetarian we meet Selwyn Image, bright from the Opera, with a quiet girl at his side. His is the joyousness strictly precise of the eighteenth century faces—he is academic, urbane, High Church and Bohemian in due measure that disconcerts neither himself nor anyone else. His eyes look rather as if Horace had polished them with his file the prescribed ten years and left them Odes.

[1] A day of blight. In the *Speaker* an article by G. Moore on *Sex in Art* that makes one feel as if one were a negro. . . .

[2] What good times men have, what pipes, what deep communings! And the best of our brains is given to conjecture of what is passing in these male heads. Yet if women seek to learn their art from life, instead of what the angels bring down to them in dishes, they simply get defamed. . . .

[1] Edith.   [2] Katherine.

CHAPTER ELEVEN

ASOLO

[A visit to Sarianna and Pen Browning at Asolo, Tuesday, *May 21st* to *June 9th*, 1895.]

[1] What a garden the country is—green to the roadside and so full of flowers, they burst through grass and leaves in one bright invasion—common as the dust of the highway, but fresh with sap and rain and lawlessness. How they sport with my fever!—and the healing greatness of nature draws close to our carriage.

Lovely peasant girls look at us—we even hear the sound of runlets—the olives are gone, and chestnuts and acacias and oaks are green above the greenest grass wherever we turn.

We slowly toil up the Cornunda hill. There is La Rocca—the timeless fortress, and that cluster of houses below is Asolo.

At the inn—Pen steps up to our window—he greets us with the generous courtesy and the very tone of voice we loved in his father.

He tells us he is engaged in trying to prevent a duel between a young Italian Count and a man whose name is well known in London—he smiles at my illness encouragingly, with rosy assurance : I shall soon be better. His smile has a semi-circular motion, running

[1] Edith.

up into the cheeks from the mouth and into the temples
from the eyes. He has the secret of jollity with reticence.
We are conducted by him to our bedroom [at the inn]
and at once introduced to Castelfranco and Bussano,
etc., on the bosom of the loveliest plain I have ever seen
—a sky come to dwell with men. He pours out his
introduction with the energy of his father—the same
uncontrollable impetus, and I am so ill, so ill—and more
than suspect the bedroom is insanitary. We are to join
Sarianna at the Lace School close by, after a rest. How
cold the stone floor is, and Pen says we can get nothing
to eat at the inn . . . I feel despair, and yet how blue
the plain, how it comprehends its cities and fields in its
blueness. We meet Sarianna on the balcony at the
School and with her Mrs. Miller Morrison, a stout ugly
woman, whose large heart gives amplitude to her expression. She has a soothingness about her. But all this
while I am faint for tea . . . at last we cease looking at
the way Asolo is founded on the hill-side and learning
where Mrs. Bronson [the dedicatee of *Asolando*] dwells.
Tea is offered at Casa Browning and we begin to walk
there. We pass the uninteresting house where a tablet
records that *Asolando* was written . . . pass the slant
market-place, with the chestnuts on a little hill above
the fountain, stop to look at the weedy loveliness of
Catherine Cornaro's castle, and later at the ferny walls
that bound the Riva's, and at last reach the " Palazzo
Pigstye " as Pen calls his country-house, under a battery
of howls, barks and yaps from five dogs. The entrance
is hollow and stony in true Italian style, but the opposite
door on to the terrace frames the Julian Alps, and in

front of the cone-shaped range brilliant cockatoos, blue, orange and scarlet, roll about their perches magnificently.

The Sala d'Ingresso upstairs is full of old chests and chairs and bronzes—peacock feathers and sunshine. The tiny drawing-room—an expanded passage—cool stone-gray, is enlivened chiefly by a couple of plumes from those magnificent cockatoos on the terrace.

. . . [1] " First of all let me note the country sounds— geese cackling, cocks. and hens, etc., but the full moment for the animals is when we have afternoon tea on the lawn.   Peacocks screech, the macaws shriek, doves come in with their cotton-wool sounds, geese chatter, the hounds bay—chickens faintly fluster, turkeys puff out their cheeks—I say in a word, it is as if Noah's ark had landed on the Casa Browning slopes and all the living creatures been turned out thereon." . . .

[2] After tea the wildest toothache comes on and I lie deeply interested in my agony on Miss Browning's sofa. Michael returns to the Inn for remedies and hears from Mrs. Morrison (at Sarianna's request) the whole Ginevra story—of that another time.

Saturday, *May 25th*.   We drive with two horses to Castelfranco.   The bowery plain is filled with sunshine —what a little city in the girdle of the walls that still glow above the moat!   And here in the heart of the bowery plain and the greenness Giorgione was born.

In the Duomo we have a shock of disappointment

[1] From a letter of Katherine's to Mr. Cooper.   [2] Edith.

when we see the picture of our dreams [1] against the plaster with the violating blue of the blind above it, no light on it, raised so high it is almost inaccessible to our eyes and appearing quite Lilliputian after what the photographers had led us to expect.

Then we command a ladder brought, and mount—we are no longer hurt with disappointment. That mother with her babe sleeping on her arm and one hand laid on the stone end of her throne for coolness or support, is part of every summer we have ever loved. The open-eyed dream of life we have when everything sleeps in the sun, sweet as it is universal—that is what Giorgione gives to his Madonna as her Grace. She is our Lady of June—full of the imagination of siesta when it is quiet wakefulness.

. . . [2] "Dear old Miss Browning, at 81, is as acute and strong as possible, and when we drove to Castelfranco yesterday, sat upright in the carriage all the way. As for the poet's son, he is a thoroughly good fellow, never so happy as when he is caressing his dogs. But his devotion to his aunt touches me; and when his father's name is mentioned, tears fill his eyes. But they are a genuinely good family here, entirely human and kind."

[3] By two, Pen and Mrs. Morrison start for Venice— poor Pen is going to break up Rezzonico [Palazzo

[1] *Madonna and Child with SS. Francis and Liberale.* Giorgione (Castelfranco).
[2] From a letter of Katherine's to Mr. Cooper.   [3] Edith.

Rezzonico—the Brownings' Venetian residence] by re-
storing her furniture to his wife. It is a hard duty from
which he has flinched. We are left with Miss Browning
and try to learn from her when the *Asolando* poems were
written.

At the Casa Browning letters have been received
from the sister-in-law, speaking actually of " outside
help " if Pen does not at once give up the Rezzonico
things . . .

Saturday, *June 1st.*[1] Market Day at Asolo 1895. We
get up feeling better and, in the market, fix on the colours
of our big Asolo cloaks and buy two shawls blue-barred
and green. At the Inn I cut open Marietta's soul ; how
warm and juicy ! In the church of the soul of Lotto
we see a hell-broth, a mess with oil being made in the
font. Marietta explains : to-day—the eve of Whitsun-
tide—they bless the fire, wood and water.

At lunch confusion—heaps and heaps of letters on the
floor (such curious things of Robert's, Sarianna says—
his copy of Shelley as a boy—the proof sheets of *Paracelsus,* inscribed to his mother, etc.). Loss of a key—a
quarrel in the air.

In the afternoon, while we are praying tea may be
brought to birth, the two poor souls (warning Michael
they are a nephew and an aunt) come in, and the poor
old woman begins to peck and rave. Poor Pen ! he is
very gentle—very, very patient. Certainly he thinks it

[1] Katherine.

would be better if no letters were written, but he is fumblingly good-tempered, while she hammers on the sore. O Age! What does God do with old people— put them in the mill to be ground, or send them to the dyers to be dyed? He must do something with them. I forgot—this morning we went to Nina's. Nina has the spirit of a lodging-house keeper—I say this as Michael, judger of souls.—When she asked for my name —I gnashed at her with my teeth; but Edith saved the situation, writing E. E. Cooper. We saw the portrait of Mrs. Bronson—" To whom but you "—begins the preface of *Asolando*; she has the eyes of a hydrocephalic baby.

[1] Written by " the Old " in Mrs. Morrison's Text-book.

" Robert Browning

Oh that I knew where I might find him—that I might come even to his seat! Job."

Rain—heavy sky—a longing of soul and body for sleep! We pack up our big box—then try to write in the little sala. It is useless to attempt a festa—useless. We meet, on our way, a babe in a glass case, like a relic. We think it is dead—but no, it is going to baptism. Sleep—sleep. . . . We are awfully dull and pace the sala d'ingresso. Now I am going to read " the Old's " article on *Tasso and Chatterton* in the *Foreign Quarterly Review* for July 1842.

Sarianna at dinner is found laughing to herself—we get her to confess—we have been talking of graves and

[1] Edith.

epitaphs and she has remembered the parody of Watts told her by Robert.

" 'Tis the voice of Prince Consort !   I heard him complain
    She is gone to that damned Mausoleum again ! "

At dinner we all get crudely hilarious—our nerves have suffered so from the weather.

Then Mick reads that W. Watson is our greatest living poet (Swinburne and William Morris have evidently departed this life since we left England !) and that Lewis Morris has been knighted—Dio mio—the grocer of Parnassus, poor man !   We feel low as mud . . . but our first lunch quite en famille goes well. . . .   Stories are told of Louis Napoleon (how he summoned Rossini on one occasion when he was at the opera, and when the great Italian, in his peasant cloak, apologised for his costume, smiled in reply, " We Kings can dress as we like ").   Pen knows the Empress Frederick well, and has been petted by her as an artist.   I asked about the relations between her and her son.   He said in the old days he hated everything that was English.   Once when his mother had an attack of bleeding at the nose—he said it did not matter—it was only English blood that was being spilt.

Mrs. Morrison says that the story of the Belgian wife is the story of a fellow art-student grafted maliciously on to Pen ; and, if the Old behaved as they say he did, he certainly has a deep blot on his scutcheon.

After a long rest we go with Miss Browning the north

walk to the Rocca, pausing under the Roman arch (that
irreverent artists call " The Shilling Shocker "—it is so
operatic and yet so overwhelmingly lovely).   We sit on a
wall above a family of hay-makers in a vineyard and gaze
at the green of the acacias on the opposite bank, till it
chases defect from the centre of the brain and heart.   It is
the youngest foliage one can see—full of the joy of Life.

[Pen had let a house at a nominal rent to a certain
N., a friend who disappointed his friendship.]
  In the evening Pen shows us all the correspondence
between N. and himself—it is curdling to see the snake
uncoiling himself in N.'s letters . . . the mean threats
the dastard used ! [1]   Pen's letters have dignity and wit
and all but the last are exceptionally strong—*that* struck
me as not quite a defeat of the enemy, but a refusal to
close.   Pen's actions have been hot-blooded and nearly
always foolish—his written words are wise and manly,
granted the position they illustrate.   We drive home in
moonlight by which print is legible—fire-flies tantalise
the darkness.
  The talk is of dogs. . . .
  We despair !
  At last Sarianna shows us *his* little Shelley, scored with

[1] The preposterous lawsuits brought by this N. against Pen hung
like threatening thunder over the whole visit, distracting them
and their host and hostess from the past, that they had hoped to
relive.
  The letters from Sarianna which follow these extracts fortunately
give a more succinct résumé of this strange affair than that recorded
in the diary, and at the same time complete the portrait of Pen most
satisfactorily.

the primitive enthusiasm of his youth, and in his age shorn by cruel scissors of its personal notes. Only one is left; in the second stanza of *Night* Shelley personified day as feminine—in the third as masculine—the inconsistency is corrected.

The book is the volume of *Miscellaneous Poems*, published in London by William Benbow, 25, High Holborn, in 1825.

On the flyleaf the Old has written " This book was given to me—probably as soon as published—by my cousin J.S. : the foolish markings and still more foolish scribblings show the impression made on a boy by this first specimen of Shelley's poetry. R.B. Browning June 2 1878

'O World, O Life, O Time!'"

I noted the following were scored with passionate strokes—*Hymn to Apollo* ; *Hymn to Pan* ; *Medusa* (" splendid ! "); *Constantia* ; *The Waning Moon* ; In *The Skylark* that verse *Like a rose embowered* ; *One word is too often profaned* ; *To Liberty, An Indian Air* (deeply marked); *Naples* ; *The Isle* ; *Far, far away, o ye* ; *Ginevra* ; *The Dirge* ; *Night* (with seven-fold marking); *Rarely, rarely comest thou* ; *Arethusa*.[1] " Unhappily Sarianna did not see that the volume belonged to us as simply as her wedding-ring to a woman. Every scribbling was alive to us, but the ' rare thing ' vanished from our sight—to be bequeathed to whom ? "

[2] Pen's suit against N. brought before the Praetor.

---

[1] From a letter of Katherine's to Mr. Cooper.
[2] Edith.

N. denies the Praetor's competency to deal with the case, because an act of friendship cannot be estimated in money, as must be done if it is to be tried at the Praefitura —what cheek! Everyone taken by surprise . . . a delay of 10 days needed for the Praetor to decide as to his competency.

Galanti, Pen's lawyer, at lunch—a small man with a small shut mouth, blonde crop of beard, long hook nose and eyes like blots made by a clever writer—that rest continually on Ginevra; Francesco Beltramini de Casati, a dear old gentleman of noble family, who lives alone with a French poodle named Ibis—a mystic " grig " of a creature—corresponds with the British Museum, writes learned books on bees and the lichens of Bassano and finds his most active excitement in his bee-hives and his café. The face is that of a modernised crusader—you have in it blue blood, idealism, obstinacy . . . and scientific fogeyism. The old dear asks us to visit his bees when next the sun puts them into a good temper.

A day of two or three centuries—these thunderous summer days in closed-up rooms are fearful—they make one fret to be dead. We go to the Lace School—see the bambini working on their lace-pillows where Pippa wound her silk. Curious to think that our poet is as much at the bottom of this charming industry as of *Asolando* . . . these little people clinking their bobbins at their blue tables in the airy upper chamber, are there

because he has lived and has loved Asolo. We buy
some lace and then go with Ginevra to the Riva of the
Bellevedere (Pen's house lent to the N.'s—they are at
Venice with the " Madre "—Lady H.).

. . . Sarianna is very tedious—repeating all things as
on a rosary, as if she did a sacred duty.   It used to make
Robert impatient ; it depresses us, for we have no vitality
to grow impatience.   And worse luck, Pen has been to
Castelfranco to secure a new pair of horses to try, and
does not return till nine, with Ginevra.   So we have to
dine with his aunt and repeat ourselves and hear her
repeat herself till our eyes sink in sleep.   Pen is much
alarmed lest he have offended us.

After Mick has had a draught of white wine at the
Inn, we climb to the Torrecella and read *Pippa Passes*
together.   Every touch about Asolo is " vivometric "
—every Italian effect of sun or thunder or season is felt
and makes one feel it ; but with the exception of Ottima
and Sebald the persons are not alive in what they say,
and the prose interludes, instead of giving the plainness
of common life, only place the truer passions of the
duologues in a setting of unreality.   The heat makes us
drowse even over the pages of *Pippa*.

Pen shows he is the son of two poets when he talks
about his native Tuscany—the blank walls, so characteristic, like some strong, unamiable trait in a friend—the
touch of rose or oleander connecting them with the sky,
the fret of olive-shadows on them and below them dust
inches deep as snow is. . . .

We say how Browning is the first poet who has given
Italy as a country to England.   Byron raved with

romantic sentiment about it, but Browning loved it
with a man's passion and compelled its life into his
poems.

"*Up at the villa—down at the city*"—" how Tuscan,"
breaks in Pen, " not only is the landscape local, but the
man is Tuscan—just as Fortù is Neapolitan. Yes, I
understand you; my father has given Italy to England."

. . . We go on to talk of the worship paid to the Art
of the Old Masters by England and what a blinding effect
it has had—we are so stringently academic. Nowhere
is there more talk about the colour of the Old Masters
and less power of seeing splendour of colour with open
eyes.

[Pen.] There is great difficulty in treating Italian
landscape in anything but broad sunlight—all the
changes are short as seconds; evening is exquisite
and over before the brush can fix it—just an instant
when things float and have golden haloes and it is
night.

Pen is most touching in his sensitiveness and humility.
He says he is a failure, and yet he has the artist's temperament and a delicacy that is finely touched. The amount
of misunderstanding he has met with and his own sorry
sense of his personal deficiencies has driven the poets'
son deep within the shell of Barrett common-placeness.

> All I could never be
> All men denied in me [1]—

these lines are a statement of the best in Pen Browning.

[1] Rabbi Ben Ezra, St. XXV.

His eyes are still his mother's—ardour and timidity almost bewitch in them—yet they are lost under fat brows and tortured with rheumatism. He has his father's seriousness, thinks about life till he is on the road to madness, and escapes with jocund instinctive habits of life, like those of a squire. He looks masculine, and is absent to the limits of rudeness; yet never really overbears, never offends womanliness, and vibrates in consort with any refinement of mood or speech or act. He has a painter's tact of vision and power of making a cosmos out of commonest things, without having a painter's vitality of touch. He certainly has no " tactile imagination " and no suggestion of movement in his work—but a great sense of the inherent worth of all he would portray—one feels his eye has been on it and into it. There he has benefited by his French training.

We agree that in Paris we realize that the senses are alive . . . and that therefore we are in the air of Art. However vulgar, terre-à-terre and irreverent French painting may be . . . Pen is very proud and therefore suffers internally—every blow is an unseen bruise: he finds consolation in his dogs and in the crisp gossip of Ginevra. He has an irritable temperament and a patient heart . . . he is never anything but kind to Sarianna when she is tactless and repeating herself . . . his high birth from poets makes him nervous; his personal humility brings as it always does patience.

He is very obstinate, and force only drives him into stubbornness or in the end retaliation. He can be led by strength if it is deferential or if it is kindly (by

Ginevra and Mrs. Morrison, who was defined by Miss Lee Smith as " being comfortable as the day "). He appears to have little head for business though great power of treating life architecturally.

Poor little man !—his sighs are awfully vacant . . . not rich as some sighs can be—and it is so odd hearing them, to look at his beef-red face, baldness and fawnish smirk, combined with the heavy sensitive eyes, half caught through their slits. He is moody as a poet proper and absent as a Cooper . . . or as Robert Browning. He loves his father honestly—acknowledges how well it was that he should die before age imprisoned him and, while praising his work and working his will, yet as a son Pen does not deny strain in the relationship between himself and his father. It is piteously comic to hear how the good dinners at which the poet ate all he liked and drank port wine from the beginning, told on the boy's Greek lesson next day—on the Thucydides and Homer. The Old believed in literal translation, Pen in the free use of idiom ; the father held that no music should be played without notes, Pen thought that music played by heart had the power of recitation, and that memory is a more important quality to strengthen than exactitude. Pen always hated lessons—one fancied with the peculiar repulsion of a father-taught son. The Old was evidently intolerant of faults and forcing in his culture of virtues. He could write his poetry while Pen was practising, and run up to the room above to correct errors without breaking his inspiration (or perhaps one should say intellectual labour).

Pen hates Mrs. Orr's *Life* as we do—the puling

invalidism attributed to a man who never stayed in bed till he died in Venice . . . his son, who was at home with him for twenty years, never remembers an illness overtaking him. Such being the case, the ailments of age would have been an humiliation to him—would have put him in a cage.

. . . Somehow Sarianna's unlovableness weighs on us now we must part with her, and Pen's neglect of his promise to go up with us to the Torrecella Tower is somewhat chilling—especially as he takes a ride instead. But it is useless to think that Brownings will act gracefully; they sometimes speak so, but are far too absent and self-absorbed to carry out their words. Even our poet was no exception. We look on the hills and seaplain of Asolo with some feelings of disappointment—the loveliness is unsurpassable, but we have not met the live force of its poet as we expected . . . we have not even got near any truth of his life, as we tried to by question and schemes and even by importunity. We have again been by the current of events and not in it . . . outsiders in a deep sense, though we have read Pen's most intimate letters. . . . We have lived in a haze of the struggle for existence nearly always, so that all the happiness that depends on the body has had blurred edges. We have had two moments of spiritual clarity . . . but we have often been dull and emotionally we have been inactive; while the beauty of Asolo has so crowded our eyes, we have had no intellectual or artistic life. Pen confesses that Asolo makes no pictures —it is so uniformly exquisite. . . .

Asolo-Veneto,
July 6th, 1895.

My dear Michael,

[1] I enclose the lace, and you shall very soon have the photographs. Pen is too fastidious and is satisfied with nothing less than perfection, but never mind him. I shall insist on their being sent, and Ginevra will work them off as soon as she can. . . . You sympathise with our vexations so I cannot resist the temptation of sharing them with you. The trial was put off on Monday last because the Praetor was ill, and yesterday when it was resumed, he announced that he would give his decision as to whether it came within his jurisdiction within a month! You see our enemy and his lawyer have completely changed their defence. At first, it was that N. had a lease and had paid rent—now it is that the transaction was a matter of friendship not to be judged in a small court, and also that the value of a house is estimated by the taxes levied on it, and the Belvedere is valued at three thousand francs a year. Now the Praetor's authority only extends to matters amounting to one thousand francs. I wonder N. is not ashamed to acknowledge he pays (or promises to pay) five hundred francs for a house furnished, which he values at three thousand unfurnished. He is anxious to get the affair into the court at Treviso, because there it will *never* come to a conclusion. This morning he went off to the mountains with his family, I suppose for the summer. . . .

[1] Letters from Miss Browning.

July 22, 1895.

. . . The interminable trial will never end. Six adjournments already. The Praetor has decided that he is competent to judge this delicate case of friendship, and will do so in a month. If given in our favour, as it probably will be, the adversary can again appeal, and not only that, he can take forty days before he makes up his mind whether he will appeal.

August 13*th,* 1895.

. . . Pen grew so sick of the adjournments and of the repeated recommendations to have " pazienza," that he took the law into his own hands and entered the three disputed rooms, the keys of which had never been out of his possession. One of his men now sleeps there every night. This will only increase the number of lawsuits—for violation of domicile; but it had the desired effect of driving out N. . . .

January 3, 1896.
MY DEAR DOUBLE STAR,

Thank you for your bright flash of Christmas greeting —may it lighten the coming year with its rosy augury. . . . Do you sometimes think of little Asolo ? I must tell you something about it. Owing to last summer's bad weather, the crops are bad, and there is much distress among the poor. For the first time the experiment of a soup-kitchen is to be tried, and the Municipality having voted Pen to be a member of the committee he is trying his best to make it a success. He has already got the name of " Cuccina Economica " to

be changed to " Cuccina Popolare " ;   the former suggests
something cheap and bad—he is really anxious that the
soup should be strong and nourishing, that the idea of
charity should be got rid of, and the hard-working poor
should look on it as a privilege to be able to buy superior
food at a low price.   Pen met with a slight accident a
few days ago—he sprained his leg, on horseback, but
it is better now.   He is much annoyed, and I need
hardly say I am still more so, by the reappearance of
N. a few days ago.   He has taken the house of the
bad priest, just opposite the Belvedere.   The first sign
of him is the following.   Pen agreed to let him off the
money he owed and allow him to stay on till the end of
the year (always without payment) on the condition of
" withdrawing and deploring " the paper he sent out,
acknowledging that he had never paid any rent for the
house, and withdrawing all lawsuits.   Pen was desirous
of avoiding annoyance for Ginevra and especially Dr.
Biadene, by being summoned on this ridiculous accusation of housebreaking.   But N. has shifted his ground—
the lawsuit is carried on in the name of his two paid
servants—Pen also is accused of breaking—and dear old
Biadene, the mildest mannered man alive, who would
not, I am sure, brush a fly off his coat, without saying
" Scusi "—is charged with knocking down a girl and
kicking her on entering the house—though she never
recollected the fact till some months afterwards.   Of
course this is absurd, and especially towards Biadene,
who has been Sindaco of Asolo for many bygone years.
The present Sindaco is devoted to Pen.   My doubly
dear Friends, I tell you all this because I like to think of

you as feeling interested in Robert's son, the apple of his eye, who really is worthy of his father. How his brave mother would have supported his refusal to throw that poor orphan girl overboard! and in Robert's name I thank you for your kind belief in him. . . .

March 21, 1896.

. . . We are in good health but our local news is chequered. Good—that the N. lawsuits against Pen, though dragged out by adjournments to the utmost extremity, have all failed. He prosecuted Pen for detaining an earthenware flower pot, value about five francs—luckily Pen held the bill and receipt. Then came the accusation of housebreaking with violence against Pen, Ginevra and Dr. Biadene. The adversary made every effort to get it tried at Treviso, instead of Asolo, but gained nothing—as it was quashed, with very severe comments on its maliciousness, and the others were condemned to pay all costs. But now comes the worst news, that N. has bought the large house (with eight columns) at the top of the street, just as you turn off to the Torrecella, and is fitting it up luxuriously, to give balls and festas to the inhabitants of Asolo.

I don't know whether you heard of the grand Charity Ball for the Croce Rosa (Red Cross), for which Pen lent the Rezzonico to the Municipality of Venice and the Lady Patronesses, most of whom were his personal friends. It was the most magnificent fête given in Venice for more than a century, and they realised about 17,000 francs. At the beginning of the year Pen was made Cavaliere of the Corona D'Italia. . . .

Robert was clear-sighted.   I rejoice in your success as he would have done.   Let me hear from you, everything interests me.   Our (Pen's) kindest remembrances —Always

> Your most affectionate
> SARIANNA BROWNING.

CHAPTER TWELVE

DEATH IN THE MOUNTAINS

[James Robert Cooper, Edith's father, was staying at Zermatt with his younger daughter Amy, when, on June 24th, 1897, he went out from the hotel and never returned.]

(Michael's words, nearly two months after.)
Friday, June 25th, 1897.

A rose-morning in June—a telegram came to me, brought in, through Amy's tenderness to her sister, by a Quaker friend, a neighbour—" Am afraid father has met with an accident." I went up the stairs. I heard the voice of my darling—" Master ! "—in cooing, gayest call, and I had to break the news. . . . We were only spoken to those days by telegrams and the one true Quaker friend. First we heard of a reward offered, then of Italian navvies . . . at the thought of murder— well, there were a few moments then, when I felt as if the walls of reason would give way before the pressure of my passion . . . but all the while I could not move. Mechanically I sent word we were ready to start . . . but I knew well I should break down on the way. Last of all came word from my little precious Amy, saying that the Valais Government, whom may Heaven requite, were trying to force her to say she had given up the possibility of crime. At that word and also because I found that Zermatt was going to be abandoned, as if there were nothing else to do, I arose. And Henry and I, in a dream, travelled on past the rushing Rhone and past the wild, singing Viege [Visp], down in the eddies of which we believed that sweet grey head was hidden— we went and met; our beloved little Amy stole back to her prayers, while Henry and I went on the traces, following every conceivable route, questioning the railway authorities, questioning the mulemen—only at the end did we feel this death is in God's keeping. Our Sophocles taught us patience. Thank God for literature, the literature of the dark days, with its long reaches far into the world to come.

[Back at Durdans, after three weeks of fruitless search, Edith writes to Amy—not her sister.]

" It is so impossible to realise here in the home round which he has twined his whole life in love for us, thought for our future, toil for our pleasure, that he will never see the plants we had set in the beds for his eyes, the melons reared for him, the noble roses he gave. With all his faults of mood, his tenderness, affection, simplicity, sweet paternity, chivalry, poetic temperament and beautifully grained ripeness, his trust in God and his loved ones, made him indeed dear and irreparably precious."

FALLING LEAVES [1]

To hush within my heart the beating cry
Up toward those hills, I cross an English street

---

[1] Michael Field.

To gardens over which the lindens meet :
The leaves are falling—ah, how free to die !
The leaves are falling, life is passing by,
Patient, they hover slowly to my feet
Yellowed with the dead summer's treasured heat :
Soon will be garnered safe from every eye,
And honey-mingling life among the trees
Be as it had not been ; as seconds fall
They seek their graves in earth, by twos and threes.
And, as I watched them dropping, something stills,
Heart of my heart, that over-bitter call,
As for one lost, to thee among those hills.

[Throughout the weary time until the discovery of the body in the Wittiwald, on October 25th, they were haunted by the belief that Mr. Cooper had been murdered. And indeed, even when the mystery had been solved, doubts would occasionally still harass them in the years to come. When the body was found they immediately returned to Switzerland.]

[1] The day is golden : on top of the Riffel the sun shines through the trees till they are apparitions of light. At Findeln it is clear that the darling went straight on—it is the natural thing to do ; indeed, some children saw a gentleman go beyond the chalets of Findeln, turn after some distance and retrace his way on a higher path by the little lake : then he could be seen no more from the valley. We follow this track and after climbing to the slopes above Findeln we lie down in the juniper to breakfast with our guides. I have not the very least hunger and oh, I rejoice, for he would not have desired

[1] Edith.

this bread and meat spread so hatefully before us on his very route. I suffer, under my fixed will not to suffer as those without consolation. These forest slopes are very beautiful—here and there snow lies under the ambered greyness of the larches, and always there is the great vision of the mountains above, solid and yet unearthly—very stone and building of Vision. It is plain we are in his footsteps till we come to the chalets of Tufteren—we have been the glorious way he trod : but after Tufteren all is confused, haunting. . . . It is strange that seeing Zermatt very much to the left he did not descend by the path below. . . . He may have done this and in the wood taken a turn of the path to the right that leads near the top of the rock from which he fell. Or he may have gone higher up to the top of the whole declivity and descended painfully on to the rock, or he may simply have struck into the forest as we did and, growing nervous at the late hour, descended. He could see Zermatt nearly the whole way and from above the fatal rock, which he could have easily reached by three o'clock in the afternoon or even earlier. Did he think he was still on the Riffel side ? Did he want to find a path that would lead him down into the valley ? Why, oh why did he go so far East, Zermatt before him— just on to the tract where search was given up as utterly needless ? The mystery is as deep as ever—it will be hard to keep the mind from hunting, hunting . . . but the mystery has no future in it, no anxiety, and in the name of life we must strive to cease asking. We get to within thirty minutes of the great rock down which he climbed—there, till next summer, we have to stop :

we cannot safely get further without nails in our boots and ropes. The pine-pins all on the ground are like ice to tread on. We descend with wounded feet.

Isador [the guide] tells me he must, from his position, have turned in the air as he fell—concussion must have taken all consciousness at once, though not a bone was broken, save the jaw in one place. The watch-face was intact, so the hour of ten at which it stopped may be no index to the time of the accident . . . but no more, no more !

[November 30th, 1897.   In England again.]

[1] We leave our guest Helen Sturge and drive in an ice North-Wester to Gatton. The distances are beautiful, strong earth against clear-minded sky, the sun is an athlete, the wind another ; the armies of beech-leaves take the slopes with a running march, the sheep are close together, all wool and no space between. On the churchyard path yew berries, above the Mother's [Edith's mother] grave the green fresh wood of the moss rose he planted and trained. We walk backward and forward among the swirls of ice and wind, blithe in our souls from the sun and the joy of having come to plant Alpine roses at her grave in memory of her lover. . . .   The Alpine rose presses close to the English mound.   How blessed is piety towards the dead ! The ancients understood to the depths that virtue, composed of justice and tenderness to those who are no longer living.

[1] Edith.

[Edward Whymper, the famous Alpine climber, had interested himself in the disappearance of Mr. Cooper, and had carried out inquiries in the face of local indifference, writing to *The Times* and insisting that the mystery should be cleared up.   The local people of course feared that unsavoury details might react against the popularity of the district in the eyes of visitors.   Though the actual discovery of the body was accidental, the Michael Fields felt deeply grateful to him and in December wrote :]

DEAR MR. WHYMPER,

We are all delighted to welcome you on Monday. . . . I am not surprised though deeply moved at what you say about repayment [they had offered to reimburse his expenses and he had refused].   A friend of mine who has encountered sore trials abroad said to me a few weeks ago, that relatives had ever failed her, and the people of the country had failed her, but always some one person had come forward—" a divine stranger."   These were her words, and I thought while she said them that we too had met our divine stranger—happily one no more.   You have wiped away from my mind a very black page against humanity, by your action and the great spirit of your action.

Always in gratitude beyond any return,

Yours sincerely,

E. E. COOPER.

He (Whymper) comes fresh and gapish from half a day's Turkish bathing.   He fights a tendency to stoutness with the patient force that got him to the top of the Matterhorn. He is a curious triune being—one-third hero, one-third old bachelor, one-third mysterious man of business and lecturer.

His head is combative—some of the rock of Bradlaugh's head about it, but with refinement softening the fierceness. A great scar on the right temple marks him as a soldier of the Alps ; the hair is a well bathed silvery silk on the skull, the eyes are blue, reticent of glances, but each glance is frank and has the modesty of genuine manliness, though there is a whimsical care for recognition, as an homage to personal force, in his nature. The nostrils are loops, the mouth a thin rock fissure—thin with volition not meanness. The features will not stamp memory—each time they are seen they are a surprise. They give the sort of vague impression one would have if a giant were smothered in rose-leaves. The smile comes rarely but it is royal, the gift of a king when it is bestowed. Like all people of fine strain who live much by themselves his talk is often on the things he likes to eat and drink and he has many fads. His sugar must be sifted that he may have only a suspicion of the fattening sweet in his tea.

He rolls on the couch, bows over Musico and kisses my little hound. When the hour comes for dressing he asks whether we have a strong desire to see a black coat—" I don't think it a pretty thing to see, but if you wish it shall be put on." We pray him to do as he likes, and he wears a grey suit to dinner.

He likes his dinner ! I have paid 8/- for his golden grapes—the only other fruit, tangerine oranges ! In the midst of dining he breaks out, " Now don't give me tea to-morrow morning." We are instructed in the kind of toast to offer, "And an egg?" Michael suggests. "Two eggs." Michael and he have their weed together and a suggestion is made that he should get us, the infirm, to the top of Mont Blanc, for a contract—dead or living. "And the dogs?" "That, madam, would add considerably to the contract." When Michael leaves the room Whym. asks if she has been married. At the negative answer he appears astonished and remarks, "I don't know why I should think so, but she has the appearance of a married lady." . . . The hero of the Matterhorn is not punctual at breakfast—the coffee grows cold, the toast grows cold and the eggs grow cold!

All the morning he is studying our Swiss bills, disentangling them as if they had been sent to him. We take him up Reigate Hill; our discourse is simple and most friendly. When he goes after lunch, we miss the only guest who has given us the feeling of wholehearted sunshine all day.

CHAPTER THIRTEEN

OXFORD

[On their return, after their first journey to Switzerland, they found Durdans so distressingly full of memories, that they spent some time in Oxford.]

[1] Worcester House—our bold attack succeeds. The kindly Rufus, the Don-publisher [Aldus Daniel] receives us with directness and sympathy. He is interested in our tragedy and listens while a demonish love of a poodle crushes up against Michael. We cannot leave Zermatt by way of a remark on the poodle ; so we escape by dwelling on the healing influence of Oxford, and then ask our questions—whether he would publish the Masque [2] with a few sonnets and lyrics. He hesitates— because authors grow impatient of slow workmanship— Austin Dobson summarily wrote to know why he had no more proofs. The Don replies, " Because I have had influenza," and summarily gave up that author. Into the midst of his hesitation Daniel introduces his beautiful books (all wife's copies). We look through Bridges' volumes and are passion-stricken with his selection of Keats' *Poems* and the lovely portrait of Keats by Severn, that seems to have caught the expression of his face when in intimacy with his Muse. Tea is brought in by Buttons

[1] Edith.   [2] *Noontide Branches.*

and during a half-hour of minutes stews and stews
in its own strength—but the rubicond Aldus has no
sense of the Satanic process he is permitting in his
tea-urn.

He has a satyr's forehead, a Don's voice, small, faithful
eyes, spots of blue, made with a single touch of the
painter's brush, a redness like the beginning of autumn
on the creepers of his College and the remains of sanguine
hair and beard. His manner is like that of some dogs,
excitable and warm-hearted. We like each other and
the air is harmonious that we three are breathing, when
in bursts Mrs. D. from her district visiting—a positive
lady with pale hair, a sailor hat and east wind voice,
who boasts that she is a better business woman than
her husband is and has made " lots of money out of
that *Keats*." . . . He tries to lay a plot for getting
us the *Keats* his wife gave the Free Library—that no
one reads and the librarian considers truly wasted. It
is also proposed that we should steal and begin on
the old Don's copy of *Keats*. Mrs. D. says that her
husband is sure that a well-known poet stole one of
his books.

We ask Mr. Daniel if he will come and see *Fair
Rosamund*, since he admires Ricketts' printing—he fixes
five to-morrow. We turn to Mrs. D. and ask her if she
will accompany her husband. " Thanks " (turning to
her husband). " But if you . . . well, you know . . . and
then Mrs. Gubbins is coming to tea." " Oh, hang
Mrs. Gubbins," growls her husband sanguineously.
" Yes, do," persuades Michael, with polite immorality.
But the lady fortunately has a fixed look and Michael

lightly, with railing accent, bids adieu. Then the honest private publisher and the honest poodle dog conduct us to the door. The house is old and there are bits of antiquity in modern pell-mell in the rooms, photographs of Italian pictures ; and from the hall an open door shows a bowery garden way with its leaves on the flags.

We go up into Merton Library—how snugly dusk and there we see Bradley of *Appearance and Reality* moving about with sour eyes and unloved face. It is he who shuts up the garden—is this like a Bradley ? Our hearts are not secure from affirmation.

Mr. and Mrs. Daniel arrive in twilight. . . . I entertain her, Michael him, and Michael gets our wish granted —that the Masque is printed by him, " before the twentieth century "—her condition ! Also he lays coveting hands on the *Songs from the Dramas*, for the years of the new century, I suppose. He is full of courtesy and service. If we stayed over Sunday, he would order the doors of the garden open for us ; he regrets he has to leave Oxford and cannot take us about to see old bits of Colleges. He will, if we will come again. He promises to send more of his books for us to look over, and the President of Magdalen to renew his ancient acquaintance with us.

Mrs. D. proves, as we had half suspected, to be a blunt, rather blunt-hearted, excellent woman, fearless of poets, and therefore able to get closer than some sensitive persons dare. She has battles royal with the proud Bridges, and Mrs. W. Morris sends for her. The

snow-drift hair lay on a pillow under the hangings of
rose and blue roses : Mrs. Morris only talked of her
husband and every now and again turned her great
silver-white eyes to the pillow and wept.   She has not
long returned from Egypt and it is true she sees no
one.   This is how the world would wish us to grieve
—and we light up when literature is spoken of, we
flush with intercourse, our faces turn to the autumn
sun—and few if any think we grieve, we who have to
struggle with shuddering determination against an idée
fixe that withers life with a blood-stain ; we who realise
leaf that passes by how our dead is with every drift
unburied.

THE FOREST[1]

He lay asleep and the long season wore.
The forest shadows moved round over him
As on a dial, their ruled edges dim ;
And steady darkness holds the spiny floor.
He lay asleep.   While Alpine roses bore
Their latest blooms and withered.   Like a dream
The harvest moon's flood set the place a-swim,
And ebbed, and all was stiller than before.
Then fell the autumn, little falling there
Save some fir-cone quick dropping to the mould,
Some trundled leaf, or stir in his white hair ;
And the great stars grew wintry : in the cold
Dusk they discovered him ; the woodmen say,
" As one asleep on his right arm he lay."

[2] The Gracious Silence [Mrs. Morris], when she speaks
at all, speaks words of kindness, and she has been the

---

[1] Michael Field.   [2] Edith.

patient friend of a deformed lady of raucous voice and vicious boredom, who remarked once that Rossetti had painted everything but her greatest beauty—her kindly smile.

CHAPTER FOURTEEN

VALE

[The Boers' attack on Ladysmith repulsed, January 1900.]

. . .[1] The Magnificent has been done—the Boers of barbarous Scruple repulsed on every side. I write madly, as foolishly as St. Paul this morning. I am still drunk with the hot milk of last night—the hot milk we drank to Sir George White and those Devons.

Our beloved Queen is dying. . . . Our Beloved, our Sovereign Lady. God knows I would die now, this moment, if so she might be spared in full brain power and strength of soul till she could pray that good prayer—" Lord, now lettest Thou Thy servant depart in peace." How pathetic that our people, as soon as they knew their Queen was seriously ill, took to singing everywhere the National Anthem.

How moving too that she is said to have asked Princess Beatrice if her people still loved her . . . that last doubt of the aged and dying if they are still loveable. Loveable ! The young are loveable because the spring is still

---

[1] Katherine.

with them ; the old are loveable because God in His
Beauty is still with them.

For us the rest of our lives can be but sequels—the big
volume is closed. *Le Matin* says, " The end approaches.
Europe waits. The world is about to breathe again."
Yes, the world of small vermin ; all lice and scorpions,
all things of creeping filth and slime. Oh, that England
may learn hatred ! Hatred and fierceness and pitilessness
—that we may all learn God-like hardship and simplicity
and sternness with our children. At present they are
taught to make money—not serve either their country or
their God.

Our Great Queen is dead. I—I have no tears. She
sweeps away with her into the locked land, my life, my
youth, my breathing. I have no allegiance to any other.
I love her. She is as simply my Queen, as God is my
God. . . .

The great illusion of the Victorian age is the illusion
of progress. Because at the beginning of her reign our
streets were paved with cobbles—therefore . . .

Growth of suburbs, growth of education among the
poor, an unmitigated evil—extension of franchise and
growth of free trade, unmitigated disasters—the growth
of Trades Unions, the damnation of the future.

The growth of sentimentality towards crime ; and
of science-craft (the priest-craft of the Victorian age),
insidious, berotting influences.

The synthesis of the reign—Imperialism.

The great virtue to be cultivated—" hardiness " and
the love of beauty.

. . . The deforming folly rampant to-day—when as a wretched woman versifies in the paper :

"The Queen is going a drive to-day."

The blasphemy of this lack of humour.   Death is not safe unless a smile watches the tears.

It is a pity the Queen is not consigned to her grave to-day.   There is something impious in delaying burial. It is like painting age, it is a horrible reversal of dueness. The Gods infect the land—disgust at the unlawful pause breeds farce.

. . . [1] " We did not write to each other when our dear Queen died.   We knew what was in each other's hearts ;   our early Victorian girlhood will always be very precious to us.   What nice, good and pretty girls we were.   I do not meet any girls half so nice or so serious."

[At Rottingdean. 1901.]

[2] Through the windows we preceive, " Presence plain in the place "—Rudyards that cease from Kipling and lead their children to the sands ; Burne Jones' with blue eyes that preserve a buried century.   There is a dull pressure to be gathered from the aspect of the villagers— a pressure toward Imperialism, shown by the hatless heads or Cape hats ; and a pressure toward æstheticism— long past, in straight, blue gowns, weird jackets, sim- plicity that knows itself simple.   Ammunition is kept in

[1] Katherine in a letter to Amy—not her niece.   [2] Edith.

our yard and Rudyard sends for it; our landlady has been cultured as by North End House.

Rudyard settles himself into his shoulders as a house into its foundations. There is a latent squareness in his features. His eyes are caskets for all things British. He is a Kitchener in soft stone. His children have a blue suit, a blue gown, a blue cap, a blue hood and four long, brown legs.

We call, after tea, on Miss Anderson [R.K.'s secretary] in a room, where her cat is—the typewriter, books of strenuous import weigh on her table and the herb cosmos looks with bland, violet eyes at the portrait of Kipling. We hear that the creator of Mowgli has no animals. He had a beautiful pony for his children, but the village lad was not of equal breed and could not control it—it turned and reared, and Rudyard, who is very nervous, could not bear the anxiety. We, who fear every village cur may grip Chow, have a terrible fellow-feeling with that nervousness.

Miss Anderson has no collection of Kipling books. He does not give them to friends. The people here think little of him—it is his own country. He is a good fellow to them. Miss Anderson acknowledges, of herself, *The Lesson* is not poetry and has laid the author open to attack on all sides. . . .

[1] Rudyard Kipling's rabbit died on Monday—slain by Michael Field's Chow. . . . I look forth—Chow and the rabbit are one—Chow pecks, the rabbit rolls and Chow pecks again. I am forth, I shriek and chase. He looses

[1] Edith and Katherine.

and closes again and again—finally Edith [the maid] extracts and exalts the rabbit, apparently lifeless. I return to Henry. Slowly my boiled blood cools. . . . He was but a white lump by our flaming little Minister Chow— but I am sorry death came so leisurely. . . . But the Chow ! The incident has made a man of him. I shall never forget the air with which he dashed in and drank water, like a young hero who flings aside his casque and refreshes himself. . . .

[1] We have just read that Lionel Johnson died on Saturday. One by one these young men who were about our way, when we began as Michael, have drifted down the hollow gusts of Fate to piteous graves. My ears feel to hear nothing but the fluting of reeds shaken by the wind. And this little creature with his face of a decayed angel and his ominous fragility, was the man who alone ever wrote words about our work that our souls countersigned. . . . Past all ruin and suffering and lapse that have swept him out of existence, warm to return to-day to his comprehension and his fellow-feeling with us, in the most secret and dear power that has been confided to us. God deal with him as he dealt with our handiwork ! I have asked Amy, who prays for the souls of the dead, to pray for him. Michael is just gone for a late walk by the sea. Truly this late Autumn is austere.

The first headline *Death of Dr. Richard Garnett*. Swift, swift has been his end—we had no suspicion of any danger. Good old friend to Michael Field ! I think of

[1] Edith.

him as ascended to the planet Venus. No Christianity in him—a rubious Pagan-Learning, skittish with quips and cranks. The flat blue eye and the flat, stubbly mouth, full, not of observation, but of native expressiveness, often of a grotesque kind, but definitely observable, as a tang in wine, as a herb flavour in honey. How he has been our Pierian spring of fact—true water for our Pegasus! Proof after proof has passed before that memory of Chronos, that fresh-hearted though tradition-minded criticism. Silenus and a Nibelung met in his being, a light fantastic wisdom and an industry that could move even the mountain-treasuries of the Reading Room.

How I can see him coming to his lunch in the B.M., smiling like a grotesque of the sun, his top-hat cockle-boating on his mounding skull—his cup of coffee dis-cussed with a smack of the lips! His humour, in *The Twilight of the Gods*, is wonderfully his own—not in the least literary—most personal and therefore precious of its essence—but his humour in conversation often fatigued, flowing from remembrance, not from the moment.

He was the last person left with whom we could talk about our work—our past is lonely now, as if a good old garden god had been shivered by lightning. He was always there smiling on our path; and we could evoke him when we wanted or pass by not even noticing him . . . but the smile was ever there when we turned to him. Positively there is no one to befriend Michael—no one! Well, he goes from us with our gratitude, our affection . . . our enjoyment of his star-struck wit, his courteous festiveness, his stored brain and dæmonic eye-twinkle, his colour, his old-world bulk of stature, his incongruity. Ah, what a masterpiece of strictly personal incongruity, for him to achieve dying on Good Friday!

CHAPTER FIFTEEN

STARS IN THEIR COURSES

[1] Lady Martin [Helen Faucit] is a friend of Miss Swanwick's. She read to her servants every Sunday evening,
in effective costume, from her sofa. One of them told
Miss Swanwick, that one such Sunday " had been the
happiest day in her life." Sir Theodore has heard from
many men, that in their youth his wife's acting taught
them they had souls—revealed the eternal womanly to
them. Miss Swanwick once heard an amusing effect
from two opposed methods of reading. Lady Martin
acted the part of Juliet, which she read from the play
in her hand—passionately well ; while Henry Irving read
Romeo in tones even, cold and unemphatic. It must
have been the most comic of duets.

. . . Miss Robbins came " up stage " to us, fervently
as actresses do. She is to write and arrange a meeting
with us—will she ? Actors and actresses are a *caste*
apart, however much society may relent towards them
—one cannot take them seriously, except when one is
removed from them by the footlights.

At Miss Toplady's—taking a little lunch before *The
Vikings*—a nip of what Punch calls " Nothing, the

[1] Edith.

needful." Old Leeson in the shop—a Voice enters and asks for Miss Worthington. Then a ripple about " *The Theatre* "—then Leeson's pompous confidence, there are two ladies inside who are going to " The Theatre."

" Oh, I must see them," rings out the silver visitant. " May I speak to you ? " it asks with penetrating clarity and Ellen Terry's autumn comeliness is at the door. I recognise the tilt of nose and glance at once ; not Michael : and to the flood of ripples about seats, tickets, stalls, she puts question " I must know to whom I am speaking."

" Ellen Terry," and there is immediate quadruple hand-shaking.

She confesses she has aimed too high. We shall enjoy *The Vikings*. It is so good of us to patronise her—if her friends had gathered round her, all would have been well. *The Vikings* has not been expensive—but no more pretty things for a long time (she shakes her glance at Miss Toplady's objects)—then with the spell of profound maternity on the silver volume of the voice, she says " I did it for my son—he has had his success." We heard *Julia Domna* in that passion that had dared all.

Sturge Moore has seen Sarah Bernhardt in *Phèdre* again, triumphantly holding the audience with seventy odd lines at a time. He says, " She makes one feel how utterly unreal and ephemeral current criticisms are—how certain one has a right to be that elocution and beauty will master the stage once more ; that actors will once again look towards the ideals which she had in view.

when she studied the role of *Phèdre*. Even now her performance is a reproach to everything else on the stage. We poets ought to thank her from the bottom of our hearts for such practical encouragement in a world which is stupid with opposition to our will." That is the way for a poet to write—but we have all been apologising for our existence to artists and art critics—we of the Word made Flesh.

Sarah in *Pelléas and Mélisande*. She comes, an elfin travesty of man, thin in limb, broad in hip and shoulder —the red-gold wig resting where epaulets usually rest. Under the big wig, eyes of the everlasting Lilith and lips of Lilith when she was hanging on the Apple-tree. Yet this being acts Pelléas till sex is forgotten as an accident —and the ideal lover remains. A wonderful reticence remains, très mâle, tempers her effulgent feminine power —gives a sense of mass to her passion.

The Balcony scene ! It is just the consummation of ideal passion. The hands of Pelléas are the music of " Donne, donne ! " The face deep in a joy, flooding it with the beloved's hair, that is lifted and parted and swayed and folded in ecstasy. To see the raised eyes immerge in their worship from the coils and currents of bliss and to hear the voice in its soft clamour of desire —terrible and sweet to the ear as a babe's hand is to the breast . . . there is nothing on the stage to match it ! And the unearthly yielding of Mrs. Pat Campbell's little dark head of hair completes the poem. When the husband comes and the comfort of the beloved's hair must be lost and disentangled, Pelléas remains against the wall, still in the unseen meshes—the one solid thing remaining of the dream, is the red rose crushed in his hand, that he had broken in disentangling a tress. Still stretching up his hand for the long tangle of hair, and finally not smelling, but slapping flat against his face, the rose he has torn along with the briars, he drinks in the sweetness of his doom till the rose falls in blood-drops from his face. As Michael says, nothing can express the beauty Sarah has imprinted on one's spirit as Pelléas. The lips close together from which the lovers breathe to each other the fate which approaches them. It is intimate tragedy.

At the *Criterion* we listened till we could not to Mme. Georgette Le Blanc-Maeterlinck. She is all base metal —even when effective she rings base. Her appearance —form and feature—is meretricious ; her gestures are meretricious. Her voice is simply an outrage on the brain. In this woman mysticism is judged. Her portrait laid in the *Trésor des Humbles* strips the soul of Maeterlinck—flesh to flesh—dust to dust.

Then to Yvette (Guilbert) and her *Chansons Pompadour* and *Chansons Crinolines* at the *Haymarket*. Old French music, on the old instruments, plays round her. Mme. Cassardessus, who plays the Viole d'Amour, sits like a Tuscan portrait. What style in her ! She takes applause as a social act, gravely, adequately. She wears blue of a faded tint, black and leaves edged with blue, her dark hair flat to the head and hiding the ears. Her neck is a stalk, her hands fairy small, her austerity deep.

This old music—it hums round human emotion, as the world of insects round the trees and flowers in summer.

Yvette is an artist, so surely born—so " de race "—she could do and say and sing anything. She abrogates all morality by the clearness of her perfection. Of course the songs are slight—the art of the music-hall. No matter! These songs are alive in their sauciness and charm. There is only one blot on their expression. Yvette works them up to what we dramatists would call a " curtain "—she forces the emotion to bring applause —she leads it to her by gestures that exact it, alas ! She looks engaging in her eighteenth-century dress and triumphant in her crinolines and single white-button gloves.

Four times we have been to our Midsummer Fête given us by Yvette . . . O *gaieté* !

To the Bechstein Hall—[After six weeks of illness]— a sarcophagus of vile marbles and mosaics, in which people are shut up alive from the air, inspiring the piano and violin with infernal heat round their foreheads. We stifle mid the airless coats and hats ; despairing we fly to the uttermost back where air rills now and then as the door opens. . . . The strut of the piano—not the grass-hopper leaps of the harpsichord—Yvette ! She is as we saw her in the fair summer—but all changed round her. " Where are the songs of summer ? " She has forsaken the divine platform of the Gods, for that of the concert-room, narrow, palm-formalised, with a background of

dead and muddy leaves. . . . There she is God-
forsaken, on her pinched bit of space, a ghost of lovely
summer with vile decaying browns effacing her white
. . . we are in despair!

And at first the amplitude of her genius seems rebuked,
as if the Gods were very angry with her.

La Menteuse! Ah, the wonderful art will triumph
over autumn. . . . *L'Auvergnat*—triomphe! *La Ven-
dangeuse* with its tragi-comic " in medias res." The
delicious *Belles Manières* with the fan for the attendant
cupid. Then the charm of voice and gesture suddenly
translated, the crystalline syllables with a pretty, mincing
hiss in them . . . English! She is singing *The Keys of
Heaven* with the expressiveness of *La Menteuse*. The
crowd of the unknown is rapturous, and again and again
the white form sways over the brown background, like
a white butterfly over harvest bracken. " I shall be
pro-ud if you understand two words," and she flits from
her British welcome. . . .

We have to endure Sonatas, Arias, Romances, on piano
and violin between. It is a marvel that human beings
can endure those soporific monotonies of noise : but the
audience applauds. Yvette is full of her genius in the
new song *Les Cloches de Nantes*, a very piercing old song.
She goes round with the bells as if she were a power of
the air. *The Hussards de la Garde* and *La Rue de Poitou
et La Rue D'Anjou* rouse one to that joy in life as mere
human life, Yvette's saucy songs can feed one till laughter
is youth in one's blood. Even the sentimental *Lisette
de Béranger* makes one a little tremulous, so raw and fresh
is the voice, " Comme j'étais gentille." Yvette gives me

that exhilaration I have only when the breeze sets to me from genius, a breeze that is profound yet sparkles, that sweeps tears into the heart and radiance over the face. After this terrible six weeks, to hear, as we heard her when health and rose-red summer were with us, was the appearance of the spirit of delight.

[1906] . . . I reach the Adelphi Hotel—so waspish that when we heard the barmaid, who promised us room No. 16, had let it and said she told us she could not definitely keep it, I give the lie in the rounded phrase, " It is a lie ! " But we have a grand Adams room with lotus mantelpiece ; and we have a sensible foreign dinner. Then to our cab to cross the way.[1] First sight Hardy—a waste pansy of a man, grimacing from a heap of rubbish. The hall full of little London. George Moore, white as a tree of silver sallows by the streams of Innisfree. There sat George Moore by a lady in a spring-tide of hoariness, showing his old heart in glassy reflections. And not far off the face of an angel-sheep turned into a kid's and gray with its baby old age—Max Beerbohm. Then not far off Symons with the snows on his juvenility, as if resting on a little pasture hill, forgetting it is not an Alp.

Good Heavens ! All our contemporaries—and all parched by the wind that drives away what it touches, all gray—except Selwyn Image who never had or has any hair on his spirited rosiness.

Not so many hoar contemporaries . . . old Dr. Todhunter complete from his coffin, the gigantic Bernard

[1] To see *A Florentine Tragedy* and *Salomé*, by Oscar Wilde.

Shaw really grown stately and aloof from pettiness, like a mountain under snows. What has changed him? The light-complexioned snigger that used to wander his eyes and nostrils—gone! Among the faces, this one solemnised by experience, broader in humanity than the pigmies under his forest. I have enjoyment from his aspect. Three curious devilkins all in one place at one time, Zangwill, the finer Yeats and Bobbie Trevelyan— all dusky irritants. And the women! All pose, head-dress, eyes and mouths set in shop window. . . .

The merciful darkening of the hall for *A Florentine Tragedy*—badly acted by wife and lover, over-acted by the merchant husband. The episode is vulgar and uncon-vincing and cannot bear the weight of Oscar's rhetoric. I begin to wonder what we came forth to see. The monotonous trifling with life and death ends at last. Up with the lights! And we rise to study this hall of contemporaries without recognition by word or bow, they sit before us, they move about. . . . The curtain up!—At once, what we came for. Eastern luxury in moonlight. A picture painted by Titian or Delacroix . . . no, only by Ricketts himself. Never has the stage been so wonderfully used—the picture painted by a great painter, with all the masses, lights, sparkle, glow, atmo-sphere of a masterpiece to set the human passion it symbolises. All the actors stand and keep their positions long, giving their speeches as chords in the *Moonlight Sonata*. The whole play is full of harmony and " leit motifs," of evocations, and all this character is brought out by gesture and timbre of voice. The Herod is a most Flaubertian study, but so individualised that it is out of the tone of the music that Oscar weaves dramatically. It is somewhat too clever ; but consistent and engrossing, as the sombre eyes grow hollow and the wanton mouth grows slack under the reddest red of the rose crown. In the red of this rose crown the highest note of the scarcely emerging, yet basal blood-red of the picture is struck for us—the red that couches in the shadow of the precious blue of the moon.

The other characters are in the tone of the imaginative rhetoric by which the play reaches us. Salomé is a pale, exacting virgin—thirsting for tragedy.

[At an At Home at Ricketts' and Shannon's " Palace."] Then Shannon coming up we ask him to introduce us to Herod.[1] He is an amusing creature, ingenuous in taste, simple   by   nature . . . deliciously   youthful. . . .   I found that he admired " that beautiful thing *Attila* " and with his young coins had bought it. A leaf of my great Druschki rose fell, floated and touched the ground. Very quietly he stooped and closed the petal in his hand —for that volume of *Attila* I suppose.

[The following incident had occurred eighteen months before the preceding passage.] Michael and I are walking with our dogs in the park, we see a man stretch arms towards the sky and then totter. Michael supports the consumptive to a seat . . . he pants he will be better, and at offers of help, says he will give up his hopeless aim of reaching Surbiton by foot and get a bus below, if

---

[1] Robert Farquharson=Robert de la Condamine.

Michael will support him down.   He is just out of hospital : his home at Witchfield near Basingstoke ; he is a clerk with an old mother 85 ; he has five shillings from an Association or Clerks' Provident Society—she has three shillings—from the parish.   "But all will be well when I draw my money on Saturday," he says with the persistent mumble of the invalid.   "I shall be all right when I see my old mother."

I shall long see Michael in ruddy hat, her face alive with compassion, arming the man down, his hollow face above a poor, genteel frieze coat.   I lead the dogs in front—many glances play round us.   We seat him in the Grot ; press milk on him (brandy he has refused) and are reproached at his weakness, as of nausea before a whole glass.

"You'll finish your glass ? "

"I can't now . . . but before I go."

He will have four miles from Witchfield Station and we have learnt he will not get his money till Saturday.   So Michael gives him 10/– and I give 2/– for the old mother ;   his smile is beautiful and when we put the money in a little leather-bottle purse, the ridiculous bag is greeted as a token—Michael goes out to the boat-house to ask one of the men to stop the bus—I learn our man is Scotch, his father from Dalkeith, a retainer of the old Duke, turned away by the young one.   Finally the stricken invalid, with quiet eye-dewing thanks, is supported by Michael to the bus and committed to the care of the conductor, having promised to write of his own accord, and having given his address and having taken ours on a stamped envelope.

When Michael returns she exclaims, " There is nothing like the primitive passions—what are Tristan and Iseult beside this poor clerk yearning to see his old mother again ? " And then, " He was a gentleman. How breed and bringing up tell ! " (A propos the Duke's service.) Somehow I wonder that charity does not seem to bring that glow and pleasure it is vaunted to do. Days go by, and the man who was piteous sends no letter. We write to his mother and our note is returned O.H.M.S. We write to the clergyman.

" I am sorry to say your kindness was abused. The man John Walker is an old offender. I have had several letters describing his method of feigning sickness. I wish he could be caught."

So that smile, when the leather-bottle purse was put in his hand, was like Cesare's when he wooed the Condottieri into the trap at Sinigallia. John Walker and Cesare Borgia were equally perfect actors—well, I am Machiavellian enough to call each masterpiece a " bello ingano." But the blow is very shrewd to Michael's humanity, and she burns to think of the deceiver on her arm.

We tell Ricketts of the Impostor : the beautiful Southern eyes hold their gravity and Michael is not teased, till she tells of Tristan and Iseult—so poor before the primitive passion of the clerk for his old mother. " Oh, but Michael, Mama is not the first link . . . some events precede ! " And he laughs a laugh like a flight of birds. He is glad the man should have been an impostor, rather than a real case of the terrible pain and illness in the world. Far better the acted than the real.

And we pay 10/– to hear Sarah—why not give 10/–
for the marvellous performance of John Walker?

[Eighteen months later a visit from Robert Farquhar-
son.]

In the garden by the evening primroses, he suddenly
said to Michael:

"But you are so good—my mother says you are so
good to tramps."

M.   "No, I am rather afraid of tramps.   There was
an impostor . . ."   Michael pauses, fearing to tell a long
story.   "But does your mother know me?"

H[erod].   "No, she does not know you."

M.   "Then how has she heard?"

H.   "She must have read it somewhere."

Then at dinner he spoke of never impersonating
anyone but the senile or effete—"I have acted every
disease."   Again at the end he spoke of hospitals.   He
seemed disconcerted and watched Michael, not me, as
I read of Tristan's [1] disguise, "A hell-burnt, hideous
fool."   The scene almost had, it seemed, a repulsive
effect on him.

Also when we met at first at the Palace he turned with
rude abruptness from us, and all cordiality would have
been lost had I not rescued it.

We believe now, that in youthful audacity he tried
the effect of his acting from hospital studies on people
in the public parks.   Hence the letters received by the
clergyman.   If this should be so, life would be stranger
than a dream.   I said if John Walker were an impostor,

---

[1] *Tristan de Lovnois.*

he was one of the greatest actors who ever lived—indeed
he was a worthy companion picture to the Herod in
Salomé.

Herod writes (we had asked him to come over and
visit the tombs and dwelling-places of the great [Rotting-
dean]) :

                                                    1907.

Most dear Michael,
   Your invitation that I may leave the horrible streets,
for rocks where you are happy with the colours of the
sea, and wind from the wings of rooks, is very kind and
beautiful, and I should be most delighted to ride in the
train that dear and kind Henry tells to me, but would
you let me come next week? My mother is ill and
our house is filled with horrible people, so she needs me
to amuse her, poor person. . . . Thank you so much,
one is longing to see you, for it was but ghosts of each
other that met in good Mr. Ricketts' house, and ghosts
are tantalising.

                              Always yours,
                                   Herod.

   I Tatti [the home of their friends Mr. and Mrs. Bernhard Berenson] has seen something of D'Annunzio and
Duse. They live with an olive walk and a door between
them. Duse puts on her gloves to visit him—Duse
whom he has taken as his mistress before the public of
the World! There is piteous comedy in it.
   Carlo Placi arranged the first visit (Norman Hapgood

was present and an Italian Countess). The moment Duse learnt Hapgood was a journalist, she took possession of him with hard determination and only talked business—he must help her American tour. All were disgusted. But little D'Annunzio, his legs not reaching the floor, began to talk, and as the lovely voice and crystal Italian reached the listeners they were subjugated. He expounded himself: his life is built on two masculine principles, Istiuto and Orgolio; and on two feminine principles, Volunta and Volutta . . . Bernhard, listening with a face of disgust broke out, "And where, Signor D'Annunzio, is the intellect?" There was a pause over all ears. "I am the intellect," replied the truculent insect in his bewitching tones.

Bernhard and Mary called on Duse. They had to go to D'Annunzio's house to learn the way, and were conducted by a terrified little maid to the wall door, after giving a promise not to betray her guidance. They were admitted into a rose-garden, where was Duse, as a shepherd, able to call each rose by name. Roses, roses everywhere. The guests were at once questioned as to how they found the door—"Wandering down by the wall," fibbed Bernhard.

Duse was very sad and shatteringly expansive. She had told D'Annunzio she was getting too old for his parts and he had acquiesced tranquilly. The guests lessoned her that the young must have their chance—so they lessoned Duse in an *Il Fuoco* mood.

Again—Mary was in I Tatti garden when Duse looked in and asked to enter. She had heard that every week the Berensons have a Bach evening. Might she bring

D'Annunzio ? She was starting next day to Russia (to earn him money). He had been absorbed in his work —cold to her. Music might refresh and soften him. The lady of strict principles who conducts the Bach evenings was *induced* to come and play.

Duse soon wearied of the music—once she wept, her face was distrait. D'Annunzio was profoundly inter-ested. When the music stopped he still remained, talking till after midnight, while she wrung her fingers with impatience, tapped them on the furniture in vain. This tragedy of a woman whose sex has drowned her very self is piteous hearing. What will be the end ?

[Two years later.] D'Annunzio, having left Duse, is now in liaison with . . . She keeps a fine stud and D'Annunzio rides. The manner of their riding is thus : first comes D'Annunzio looking neither to right nor left as he passes over the bare Tuscan country—then, by and by, a man servant : a pause : then the lady in white, riding on with not a glance on either hand—then, by and by, a man servant. The cavalcade takes an eighth of a mile.

We went on the 23rd to see Duse in *La Gioconda*—she walked through most of it—she spoiled the triumph and meaning of La Gioconda in the studio scene, by selfishly disturbing the values . . . in the last scene, in spite of the repulsive, accidental base of the act, she was pathetic as Euripides is pathetic. It was Greek, it was great, it was fearless in the evocation of agony and royal in the absoluteness of the means by which we felt it.

D'Annunzio has almost spoiled Duse—she is a queen-
slave now and sad with her discrowning as Hecuba.
The perpetual dolefulness enrages one—it robs one of
the variety that gives its lights to a solemn method.

CHAPTER SIXTEEN
THE TWENTIETH CENTURY

[1] In pursuit of God-like hardship, Michael has started for the first Dolmetsch Concert . . . with a great gulp of Vino Santo she tears herself from Chow and me. We have been laughing, laughing at the wild unpreparedness of our toilet for evening display—Michael says, " Of course if we were asked to a dance of night witches, we could wave our torches with the blithest."

We have been out of the world so long, we are like Byron in Italy when going to an Englishman's party after his exile. And we are so timorous before the insuperable midnight—its cabs, trains, solitude.

As I sit down to my lonely dinner, Whym in his chair, his eyes exclamatory for his Miss, this telegram feeds me : " Borrowed umbrella, fichu, high bodice, comfort, tea, blessing."

[2] It was horrible leaving Henry. I left him in bitter wind. In town violent rain set in. At my tailor I tried to borrow an umbrella, and it is characteristic of London that the great house did not possess an umbrella. Carlyle should write of it—the wearied soul from the country asking the hospitality of that hooded staff—the consternation, the dismay—the final loan from a neighbour. In my club there is no soul. I roam the dark and empty

[1] Edith, 1901.   [2] Katherine.

259

rooms. I cannot dine. I play with a little soup and threaten suicide.

The concert-room is low, lighted with sconces—set round with instruments. The instruments are wrong in decoration. The painter sets his room round with pictures, but the musician's art appeals not to the eye but to the ear. The violin, the pet dog of a lifetime, may be tolerated, but he is best in his case when he is not in his master's fingers. Dolmetsch's face is too flagrant with genius. Even the godhead must be tempered. And the human creature, good to contemplate, is not a plain joint and greens, but a finely ordered dinner of several courses and delicately blended diversity. Even the poet must be a very distinguished and attractive personality, without his wings.

The room was full of faded Victorians, but not my Victorians—mine were of the season before last. Not an Image, not a Horne, not a "little Arthur." One felt that Pater was buried very deep. . . .

[Another concert.] In the Dolmetsch concert-room I have passed some of the most acutely miserable moments of my life. . . . If the instruments sang I should be content : they buzz. There was one little French song that rose up, a thin little plaint to the heavens—then the infinite self-absorption of the bees began again. Occasionally I caught the dark, milk eyes of Dolmetsch— they are distinctly allied to milk—resting on me. The audience is the quaintest I have ever met—misshapen, defeated, ugly people, manqué every soul among them, asking of life to be insignificant. I did not see there a happy face or a sad face or a human face—small, braided monsters of the Néant, row on row. The ideal of the Dolmetsch family is the grin. They are very good-humoured, lovable probably to those who are near them. Dolmetsch himself confounds process with result. The executant must charm by his music, not by the curious properties of his instruments.

And after all this bitter comment, this Miss Austen music does engage one. In a Japanese garden and if one could be sufficiently small—one would be caught by it, as one would like to learn the notes of the birds.

Last week I met Dolmetsch . . . he was infinitely amusing on the six cottages he inhabits on the banks of the Thames. He is full of the happiness of catching his fish, waiting for his eggs. . . . I have a dream of buying Janet's spinet for Henry and of Henry's thrumming little tunes to me. It will come to pass.

I have named one of my MSS. books " King Edward VII." We have gummed into it a portrait of the King, part of a group. He is standing by a little Lady Duff-Gordon, or, as we interpret, standing, cap in hand, before the infant muse of the twentieth century. We take the King as our tutelary deity—to keep us genial, simple and humane—to preserve us from being literary—to give us something of the breadth and wisdom of Dryden—of Pryor.

[1] Yeats and Tommy [2] come.
The first motion of Yeats is to seize a book for bread

[1] Edith.   [2] T.S.M.

and support in his shyness. . . .   It is Ricketts' *Hero and
Leander*, and there is not another book in sight.   We
leave him to recover : then Michael shows him the river
and the pendant [designed for them by Charles Ricketts,
a portrait of Edith Cooper, now in the Fitzwilliam
Museum, Cambridge].   The miniature he finds most
lovely, but does not know which of us it is.

His shyness makes Tommy more familiar.   The
stranger manifests that we are somewhat intimate after
a year's friendship.   It is an easeful truth.

At dinner Yeats is fearfully shy at first, doctrinaire and
" causy," but gradually he becomes warm and vivid in his
monologuing.   He is dark, with a Dantesque face—only
not cut in Italian marble !   His hair dribbles in a Posthle-
thwaite manner on his brow.   I wanted to give the order
to Lilias to bring grape-scissors and cut the locks.   His
eyes are abstract and fervid : when he speaks of spiritual
things and shakes back his forelock, there is a smile like
an atmosphere on his eyes and brow.   The mouth is for
speech, speech.   The hands flap like flower-heads that
grow on each side a stem and are shaken by the wind.
At first the gesture spells one ; then it irritates, because
it is a gesture and is not varied.   We put on our smilax
wreaths.   Tommy looks like a primeval forest god—
terrible—the source of panic and of the cruel laughter of
simplicity.   Yeats feels he is wearing spectacles and the
twine looks conventionally poetic on his hair.   Then we
cast the wreaths on to Whym Chow's neck.

Yeats is not of us—he is a preacher.   He preaches
some excellent things and some foolish things.

He knows our plays well and seems to care for them

with insight.   I was not prepared for this, but Dowden
fired him with them in youth when he was at Dublin
University.   His wit is rhetorical—not the instinctive
mischief and drollery, the moment's wild happiness in
some contrast, that is so engaging in Tommy.   He is
an evangelist, quite sincere in his exposition.

We have some amusing glimpses at George Moore—
calling in a policeman to know if the law requires him
to eat his landlady's omelette ; or gazing at the amateur
Dublin actors of the Clerk fraternity and pronouncing,
" Well, you are a seedy lot."

Yeats reads a little prayer to the Psaltery—a most
charming poem.   All the Archangels appear in it with
shoes of the seven metals.   Also he intoned as if to the
psaltery Keats' *Bacchic Ode.*

Yeats says that in his first review of us, written when
a college youth, he remarked we did not dream or saunter
enough.   Poor George Moore, who wails over the way
in which character becomes faint under Yeats' handling,
would find in this lack our safeguard.

We have been saying we envy men their conversation
with each other.   " Men don't talk well to each other
—they talk well to women.   There must be sex in good
talk."   Tommy, lying Pan-like on the settee, echoes this
with fervour.   " A man has no ideas among men—but
he goes home to a cook or a countess and he is all right,"
sings Yeats.   Therefore he is a believer in many flirtations
and believes Goethe's wisdom was born to him of woman.

[In Italy.]   We started off to call on Vernon Lee,
accompanied by Miss Crutwell.   Such a walk !   A grey

sky making the wheat of the " poderi " glow green into one's very brain . . . on the ground little asphodels. We passed the stream where Boccaccio and his ladies sat in coolness and told their tales : finally we arrive at Il Palmerino.   We saw a *sibyl*, in a tailor-made black dress, vine-dresser's hat and apron, sowing seeds.   It advanced—it was Vernon.   She looks fifty ; she is thirty-nine.   She is very ugly ; the face very long ; the eyes with a look of greed for discussion.   Yet there is much suffering in the expression, or sadness that one pities.   The features are restless and have a sort of ghastly good breed.

The bosom-friend of Vernon, Anstruther Thompson, is a splendid example of the thorough-bred English woman, to whom dogs and horses are as familiar as books to us—a noble, handsome, easy woman, she too is strapping tall.   The tiny house has no charm ; it is too crowded and awkwardly disposed, and, like its mistress, has no central unity of purpose.

Vernon was very stupid in what she said about art— about Huysmans—while the poet sat in dual quietness and the metallic conversation went on.   Then came the return : a huge sheep-dog accompanied Vernon—these Italian watchdogs are the terror of the " poderi " ; we say they are the form in which devils now appear.   We were nearly at the top of the hill when the dog of Vernon's great enemy sprang from a wall.   Terrific noise !   The dogs close under the vines : the three immense tailor-made women rush in with sticks : Vernon's appetency for the fight, the dominant long back of Anstruther, like the leaning tower of Pisa over the combatants, and our nice Miss Crutwell's violent promptness of visage, remain with me and will for ever. Diabolic howls, black arms grasping tails, calls for " acqua ! "— a peasant woman with a vine hook—a coil of brute fury in the wheat . . . and we fly down the hill, down, down ; shamelessly, quakingly we seek holes in the hedge. At last on a little knoll the creators of *William Rufus* and *Canute* exchange a dialogue.

Michael (distracted). What are you afraid of ?

Henry (in calm silver voice). Oh, I am afraid of being killed.

Michael. Don't stir ! I forbid you.

And there we stuck till a voice, cool as a man's, called, " Do come on ; we shall be so late for dinner." " No," says Michael, " I'll not pass those dogs till they are chained." "But they are," contemptuously adds the voice.

Michael and I shake with inextinguishable laughter when we think of the fierce tail-gripping women, all teeth and courage and pugnacity—and of the timid poets, the worshippers of Vikings, trembling lest an infuriated cur should fill his mouth with their cheeks. I saw the flamelets of pomegranate leaves on their wild bush, ruby flamelets, and gathered the mealy white heath.

We drive to Upperfold, Miss Kinsella's house. I am a little disappointed—I had hoped for a French convention in the rooms ; they are merely full of French furniture. But the wonderful Miss Louise has a strange daring with colour. She has put up some murex-purple curtains, embroidered them with green, and has the stern

intention of threading them with red. Her dress is
audacious—but a little spinsterish—I mean a little
narrowly designed, to please herself. If she were not
so regnant she would be hooted. She is all pink with
mauve and white hat, veiled in arsenic green and topped
with rose-red daisies, and one looks at her, fascinated to
look—one's rebellion stamped out by the fitness of things
diverse. She speaks prettily of the advantage of being
educated in France. It gives one perpetual youth ; for
in France young people are understood, in England the
men and women only become young when they are
middle-aged—so to pass from one to the other is not to
grow old. She loves eighteenth-century French life—
when women made a world, and men were the raw
material of their art—when a peasant's son could be
discovered by a woman's penetration to be a genius,
could be fostered and placed in the world she governed.
Even now to pass from France to England is to pass
from woman's interest wholly to man's, and it is a coarse
change. Louise wakes every morning to wonder why
she is so happy and to discover it is because she is unmarried. She is not lovable, she is not a good hostess,
she does not evoke like a French woman. She sits, a
smile round her even teeth ; and her eyes are sweet in
their lashes as bits of sky rind, the fringed boughs of
trees. Her skin has a dry colour that supports all the
truculence of green and pink and mauve on her head,
certifies that Whistler admired such ventures. She is
ornamental and empty—in the last resort. She is a
challenge rather than a person. She has the brightness of
a trumpet note and the ring of it, yet all the while she has

the aspect and mode of the spinster. She is most singular in the pride of her dizened virginity. At times she seems spectral, as dragon-flies can seem.

. . . Santayana's mother. Curious Americans asked the old lady what she did, how she employed herself. The old lady said she always found plenty to do. But what? " Well, in winter I try to keep myself warm and in summer I try to keep myself cool."

Roger Fry, his wife, and Mr. Dickinson of *John China-man's Letters* and the *Platonic Dialogue* come to tea. There is a charm about Roger Fry—the bouquet of a special kind of red wine. He has humour—so too in a crotchety way has Dickinson ; and gaily goes the time over the toast and strawberry jam. We enjoy our allusive, literary English humour, fantastic, full of tolerance and banter. We are so glad no American, Jew or Alien is among us.

Dickinson is deeply interested to hear of my vision of death as a grey coast I reach, detached consciously from my body. He has never had the vision himself, he learnt of it from a report of the Psychical Society.

Dickinson believes that fundamentally he can only understand, and therefore like, Englishmen. Dickinson is a gnarled apple-tree, bearing the ripest fruits of a University.

We are sad and rather ill while the day clears slowly, and suddenly is a happy child, good in every impulse— a blue afternoon on which trees look quite different.

Mary [Berenson] brings Mr. and Mrs. Houghton of
Florence neighbourhood. Two people on whom the
spirit of happiness—like an earthly form of the Holy
Ghost—rests continuously. They are full of beatitude
instead of hatred. The husband and wife have outgrown
the barriers of sex and become so much alike, they are as
brother and sister. I have seen this kind of marriage,
unattractive because it is confusion, the distinctness of
sex quality impaired. He has shiny pond-like eyes, hers
are like the dark bubbles rising through sedges as a
current passes. They are sweet, aggravating people with
no firm outline. She cares for jewels—buys a thousand
baroque pearls at a time—has seen a beautiful Indian jade
necklace that is to be sent on approval to us. . . .

Mr. and Mrs. Houghton were vegetarian for eight
months after marriage. A distressed friend left a cat in
their charge. The cat was to feed on mice, but it ate
its capital up, every day laying the mice in rows, with
awful intelligence, before the pair. Then all mice ceased.
The cat grew lean, the cat grew fierce and a confirmed
swearer—the friend's cat was empty. Edmund went to
the butcher and bought a beef-steak. As it cooked, not
only was the cat ready for it, but the woman did eat of
the steak and she gave Edmund to eat. There were no
more vegetarians in that house.

Cap. Jefferson, when out with Stanley, came across the
race of dwarfs, that live on bananas in the darkness of the
great forest and die of light. A little couple, Adam and
Eve, attached themselves, dog-like, to the Englishmen.
One of these gave Eve an old mackintosh. She wound
it round her with a woodland girdle and trailed about

with a mirror, in a passion of vanity—poor little bit of a woman, with her strange cries no more translatable than the cries of a brute—while the camp of European men laughed loud. Little Adam died on the edge of the forest. Eve died a little further on in the light. Pathetic comment on my finest bit of pathos—" The shade cares for me and will keep me safe."

Following on an introduction from Mary Berenson we have had an invitation from John Marshall, partner in Lewes House with Ned Warren.

" . . . It would be so pleasant to see you at lunch on Sunday, that I hope the drive across the downs will not be too hot for you. Alas ! there are but few things here to attract you : I wish there were more."

In heat, under a hooded Victoria, we reach Lewes House—a shaley old house that might be a private Lunatic Asylum outside ; inside a British-looking man, with obstinate, blue eyes, gives us brusque welcome. A whippet flashes by. Orders are called to our man . . . we are in an oak-walled drawing-room. Introductions to Lord D. . . . and Furtwängler—instant march to the dining-room, also oak-walled, where we are pewed at our meal, the black oak table being nearly as tremendous an effort as the pews.

Furtwängler's English was like batter-pudding striving to express itself. So in pity, the violet-natured, meek Miss Marshall asked him the names of his children—they were spirited out as from the hot pan. And the fierce professor with his erect hair and small rapid eyes dined with no other disturbance.

After coffee we are wafted to a fowl-pen in a paddock.
. . . The priceless companion screen to the *Throne of Venus* is before us.   I give my ideas as to the period, the subject—" Ja—Yes," fizzes Furtwängler, and strives with English to illuminate the screen.   Then he becomes absorbed in the relief.   His hand hovers, with the science and revering happiness of a bee's hover above choice flowers, round the lovely outlines.   It was watching an action of fine art to watch this connoisseur's touch.

We find ourselves often speaking of the old house, full of mysteries . . . a lovely Aphrodite behind a dressing-room door ; a drawing by Rodin left, as if by Psyche's Ministrants, on a table ; Thanatos stretching pinions where one would expect the winged fowls !   It seems to hold invisible mysteries too—and then there is the silky-eyed whippet, all of a sudden behind one in a deep chair. A very stealthy, enthralling old house !

Once twenty white cats with blue eyes were kept in one room.   " How many cats were there, Jim ? " " Nineteen, Sir."   " Oh well, that's the same thing."

CHAPTER SEVENTEEN

SANCTA ECCLESIA

[Edith's sister Amy, had, in 1900, married Dr. John Ryan, a Catholic, and though Amy was not baptised into the Roman Church till 1907, this close contact with a Catholic circle undoubtedly played a part in their decision to enter that Church.

In 1905 they had published anonymously the play *Borgia*. The late Charles Ricketts, R.A., in the following passage describes how it had affected their thought:

" It is a curious fact that the reading this work entailed, was the direct cause of their conversion to Catholicism. The singularly humane and vivid picture they have given of Pope Alexander, had been intensely lived by them . . . Henry's conversion was worked out in secrecy, without the knowledge of her Aunt, who hopelessly exclaimed when told, ' But this is terrible ! I too shall have to become a Catholic ! '

" It enriched their daily lives and proved a source of infinite consolation when Henry became smitten with cancer. With their conversion certain traces of bitterness and disappointment in Michael, over the silence with which their work was received, disappeared ; with age she had grown less quick-tempered. . . ."

After Mr. Cooper's death and Amy's marriage, they had become passionately attached to their dog, Whym Chow. When he died, in January 1906, they were for

long inconsolable, thinking of leaving their home at
Richmond and retiring even more completely from the
world. In reviewing that year, Edith writes]

For years I have worshipped the Holy Trinity, ever
since I prayed, and Michael prayed, for the little earthly
Trinity, Whym Chow, Hennie and Michael, to the ineffable Divine Trinity—that symbol all creators must adore,
who attain to its fastness of Life. Closer than ever was
this worship when Whymmie died and in the midst of
this great mystery loomed for me an altar, as the symbol
of sacrifice, of Love unto Death and beyond it forever.
I have always disowned the Church of my childhood,
because it was destitute of the real centre of all true
religion—an altar with its present Deity—and because
the Dead had no portion in its services and there was
no universality in its rites.

The Bacchic joy of Benediction was shed on me years
and years ago at the Oratory—though rarely going to it,
I have loved its flame-lit gratitude.

When at Edinburgh, Michael spoke to Father Gray of
her joy in Benediction, she found it was nothing beside
the Mass to him. Feeling the centre of reality was in
a simple Breton Mass he had attended, Father Gray
immediately became Catholic on the advice of the simple
priest. He could die for his religion and is willing to
live for it. This woke a curiosity to study the unknown
Mass.

. . . Weeks of autumn went by ; Alice Trusted sent
us some small books and leaflets on the Mass—I read,
and my mind took on a glow. But we could not find

a missal we could read . . . and day by day we were growing sadder and more empty in our life of complete solitude. Then Michael (if Archangel also a spirit of vital unrest) swore she would get a missal, and in November wrote to Cockerell, who sent us a list of Charles Higham's missals. They came in selection and we took one in sheets—of immense type—a priest's of course. Every morning we read it together—it simply was my natural food. I felt that Berenson's apprehension of symbols, as the means of life, lacked in one thing only ; the will remained remote from them, and the Blessing was not wrestled for nor won. At last, on Dec. 2nd, I resolve—we resolve—our apprehension is made an act. We go together to Mass. On Saturday evening we had been as mad, and without hope, blaspheming our fellowship with reproaches—the very chaff of Hell. We went to Mass, and the prison walls of our life fell as we prostrated ourselves before the one perfect symbol, and all we love was with us, included and jubilant. Demeter and Dionysus (our lord Bacchus) yield themselves up as victims to the great Host, the Saviour of the World—" Et antiquum documentum novo cedat ritui."

Fraser's book prepared my mind for this pure subsuming of sacrificed divinities under the one divine sacrifice ; that we should offer by them " panem sanctum vitæ æternæ et calicem salutatis perpetuæ." My little beloved, my Chow, by his death, brought me to worship fully—because he brought me to realise the need of an act of Sacrifice in making the heart a Spirit, the will a creative sufficiency.

CHAPTER EIGHTEEN

MARGINAL NOTES

[1] Henry read to me this St. Andrew's Day—this piece of loathsome journalism from Bernard Shaw:

" As to the crucifixion, it was a terrible adulteration of religion, to make a public execution its central fact. The end of the Gospel story, the popular and bloody part, spoiled the beginning. If Christ had died in a country-house, worth five thousand a year, everything he said would have been just as true as if he had been sacrificed."

I write to the Rev. S. D. Headlam.

DEAR SIR,

I write to you after reading an account in *The Times* of certain words of Mr. Bernard Shaw. To my amazement I find they were spoken with the approval, under the auspices of the Guild of St. Matthew. I write, sir, to learn whether this is really the Guild of St. Matthew, founded some years ago with the avowed object of bringing more clearly home to our hearts the mystery of the Incarnation ?

Surely it is some other society, or the purpose for which it was founded has been utterly forgotten ?

[1] Katherine.

This is no matter for angry newspaper correspondence. I ask for a simple explanation of how the quoted passages, so blockish in their stupidity, can bring any believer or unbeliever nearer to the Life that was not taken away, but " laid down." Which of our words is " true " in any real sense save as the outcome or prophecy of deed ?

You of the Guild of St. Matthew know and proclaim it is Christ's action, His deed, His being made Flesh that has availed—and in the sacrifice of His Death, He is again made flesh, giving us of His Body and His Blood.

Of this precious mystery your guild professes itself one of the guardians. Yet your guild heartily thanks the author of the enclosed sentences. Their crude blasphemy (and so easy to see whence it cometh !) would be of no importance as a passage of vulgar journalism. It is confusing to see them in their present relation.

I ask very earnestly for a full reply to my questions. Our Lord Himself laid much stress upon His Death. You, sir, are minister still, I suppose, of the Church's Sacraments. Do you too believe in the merit of the country-house death ?

Faithfully yours,
K. H. BRADLEY.

[1] Two good stories from Father Green :
A woman told him she wished to be a Catholic.
" And why do you want to be a Catholic ? "
" Well, Father, eighteen years ago a priest told me I had a Catholic face." And the tiny seed has grown

[1] Edith.

through the years, till she wished to have the face of a Catholic.

The Priest meets Herbert (our old chair-boy) soon after he has met the poets. Herbert is eager in our praise.

" Such learned, clever ladies—and they write . . ."

" Oh well, what is the matter, what do they write ? "

" Oh, they write Shakespeare and that sort of thing."

" What do they write ? "

" *They write Shakespeare.*"

Father Green's face looked like a beehive with sunned hollyhocks round it—so enjoying and so busy. We must all laugh—nevertheless it was Robert Browning and not a clerk who apprehended and maintained we " wrote Shakespeare."

[With Bobby Ross at the Carfax Galleries.] For the rest, Blake has a repugnant effect on the eyes that had not seen him for many years ; and amongst the hideousness of nightmare, it seemed quite sane to hear Bobby giving an account of all the mad murderers at Broadmoor. Terriss's murderer seemed to think he had been just a little hasty. A man who had cut the throats of his wife and many children had made a stained-glass window on the subject, " Suffer the little children to come unto me and forbid them not." Fay has refused, like me, to believe, but Bobby swears as if he were in chapel. The governor had never seen anything remarkable in the window. Bobby is to come to us on Septuagesima Sunday—and he actually has the wit to see the humour that lurks in such an intention.

Bobby Ross comes—using, very skilfully, the wild

rain for penitential tears—to pray forgiveness for his failure to appear two Sundays before. We treated Bobby as a Dead-man, but he insisted on regarding our " Come in " as a viaticum. Very skilfully, with deliberation, he prepared the story that was to conquer our forgiveness. He had been to Florence—on his return his friends did not ask him about the Baptistery, about Verrochio . . . only, " Have you seen Berenson ? " This got on the nerves ; so one day he announced a dreadful discovery had been made in Florence. . . . . ! ! ! . . . . . ? ? ? . . .

BERENSON WAS NOT BY BERENSON

The sensation was indescribable. . . . No one knew what to do . . . Mrs. Berenson was packing up. . . .

The tea and cigarettes welcomed the Dead Guest suavely. Michael was fresh and sovereign in her eighteenth-century gown. I was decidedly mystic in the dusky veil with its glimmerings. Bobby is a curious mixture of wit and Catholic seriousness—only Catholics seem to know seriousness as a mode of mind and spirit. At the same time there is something illusive about this man, with his romantic kindness, and his wit, deliberate as a growth. We do not yet understand him. The face is dark-skinned—square about the jaw—a little mastiff-like ; the black eyebrows have the concave of Spinoza's—in the eyes there is the character of a dog's—something kind and fixed and not of men—yet devout.

[A letter from Bobby Ross.] " In a semi-geographical work called *Near Home, or Europe Described*, I can recall many stereos of dialectic cast in a Socratic mould :

Q.   What is the religion of the Italians ?

A.   They are Roman Catholic.

Q.   What do the Roman Catholics worship ?

A.   Idols and a piece of bread.

Q.   Would not God be very angry if he knew Italians worshipped Idols and pieces of bread ?

A.   God is very angry.

Perhaps it was a gloss such as we find even in the most sacred passages of scripture.   It was actually at Brighton, where I passed an uneventful childhood, near the Dyke Road, that I learnt from *Near Home, or Europe Described*.

CHAPTER NINETEEN

THE ROTHENSTEINS AT HAMPSTEAD

[A visit to the Rothensteins.] [1] The day was malign, as days can be in shimmering spring, we felt ill. Hampstead was a mighty mole-hill, oppressive to our hearts, physically and æsthetically. We took Eucalyptus and daffodils. There was talk of John and how forbidding breath had passed over his desire to lunch with us— then entreaty armed as command from us that John should lunch with us. He is a grand boy, shooting out his words like stalwart balsam shooting out its mature seeds. He and Michael were lovers at first sight, and as a token she was to think of engines as she fell asleep and he of Nelson. Will Rothenstein's son had never learnt so much in a quarter of an hour as from Michael in that time—and sound Imperialism too.

Oscar stories.

The kind warder at Reading Gaol thought he might turn his chances to good account—so questioned Oscar as to what he should think of various authors. " Well, sir, there's Dickens ? "

" Dickens ? " " What should one think of him ? "

" As he is safely dead you can think what you like."

" And John Strange Winter, is he any good, sir ? "

[1] Edith.

" A charming lady—he is a charming lady.   I prefer
to talk to her rather than read his books."

" And now would you tell me about Marie Corelli ? "
At last Oscar turned.

" I could bear it no mor_.   I approached him—' Of
course there is nothing against her moral character—
nothing in the world, you understand that : but as to
her books, she ought to be standing here in gaol where
I am—and I should be out where she is ! "

Oscar remarked of Watts Dunton theorising on the
sonnet, " His old law days taught him to fuss about
six-and-eight."

A cab is got and we drive in keen damp about the
Heath.   There is something spectacular about it—something strange, as if we were driving through the pages
of a story book.

At the Spaniards, we get out to the crazy old place
—a false snow storm decorating the panes—desolation
on the bits of eighteenth-century statuary and cockle-
shells—on the sheds of Eros left bare for the winter.
The student of old, we remember fresh from the Latin
Quarter, wakes yearningly in Rothenstein, as he looks
into the little sheds and remembers how he envied his
London model because she had an appointment, far out,
at the Spaniards.   Even about this place a little air that
haunts Watteau's *Fête Champêtre* is not quite away—a
breath of the transient round, the gathering place of
pleasure.

We could not live in Hampstead—but we must
cement this new friendship by visiting it for a day or
two.

We have had a note from the Rothensteins :
" We are very happy that you like John—we are so
happy that we care so much for your two dear selves."

He [Rothenstein] writes, he is shy of reading our
letters, " There is something left of ancient superstition
in each of us, that makes us almost shrink from happiness
when it comes too near, and I find I do, from great
kindness and praise of any kind. To write as you do,
shows a confidence which makes your words seem almost
too costly to accept without scruple, and I am fearful of
your finding a scratch on the surface, which may one
day deprive me of it." Speaking of the scratches for
which we blame others and the expression of false and
insipid selves for which we entertain self-blame, he says
beautifully, " It seems so odd we can so worship the
tree, and can yet treat leaves and branches unfeelingly."
He continues, " To our friends we owe the privilege of
expressing the cleanness of our natures—with them we
breathe purest air, where with other men we stifle and
gasp. My Alps—I call my friends—and the pictures I
love are the clear pools in which they and the sky are
reflected—in such there can live nothing mean, and not
to know meanness is to be aware only of what is good.
We shall wait for you patiently to join us here—we
know you will come when yourselves are as whole as
your minds."

How excellent to find a wise man who knows that our
minds are whole. . . .

The Rothensteins come. Alice accepts her name :
Noli (me tangere) [garden balsam]

Will proposes he should be our Kalim, the Japanese Dog of Heaven.[1]

M. And what would you do?

R. Bark! And keep Ricketts away from Heaven.

The shadow of a rose on water passed over Michael's face, and, of course Rothenstein, in a joyous laughing chorus, became there and then *The Heavenly Dog*.

He says we did not look when we came to see him, and must use our eyes on our next visit. He is ordering one of those Yorkshire Cheeses, of the Age of Gold, for us—it has to be required of the Dale three sacred months before use. This is a real gift—grown out of the desire in another's heart and presented to that other's hands.

Talk brilliant. . . .

Alas! Too long unrecorded. All is gone from that treacherous white sand—Memory. All except Will's joy in the Seal of the Chapter of Aberdeen—a closely imagined Nativity on our altar; and his acknowledgement that the symbol of the Trinity is the greatest symbol in the world.

[2] A most happy visit to the Rothensteins. . . . There is a sort of blessing over that house, traceable in the end I think to Billy. It was good to wake to children's voices, and looking down from a great height, from our bedroom window, to see the father sweeping the

[1] Sir William Rothenstein in his *Men and Memories*, Vol. II, p. 113, refers to this meeting. " The ugly dog (Binyon told me too late, that he was not a dog at all, but a lion!) that guards the Chinese Heaven I suggested as a name for myself. . . ."

[2] Katherine.

lawn vehemently, his small daughters toddling about the dew with bare feet.

" John," I ask, " do you play by yourself or with your sisters ? "

" Oh, with them. I do not let them interrupt me at my work. Is that right ? "

How illuminated is John on the Doctrine of Sisters !

[1] A welcome so friendly—Noli's, as when a perverse bee hums. An ugly house recreated. The large room in colour like a firwood when the cones are yellow—hung with lovely Rodins, Rembrandt drawings, Puvis drawings and little things by Millet.

Over a dinner such as " real " people like—of good creatures of the earth presented to the palate, with due respect for their own clean quality—Billy assures us with the seriousness of a voice from the hold of a vessel where it is believed there is no survivor, that he never lived the life he was credited with. He was hurled from a provincial grammar-school into the midst of the vicious, dazzling life of Paris, introduced there by his discoverer, Conder, and he tried to make himself accept life as it was to these Brilliant Ones. But as he himself put it, in an epigram on Arthur Symons : " He got up every morning with bad intentions and broke them every night." Hundreds of young men are in this state, enchanted by the vicious estimate and yet deep in the ultimate recesses of their wills, guarding a good they are ashamed of and love inveterately, as is proved by the fact that they cannot sin deeply, though they are

[1] Edith.

near all the bravery of Satan. Bill
amusing on this phase of a man's li

He told how when Margaret Wooc   o
see student life, the English students   ag
the Dean's daughter, and arranged to   o a
café and each have a model on his knee   and
rave : but when the quiet little lady came,   was no
ragging. This play at vice dropped down like bunting
stripped and rolled on the ground by a breeze.

Billy's Jews are as perfect as Anatole France's Priests.
From within they gather us to their passions, their
central emotions. God gathers us so when He would
impart His tenderness or His influence. "Under the
shadow of his wings." "As the hen gathereth her
chickens." Great art does this too by its symbols, by
persons, by powers, by eternal moments.

Billy is great, when his brush "draws in" his Jews.
His actual colour seems to me unrelated to the inspiration
of group and mass, outside the emotional vitality, and
in this differs creatively from Rickett's, that as colour
helps the fiat of the Drawing with another kind of fiat
—like that of our Blessed Lady to God's.

We are in the summer evening again, driving fast to
Will Rothenstein. There we are entertained on most
apt wisdom (alas, the form and substance are gone under
the indefiniteness of the heat). I remember lovely trees
of a garden, Noli's purr over our Kate Reilly hats—and
a supper. Suddenly, "Do you know what you are
eating ?" I ask Michael, regardless of my host and
hostess. "It's a fowl you're eating." And the day is
Friday. My question a masterpiece of incivility.

CHAPTER TWENTY

DEATH ACROSS THE SEA

[Edith's sister had gone to live with her husband, Dr.
John Ryan, at Grove House, Milltown, Dublin, in 1906.
The Michael Fields had been over at least once a year
to see them. In January, 1910, Amy was taken ill.]

[1] It began with a scrawl from our Little One, written
on Friday, Jan. 14th, that she had " Influ " and fever.
I remember saying in the sacristy, that she and I recognised that Nature and Grace were against our winter
visit to Ireland, and now it was shown we should all
have influ ! Yet I was anxious enough the next day to
pray in the Holy Name for her safety.

[The news from Ireland becomes more disturbing.
Michael telegraphs she will come, but the start is post-
poned.] January 19th. Telegram : " Most dear love
from Amy after good night. Temperature better but
woefully weak. I think crisis possibly coming." Flocks
of little birds sing in my heart. . . . There is no song
like that of many little birds in my heart.

[They start for Ireland though the news is still reassur-
ing.] Through the excited journey—the permanence of
the movement of the express—the hopes, the thoughts

[1] Edith.

285

of love and fear. . . . Sullen darkness—the spring of electric blaze to read by—Chester and more tea.

Wales obliterated by darkness—nothing to be seen but some huge storm clouds of ' slick ' blackness on the obscurity. A roar as if we were shooting along a lion's throat, and we are through the Menai and in Anglesea. The darkness seems to have sunk like the chest of a corpse and settled itself into the flats of Anglesea.

[They arrive] . . . and then on to the platform bursts Johnnie, [Dr. Ryan] not so vivid and pink, a still form of usually effervescing wine . . . we ask "Is she better?" A torturing, non-committal answer; but we are satisfied she is not worse and surrender ourselves to the mysteriousness preserved as to our future. . . . Johnnie says we are to stay at the Hotel, by Amy's previous desire, as she must not hear us come and there are no bedrooms to offer at Grove.

[Later. At Grove House.] We creep about the house and settle in the noble drawing-room. The crisis is expected during the night of Friday—so there is no question of return to the hotel. Pussy's drawing-room is disordered by sofas and blankets and pillows—her beautiful drawing-room with the birds and garlands of the eighteenth century, so delicately suspended over the confusion as ceiling. I see the chrysanthemums among the veronica leaves are dingy. I whip out the neglected flowers and leave the veronica leaves I taught Pussy to gather for her vase. . . .

The hours settle into days—the days of old centuries. Never was there such measure of time weighed out to us. . . . The pain is on the core of love and we simply demand it should end and the doctor mutters no demur. Where is his hope? Michael goes first and the Little One smiles.

"Michael who is very happy has come to the Little One who is very happy."

"Oh, very happy."

"Yes, very happy, it is our secret."

Johnnie says, "And you are very comfortable at your hotel?" And Michael says "very," but that no more concerns the Little One. Then I am sent for. O, Little One—she is indeed the characteristic Little One, but so pale with harassed pallor—the nostrils sharp and breathing a breath whizzing and sounding like flight on flight of warlike arrows—the little mouth shut firm—the round brow and fine eyebrows just creased with trouble. The eyes deeply intent and clouded with fever. . . . It is impious to feel as I do—panic at a loved one. But, with words of "Little Pussy, Hennie is come—it is Hennie come to the darling," I reach the range of her attention, penetrate the absorbed brooding over the dreadful arrow flight. . . . Then a smile . . . the lips curve, deprecatingly sweet and the eyes are filled with the charm of those whose light is the Light of the City of God. Recognition is there, passionate love is there, that knows nothing of how or why the beloved is apparent, but receives the apparition with golden Lauds. . . .

The giant hours stretch into evening, at last they achieve night. . . . (A priest comes) Little One does not die—   The priest goes—but Michael still holds her candle, and will hold it as the eyes turn towards it sometimes.   The Nurse wants to get the candle extinguished and Michael distanced from the bed.   Johnnie comes to me distractedly.   He cannot ask Auntie to quench the candle.   Will I help?   So I creep upstairs and find Emily praying outside the open door.   I get her to go in and tell Nurse quite simply to say she wants the space round the bed, if Michael will put out the light.   Of course Michael quenches at once—but I shall always see the resolution and fidelity of her form and of her little, candle-bearing hand, as she recites and illumines. . . .

One of Amy's poor, with streaming eyes, walks with me from the Church, " What shall I do without her! No one in the world has been to me what she has.   I shall never forget her."

And I slip upstairs without Nurse's consent and come close to Michael, who has never budged, and very near the Beloved.   I am in my hat and it seems to arrest the sweet smile into something more precious, attention —poignant recognition, giving an eager pain to the gold of the smile's gold . . . but my Pussy had seen her " Hennie-boy " and knew that the Channel was not between us any more.   Then begin the hours . . . . antediluvian hours . . . before history, when everything is not save the dragons are—and the dragons are the powers of Death, of the Grave, of Separation and Corruption, of audacious Hope, of the Familiar become Alien, of a dear one's Proprietorship become uncertain —so that Pussy's seems on the edge of rebellion.   These hours are monstrous . . . The Consultant is almost hopeless—but suggests a slight operation. . . .

Then Emily comes in to say there is a change and we are all sent for. I go up stairs to see Death—rather Dying—it is cold round my heart. A forsaken egg in a nest is my heart. Johnnie is close, kneeling close and in a lovely voice, the very honey of Love in the clefts of the awful fastness. . . . The nurse makes Little One drink—I hide my face. Then she says, " You must leave the room now and leave them together." I could murder the woman, making hatred rise in me at this solemn moment of Love. But I only say, " I remain. He wishes it." (Why, Johnnie had even arranged how Auntie was to hold her hand to the last and I to be where I could see her eyes to the last. . . .)

The breath is now less high and tense. I kneel not in sorrow, but in the wild endurance of a fascination. . . .

The Priest begins his wild, intent Latin prayers, litanies and absolutions—with a velocity in them, of an anxiety in having to let things of immortal value compete with time, running out fast from a human soul. . . .

O God, who made her, the nostrils are tense for breath and there is no breath—they are cut off from God's breath, as if they were chinks in a rock, that birds might flap into . . . and unguarded . . . fissures not nostrils. The little mouth, firm and closed after strife, as during its continuance—a little dark and as hopeless to open as a chest, the key of which is down under fathomless sea —unless a new key were found ; and this cannot be ; for there is no worker on earth who could fit that ward.

The eyes are almost unchanged. This battle being fought, there is no radiation—it is done. It seems such a small thing being merely done.

We gather in the drawing-room and John with a note of triumph reads prayers for the departed. . . .

I had no idea Little One had such beautiful hands, tended as a priest's hands and for holy work—to deck the altars, to lay out the vestments, to touch the sacred vessels. " I have seen the hands of many Protestant ladies, but they were quite different from these Catholic hands," Bridget says, venerating Pussy's. That clasp of the crucifix—what a joy ! The supernatural gripped by the corruptible.

I have seen her lie like that on her bed, when tired, in an afternoon sleep. But this Pussy—in timeless sleep, yet corruptible sleep—not the dear, fleeting soundness of rest, that Pussy was asleep. And this majesty is so small in compass. If she could move one would adore her. She is motionless and one says the Credo and Pater and feels one must leave the inveterate repose. . . .

The eating and drinking in the house of Death ! It is part of the monstrosity of Death's interruption of Life. I can have no abandon, I would I could have abandon near the Holy Dead. . . . The weird Sunday dinner, Henry carving in Little One's place ; and the Nurses that the Christian in me must love and the human being in me hates, to be served first—for they are both come on pilgrimage to the little lady who in a day or two has won their hearts, through all their officialism, and they are going to stay in the Death Chamber while Milltown troops to the bedside of its saint.

Johnnie wishes her to rest near us—wishes her to be brought on the waves back and to lie in the little Vineyard Church [Richmond] where she was married and to be buried at Mortlake under the tabernacle—in the cemetery where wild Sir Richard Burton lies under a stone tent. Death always comes to us with the poetry of an event, big with battles for the soul. . . . We have seas to cross ; our dead have to be left in the snow mountains, or be borne over the ocean. . . .

I had never seen an open coffin before. It is shocking beyond speech—a shriek is the right and natural expression, but I am never natural and I do not shriek.

The morning is so pure in light and frost ! The day has that insouciant chastity of the Irish nature that makes Irish skies attractive in gay cleanness.

Mortality stifles one. Hardly at first can I get my thoughts clear of the taste that lies on my tongue. Then the young priest sprinkles the dead for the last time and there is a fumble to find the words he should read . . . and we talk of the journey and the hotel we shall seek in town . . . and the Jesuit is pressed to have more ham and eggs which he takes with appetence— his clouded eyes giving to us a level consideration and appointment. So, in the sunshine, scarcely looking round at the Irish home as we leave it, we part again from old Grove. . . .

[In England again. They arrive at Richmond by the

workmen's train in the early morning and go straight to Church and later to the cemetery.]

The grave-digger is already at work—Michael bends down and kisses the soil for what it is to take to itself. Perhaps the little priest is astonished, but he keeps his " Well I never ! " in his own sympathetic quietude. . . . And I hear Father Jewel say with infinite concern, " The body is here." . . . But I turn blank, the coffin becomes a stranger. . . .

[After the funeral.   Lunch at Paragon.]   My Faith ! For a moment I lose blankness.   But it is better for us all to be together—it fosters our humanity.   Johnnie speaks wonderfully of looking out toward the prow and seeing her riding on over the waves to take possession of her grave and to say farewell to the Church of her nuptials.   He had never had such a sense of speed and freedom.

CHAPTER TWENTY-ONE

A LAST TRIP ABROAD

[A holiday at Boulogne, where they are joined by Father Gosscannon, Edith's confessor: August 1910.]

[1] The little bloused commissionaires surround Goss with their gesticulations and farragoes of speech, as if they were winding worsted round a spool. And we are abroad !

The trails of smell. . . .

The shambling along of life . . .

The pariah look of the dogs . . . the men with their clothes tied on them as if they were scarecrows above the crops. The women a little more pompously self-sufficient, with brown skins and " an air," though they may be sadly battered by life. The curious shops, that give the impression of being there for the needs of a smaller kind of animal than the English kind and one that eats more lightly.

I remember how, many years ago, mother saw Our Lady of Boulogne carried down to bless the sea and told me, a little child, of it, as if she had seen a moving rite of Brahminism. How my heart's prayers are for that beautiful young girl, strong in her virgin simplicity of soul, whose eyes beheld and saw not ; were half-enlight-

[1] Edith.

ened when she was a young mother and was baptised a Christian ; were darkened again by heretic obduracy and pride, when she became the hardest of heretics, an Unitarian ; and then gradually, as death came on, were enlightened and grew soft, as she bade me read George Herbert's " Christ my way, my light, my truth "—and in the hour of death, glowed as she murmured, " I feel on the brink of such revelation." Beloved Mother !

. . . The French bed ! The solid comfort for limbs and fleas ! . . .

I make up my mind to act to Goss with the simplicity of friendship. So we call early and find him and his friends in the courtyard of the " Bourgoyne "—so quaint a courtyard—Irving set it on the Lyceum stage. The familiar faces have the free cheer of being abroad on them, and Gossie meets me with a smile that blesses and yet is " calin." He takes us to the Fair. A huge Frenchman (huge in mass, not in height) sells us bowls for " café "—to be used for French breakfast at Paragon. Michael asks for " quelque chose pour les oiseaux." The vast monsieur seeks and advances like a solemn walrus, a tiny glass bowl on his chest, " Voila ! pour les oiseaux." The absurdity of the scene catches and retains Goss. His eyes fill with elf mischief and he laughs constantly during our progress. Just as the Irish hills take the light differently and more delicately than other hills, his eyes laugh and smile with finer quality than other eyes . . .

He comes to tea, to meet the profound Susan who is staying here with brother and sister. Susan is like beef essence. Her human profundity of sense and wisdom is too untempered, and Gossie, through the guard of his immense caution, yet allows distaste to escape.

He comes in to " café," a very welcome moment, especially on abstinence day. All afternoon he has been walking with his friend he calls the " galloping Major " on the breezy cliffs between Boulogne and Wimereux, and he comes in as if intoxicated, the Celt in him heady as the wildness in a March hare. He has got, at her request, a little French Prayer Book for Michael. This he gives her, with an irresponsible, resonant laugh, that has the sound of waves round flotsam, " Don't speak to me of confession ! Not now."

As he enters L'Ancien Palais de L'Evêché, he cries out through the echoes, as a supplement to " un café "—" du crême ! ! ! " It rings out. " I ought not to shout in this holy place ? "—such innocent Bacchanalianism of the wild sea-air ! One has, however, to be careful—he is exalted and could be quarrelsome in a minute, if he were not such a Child of God—a mere child.

Saturday. The two lady friends, the " Galloping Major " and Goss come to tea. Michael had to withdraw at five, to reach St. Nicholas, where she is brave enough to make her first French confession to l'Abbé Sauvet. She has had to learn her sins by heart.

In a surge of wind we gaily take La Route Nationale and drive on and on through Boulogne, beyond the walls, by the burnt-out Jesuit College, with a view of Napoleon's monument and a wide country of wolds and little groves, big enough as country for the wind and cloud and sun rays to take their " vacances " in. The Irish eyes respond to this breadth of delicate earth and atmosphere. We talk of the nothings of mere transit . . . the curly red of the old farmhouses—of the girls veiled for the procession we have left behind—of anything that is driven into our heads. M. le Cocher sings English songs that Goss hears at the Church concerts, and he warbles them alongside, or breaks out into French ditties of his student days. One about the Duke of Marlborough he gives with sweet rollick. And the passers-by look round at Monsieur le Curé and his ladies. The cocher stops at a wayside cabaret and leaves his horse to stroll the rails of a light railway. We call and protest. He presents madame with a great posy of dahlias and autumn flowers ! Then there is the running quarrel with him as to what we expect and he intends. La Route Nationale runs through the vast copse of the Forêt. There seems no way in and, almost despairing, we strike a sentier. But it is damp and close and the alders almost take it to themselves. Michael and I begin to get anxious lest the expedition should be a failure and lest Goss—as the inaugurator of it—should become discouraged and vexed. I make the most of the centauries closed up, moist, of the bits of crimson dye on the ivy, or carnelian on the leaves of the self-heal. Goss at first only wonders at our Sylvan babble, and we propose a search for a broader path. This he soon finds, guided by Michael's woodland wisdom. All the flowers of the wildernesses of the country grow on earth beside our way—calamint and geraniums, agrimonies, cudweeds, willow herbs—all the dim, fresh creatures of the hedge and grass, in their autumnal flower; and Goss hears us call them by name and as we gather, caress them. He walked into this forest with the Major and they had only noticed it was extensive and a real forest . . . Now it lives along our way ; and as we gather and name and welcome the flowers, he grows aware of a new world emerging around him, and he hears the wind come out of the profound foliage into the near trees and tell them great monodies of the whole forest; and he grows responsive to the duskiness of the light in the shadow or to its sudden captures from the sun. Eagerly he gathers where we name and marvels how we know this sweet forest lore. We come across parties of country people pulling down ash-leaves for a drink—filling bags with the fantasies of the ash-leaves. And following Michael's instinct for forests we come into a path of grass—the veritable green sward of the fauns. It is a beautiful thing to watch the haunting Irish poetry come into present possession of the priest—the great, immeasurable seductions of a forest gain him in the company of poets. His eyes capture the sun in rays like the shades—his voice has a freedom and freshness of the golden age. A highway appears—he tosses up his cap, not as high as a layman would toss it ; in a childish, ineffectual way. " Vive la Route Nationale ! " But the carriage waiting and full of umbrellas is not ours. We wander in marshy underwood, struck firmly by the setting sun—gather little silver oak-leaves, and then I find in Gossie's hand the mint I had gathered and given him, a spray of little silver oak-leaves and the pagoda of the self-heal's fruit—such an ecclesiastical bit of wild wood ! We must retrace our

way—all the way the trees grow gentle and immeasurable
in their Paganism, and flowers have a note of colour that
belongs to the ecstasy of sunset.   There is something of
treason in the silence.   The frolic spirit of Goss changes
into fay-struck innocence—a sense of being led on into
marvel.   As we drive home, the sights of transit again
prompt our talk in the wind—but an aerial music has
passed over the cadences of the divine office in Goscannon's mind.

He comes in to tea enravished with his holiday . . .
then Michael challenges him to stay one more day . . .
" No, no ! "   He makes resistance.   It is the instinct of
the priest, who is so dependent on others for means,
not to make himself cheap.   He alleges with grimaces
of bonhommie, " Mes plans, mes arrangements."   Then
Michael becomes the French woman she can be, and purrs
out a taunting, cajoling, scolding tirade of French.   I did
not know she could do the Gallic persistence of tongue so
well.   [He stayed and they had another outing.]

Laughter springs and dances in us all.   Across the
stream one willow herb affronts us with pinkness.   The
colour is salient and provokes attack.   " Shall I leap ? "
says Goss, drawing up his strongly built frame in
form for a jump.   " No, indeed you must not think of
it," I say—regarding the ill-nourished unpractised limbs.
He comes away from the mill-stream of flaunting willow
herbs.   " I could have to save my life."   This ineffectual-
ness, in natural ways, of the priest, is one of the pathetic
aspects of their self-sacrifice and adorable vocation.

[In the Cathedral.]   Little do we realise what Goscannon's determination to give us Holy Communion will require of us. In the Dome Chapel a preacher is declaiming ; in the Cathedral pilgrims are chaunting, " Ave, ave, ave Maria ! " On Monday we had followed Goscannon to the Altar of the Sacred Heart, where he had to vest at the altar and was served by the old host of the Bourgoyne. Unluckily quite a number of people gathered, and a terrible fear absolutely distracted me during Holy Mass, that when we knelt to receive Holy Communion, they too would come and kneel. They did . . . I could see the distraction and irresolution the situation produced on the priest. At last, as the absorbed old man tactlessly refrained from speaking to the people—Goss turned and, quite white, gave us absolution and brought the two consecrated Hosts to us : then a gentle, firm voice said, " Il n'y a pas des Hosties ici." There was amaze and anger ! Then someone said officially, they could all receive at the Lady Altar. Most rose—one stout and heavy woman, with an expression of disgust, that in some French women expresses wrath, shrugged her shoulders and said, " Non, c'est égal." Oh, my Lord ! I was so sorry she blasphemed through a grace that had been given to us alone.

[Goscannon is returning to England.] We send him on to find his bag and stand awhile at the steamer's side, in confusion of third-class passengers, and the career of boxes and packages . . . He runs down the gangway to tell us he has his ticket safe and to babble the moved nonsense that becomes speech, by the side of a boat or train. The ropes begin to creak and we make him ascend.   He stands above us and we come near to the parting steamer.   " Now we must hear you say ' Adieu, charmant pays de France,' " says Michael energetically. This he does, with elfin language in his eyes—" accents strange " of loving us true.   " Now say, ' Te quitter c'est mourir ! ' " persists laughing Michael, " You must say it "—" Te quitter c'est mourir ? " he says obediently —" But it is not France I mind leaving behind." Courteously and gently his eyes rest on Michael and then, as the shade slips on over a dial, the dark, parting eyes are come to me and rest on mine with the most perfect love, consecrated and tender and whole. . . .

CHAPTER TWENTY-TWO

PRELUDE TO DEATH

. . . [1] I am going back, though I write in the present, after a fortnight, the greatest in experience of my life. Feb. 6th, 1911. The doctor had examined me and been silent. . . . He comes and asks for Michael. As she is at the Vineyard, he comes in and talks burly cheerfulness to me. But I face him, tell him we are Catholics and must face reality, and conjure him on this ground to tell me the truth. " You think I am suffering from something serious ? "

" Well, as you have put it to me the way you have, I am bound to say I do."

" With cancer ? "

" I believe so. It is my opinion."

" And it will be fatal ? "

" Yes."

All this time I feel like a marble temple in ruined and immovable cold. I learn more and more about this internal cancer, about its terrible indecision, and, every way of it, horror and disgrace. I am undone before my own face, as death undoes one after He has covered one's face from earthly life. There can be no removal—only a hideous operation of alleviation from what has to come.

A ring—she comes, and her voice is of Dominican and

[1] Edith.

Apostolic joy—she has got an old convert, who had
grown negligent in his religious duties, to ask for the
cleansing of penance . . . I cannot speak—she sees my
speechlessness as an awful vision, far beyond anything
heard ; her questions rive it.   To tell her, " The doctor
says I have cancer ! "   To see her grow deadly fixed.
. . . I realise how infinitely distant from the love I have
for her, are all, even the tenderest other loves.   The
fear of death made me cold, but the thought of losing my
life on earth with my beloved, brings warmth and tears.

But I forget . . . I send in the afternoon for Goscannon, with special urgency.   He comes at five—the
candles are lighted ; as I enter he says briefly but with
intent, " Well, what is it ? "   My throat tangles—at last
I untangle it to say, " I have had a great shock."   I do
not see so much as feel a great anxiety settle over my
confessor.   I sob out the terrible doom . . . so he
shelters me with his trust that I shall have peace at the
end.   He is sure I shall have peace.   All the while I
was speaking of my doom to Goss yesterday, I had firmly
maintained it was a just and merciful temporal punish-
ment for my great, flagrant sinning.   I knew I deserved
it.

[A visit to a specialist.]   He seats us, asks me about
my sufferings—when and what they are and in three
minutes has announced, " You are an artist or a writer ? "
In that place, everything said about one's disease is a
jagged nail driven through one's pride.   Swift indeed is
the investigation—the touch smooth and supple and
judicial.   " That is soon done.   Now while you are

arranging things, I will talk to your Aunt." They go —I know his opinion, and, clutching tighter the little crucifix I have hidden in my fist all the while, I say to that dread knowledge, " Thy will be done—Fiat voluntas Tua."

CHAPTER TWENTY-THREE

A MOTOR JOURNEY

[They had been in retreat at a Convent near Clacton-on-Sea, Oct. 1st, 1911.]

[1] Then we try to eat an early lunch—but the terrific, chill wind and the long loathing of the convent food and of the smells of cooking from the little servants' kitchen, make me very sick, just as Drury and the motor arrive. Joy to see our swift deliverer from the convent. Then off in the sword-play of the wind, but behind the shield of our windows.

At Colchester an Inn is sought, where we can get a fire —vain! But at Ingatestone the host of The Spread Eagle says, " No fire, but we can light one." Sense and Inspiration! We enter the Inn with blessing. A nice sisterly daughter of the house lights a blaze and waits on us. She shows Michael some nice bedrooms, " If you ever want to stay." And something shoots through Michael that she will want to stay—but she resists the thought. We start, and only half a mile further on, the motor absolutely refuses to move. There is stir and fume of absorbed men about it . . . it refuses to move. The chauffeur's boy fetches me a closed cab, and we are back at The Spread Eagle, to our fire, and having scraps

[1] Edith.

of invalid food served by the sisterly daughter of the house. We want to take a motor on at once from the garage, but Drury persuades us to wait for a car from Richmond he has "phoned" for, and he assures us it is on its way and will be at Ingatestone by six. But we listen for the whirr and clack of a motor and only hear horses' feet, till after eight. Then it comes and there is delay till 8.30; just as we are going to start we see a stranger in charge. I protest that our agreement was that Drury should drive us from Clacton to Richmond, and I adhere to this. The other man simply sits on and pours out insolence. We can come on with him or not —but he will drive the car. He has a wife and children —he doesn't care for us or Mr. Smithers (his master). I am very angry. I don't say what I should not, but with a violence that is disgraceful, especially after retreat, I refuse to trust myself on Saturday night through London with a man who has behaved so insolently. I order the luggage off the car and we ask for—a room at The Spread Eagle! My heart is so wildly disturbed, I pray not to die through a motion of anger, and make an act of profound contrition.

A car and a gentleman-chauffeur has been ordered over night. (Drury who was without fault and the wicked stranger started home in the night, towing the inert car behind the other.) By nine we start into the dazzling, awful East wind—the radiance of the earth, the wide look of a Sunday morning—how we enjoy the drive till the wind closes down over the sunshine as we reach London —nobly empty; such grand heights of houses, such vistas contained by brick and stone; such atmosphere up slopes and down valleys of masonry! All still, almost as if rural. "And a river flows on through the vale of Cheapside."

We pass De Vere Gardens, we pass Pater's London home, and Miss Vickers' Kensington house . . . many are the dead; and they were faithful and good to us. May they rest in peace. And we are back at Richmond in two hours' time.

CHAPTER TWENTY-FOUR

RED LETTERS

[1] Words about *Poems of Adoration* from Gordon Bottomley that make light shine about the heart. [Oct. 1912.]

" I wanted to read *Poems of Adoration* before I wrote ; too many weeks are gone since then, but often I could not write at all ! Michael bade me like *The Dance of Death*, and I do think it beautiful with the strangeness that is to me the root of beauty. But I love more the first fourteen poems in the book, the poems from *Venit Jesus* to the end. *Real Presence* seems to me one of the quite supreme things in its order, and in many of the poems again and again there is a wild (in the sense that an anemone is wild), pure energy, a startling closeness of expression to sensation which go past Patmore and F. Thompson right to Crashaw's side. But it is a book of rapture and purgation . . . Oh, *Macrinus against Trees* is delightful and true in more ways than one.

And the cover ! [Designed by Charles Ricketts.] O Michael and Henri to be envied ! How happy I was to see the lovely lines playing together in crystal-clear chimings again, as I first saw them when I was a boy and thought there never was such a master of line— indeed there never was and there is not.

[1] Edith.

307

O don't think me naughty if I say how delighted I was to read in the colophon that one of the poems had appeared in the *Universe*. That is where we should all like our poems to appear."

We hear that Bishop Brindle of Nottingham, coming across the line, " Pearl of great price, within the monstrance set," asked Sœur Marie du St. Sacrement, " Who wrote it ? " Hearing of Michael Field he gave the military command, " Write and tell them I want the complete set of their work. The bill to be sent to me." Of course the Bishop was supplied at once with *Wild Honey*, as the turning point from paganism to the great " Ecce Agnus Dei " vision of St. John the Baptist—and *Poems of Adoration* as the first-fruits of our Catholic life. I explained that as converts we wished our pagan past to be left to itself—I speak of my illness and ask for the prayers of a Shepherd of the Church for Field and Michael. Fancy even a soldier-bishop with *Attila*, *Stephania*, *The World at Auction*, *Julia Domna*, not to mention Borgia and the works of the author of *Borgia!*

On Monday, 13th January 1913, I had this exquisite letter from the Cathedral, Nottingham.

MY DEAR CHILD,

I am very grateful to you for the beautiful books : and yet—may I say it—I regret that you were asked about them ! I might perhaps have obtained them through some of the booksellers who send me their catalogues. I am not too proud to accept a gift ; but *Wild Honey* has been used : it has little words here and there which show that it has been a friend to whom you talked and I feel

like the thief who has robbed you of your companionship! So please forgive me! What compensation is in
my power I will gladly make : on Thursday I will offer
my mass for you both ; and you shall have daily a
memento. Most of my fifty years of priestly life have
been spent where pain and sorrow have their home, and
I have learnt to see how God purifies the life of his saints.
Good-bye, child, and may God bless you both.

Yours in J.C.,

ROBERT, Bishop of Nottingham.

The soldier-bishop is very gentle and exquisitely
intimate in refinement of touch. He " roars us like a
sucking dove." What a happy error to have given him,
unknown to me, that marked copy of *Wild Honey*, that
was the last in the difficult depths of the soldier's kit box
under our bed—sought out by Josephine. And that
little gossip of the poet with his poems has brought us an
especial mass and a daily memento at the Altar by a tender
Shepherd of Christ's flock.

CHAPTER TWENTY-FIVE

FATHER VINCENT MACNAB

[In the following pages are some glimpses of their intimate friendship with Father Vincent MacNab. From Edith's first recoil in 1907 till Michael's death in 1914 they looked to him increasingly for spiritual and intellectual guidance.

The passages, though fragmentary, may suggest their intense absorption in religion, and the boon they derived from frequent contact with a cultured mind in sympathy with their difficulties. All the entries are by Edith; though Father Vincent was Michael's confessor, her reports are too personal for present use. In 1911 they became Tertiaries of St. Dominic.]

[1] We journey to hear Father Vincent at Our Lady of Victories, Kensington. I hate him from the first moments of sight—there is a supercilious hardness in the profile and the voice makes no terms for him—it echoes from a Scottish mountain valley and the gestures do not conciliate—they amaze by their popular appeal made a fine art . . .

[A month later at St. Hugh's Home.] At last he comes—there is a sense of discomfort about his approach and his advent, that always rises from shyness. The

[1] Edith.

310

mentally bold is physically shy . . . Now of himself—
the features are not comely, they are proud and rather
patently sensitive when sensitiveness should always be
illusive. But the pride and sensibility of the face are
conquered by a humility that has never flinched. Will
it ever flinch ? One looks at the orbed shoulders and the
large orbs of the eyes—no ! it will never flinch.

Michael takes me to see the great Vincent at his priory
. . . soon the elegant wasp appears, thinner than ever
without his black cowl. He is welcomed by Michael,
and Henry re-introduced, and then I am left with him.
He awaits my mind, his eyes covered with the lids ; the
lips mobile for action, living as the curves of a water-edge
—curiously are the curves fluent and yet discreet, which
gives them a haughty ease.

I tell him I have a question on the Encyclical [1] to ask
him—but first there is a moral question on which I need
his help—how to deal with essential pride of nature.

The wave curves of the lips spread and swirl, the lips
take on a little sinuosity of contempt and the voice very
low, attuned to respectful deference, address me while
the eyes rest on mine. [She refers to a judgement passed
by a confessor which I have been unable to trace.]

"I should not have said so. The fact that you
recognise your pride would sink it down from the rim
of the mould. Pride conscious of itself is on the way
to humility, as humility conscious of itself is on the way
to pride—if not already pride."

[1] The Encyclical of Pope Pius X condemning the 65 Propositions
of Modernism.

I protest. This pride is so essentially myself I cannot imagine a thought, a word or deed without it—I cannot get away from it. I fear to crush it—it would crush me, myself—and I fear to lose my fineness in giving welcome to quality, my detestation of inferiority, my choiceness of the artist :

" You see, Father, I am an artist to the finger-tips and I must bring the whole of my life to art, express it in terms of art."

" Your choiceness lost, your severity of judgement as an artist. No, it must not be lost. It has been the principle of my life to lose nothing ; even in dealing with sin—I have always found something that must not be lost in it—some aim, some love, some quality that has been followed erroneously, made a huge blunder of, mistakes that might be fatal. Find this core round which everything is mis-shapen, find the good, cut it out and save it. . . . We must go back to St. Thomas Aquinas' supreme paradox—that there are two equal and independent causes of salvation—one Divine Grace—one human man's volition. . . . The Sphere of Divine Redemption is like the conception in the sculptor's mind ; the sphere of human potentiality is like the block of marble. The art of the spiritual life consists in making them correlatives."

Then we turn to the Encyclical. I tell Father Vincent, his laughter at the modern craze for *rights*—so that we will not bear against our proud flesh a swan's-down touch of restraint—has done me good. He flushes into a response of laughter and agrees there is nothing like laughter for dealing with pride. It simply crumbles it.

But, I continue, the letter has been a great stumbling

block to me. "You see, Father, I entered the Church from free inspiration—the revelation that it was the only church in which God lived among us. . . . Then dogmas crashed on me. I had a death grip to receive them, understand them and then come out to the free Heaven again. I was just beginning to fly when His Holiness' Letter twisted round me like a snake round a flying eagle and there we were in struggle, till you brought me down with laughter."

[A year later.] "Your time is so precious, Father, I can hardly bear to take it up by telling you what I want to talk about." And I plunge into the problem : What is a dramatic poet to do, who, receiving Christ corporeally each day, must needs deal with sinners and become, as Matthew Arnold says, " what we sing."

"That is what God did. He became Man that he might teach man a new song. It was only by bearing that sorrow he could do anything great for man. So with the poet, he must bear sin."

I explain the strong physical identification I have with my characters . . .

" I should not like to give my opinion off-hand. It is not that the matter is so much serious as delicate. All I can say now is, wait long and do not put the matter by—never solve anything by fear. Christ abominates fear. And remember St. Augustine (' Ah, we are all St. Augustine's children,' he murmurs tensely), and his famous words, ' I love God and do as I please.'

I see the tragedy of your life now—the tragedy that will be there to the end. The struggle between what

you owe to Christ and what you owe to your art.   Ah,
it is the hidden tragedy that is often so much more profound than the public one.   It was so with Christ.
What was the tragedy of His mission on earth and His
death on the cross, to the hidden tragedy of His life here,
that was severed from the Father ? "

" I have always said that the artist was a lost creature
between Heaven and Earth, grasping spiritual things with
one hand, and with one passionate grasp the things of
sense."

" No—not lost !   The poets are the mystics—they
lead the way to revelation—and as long as they grasp
the things of sense, they are safe.   The Church welcomes
poets.   Heaven is full of song.   But there will always
be the delicate question with you, what you must bear
for your art, as Christ bore sin, and what must be rejected
in your material.   It is a question for you yourself and
it must always be fearlessly answered.   This will always
be your tragedy. . . .

You have always regarded art seriously, as your
profession, your vocation, have you not ? "

" Since I was a child, I began to write at ten."

" Then you must be willing to take up your tragedy,
you must be willing to bear sin and to suffer—you must
always remember Christ had a vocation from God and
bore all things for it."

I hear the school children outside as bright voices—
and thank Father Vincent : " There is no other priest to
whom I could talk as to you.   Sometimes I feel shut up
and then, at the end of a long avenue I find Father Vincent,
a door wide open."

" Oh, I must have doors all round me and open. I sometimes think I shall die of freedom." (What did he mean? That he would catch cold from too liberal airing ?)

Wonderful Vincent.

. . . Father Vincent is very lenient to pride. He quotes his own St. Vincent Ferrar. " Pride ! Oh, it comes and goes and comes again, but I don't find it stays."

[A first visit to Paragon.]   The strange, restless form ! He sits for a while on the settee.

" How cool your room is !   Cool and sweet as a dairy."

" Father !   The most perfect compliment Paragon has ever received."

We tell of Ricketts' remark that we both of us had something of the huntress about us, and the sense of concern it gave us. " A huntress—something cruel about it that would kill," he says, with bitter lips, as he ponders.   Then suddenly, " Well, a good hunter runs his game to earth.   The huntresses have done that— what they hunted they have secured.   They have gained the great prize."   And he smiles with a broad sweetness across that enigma, his face.

[In her last year Edith had spent a certain sum of her capital and felt some qualms about possible extravagance ; it had gone to make the house more convenient for nursing an invalid in, to trinkets and gifts for Michael, and to furniture and pretty things for her own room. She consulted Father MacNab on this point.   He condoned her little extravagances and set her mind at rest. Edith continues this visit.]

[Michael and Father Vincent] come up to bless the two
renovated bedrooms—Michael's living idea—the drops
and the beautiful words fall about, the happiest dew has
been sprinkled.

When we speak of the costly blue and white curtains,
with a glance at the dazzling water, Vincent judges, " I
think the Thames is worthy to be framed in silk."

Downstairs I ask him to say two Masses, that the
Beloved would allow us to give to Him and the Catholic
Church a Drama, that our life's work might be re-
dedicated and blessed as our Lyrics had been.   We talk
a great deal about the Irish possession, just now, of
English literature ; and of the great peril of it from the
infamy, cynicism and perniciousness of the Irish mind
when Faith is gone from it—Bernard Shaw, Synge,
George Moore, and Oscar, the least harmful of them all,
because he had perhaps the power of return.

Michael invites the Prior to the riverside.   He springs
down, " It was a kind thought, I almost think I was born
with water on the brain."   By the little flight of river
steps he thinks of the currents and swirls of Portaferry.

Then good-bye ; but we have been so happy we can
part with sunshine round us.   He says that he came very
anxious over me, but leaves very much less anxious.   A
wire and he will always come to us.   Dear Father Prior !
He is pleased I can praise his really good poem on Jesus
as the hireling of our wretched love.   His face looks like
a garden-bed that has received a visit of bees, when one
can speak of anything he has done in poetry—the realm
he so nearly dwells in, yet enters so rarely.

CHAPTER TWENTY-SIX

EAST AND WEST

[At Rottingdean, Sept. 19, 1911.]

[1] A telegram from Rothenstein—he is running over to see us for an hour. Just before he comes Father George appears; having just reached Brighton, he had not had time to write. Michael takes him on to the Downs, and under the windmill, I see them in the grass, the devoted little priest listening to Michael. I see a blot of a red rose in her hat. I see another round her handkerchief in her hand. It is so remote and piteous to see her there, talking of me in my suffering. O my Love! Little Father Barret is sent off to lunch at his Home, but is to come for a drive at three.

Rothenstein comes brotherly, abstract with ardour. He comes to the sick-bed as simply as to his easel. Then he tells me of his profound experience among the Hindoo Mystics and Ascetics. They seem to have every power of contemplation in four-fold might—except intellectual humility. "I could not find that in anything," Rothenstein said. The Hindoo wants to dominate his gods—the Catholic to be dominated by his God, till mortal is in union with immortal. I wish I had pointed this out to Heavenly Dog. I did not, more shame to me. We have a simple lunch and then " gold tips "

[1] Edith.

317

and coffee. H.D. is to draw the mill for us, when Father Barret comes for his drive. I tell Heavenly Dog that fear has been taken from me in front and at the sides; but I want to have all white behind me, no fear there. He says I am wonderful. His Hindoos cast all fear out of the spiritual life. Just before leaving he returns to say good-bye (he is going to America) with both hands, and he kisses my cheek, murmuring, I must still be here when he returns.

Then Michael reads some of the poems of Mr. Tagore, the Hindoo poet, whose portrait Heavenly Dog has done with infinite fineness of love, whose poems Willie Yeats has prefaced. The *Poems*, as we read them, are Mr. Tagore's prose translations of his own verses.

The earlier ones are extraordinarily beautiful, in the hinting of the mystic relation between God the poet, and a man who is a poet. Much of one's own experience is simple before one, as one reads.

Unfortunately the book palls after a while—its pantheism wearies. Pantheism is a huge and burthensome thing for poetry to carry. It is most uninteresting to the imagination, it is to the heart, dissipating; for it gives no object for Love. It demands passion for nonenity—for, to the heart, to ask it to love a vague all—a Pan, who has never had his Syrinx—is to ask it to love non-entity. Then the way of Pantheism ignores sin, evil, suffering, or vaguely trusts in nature—in sunrises, sunsets, rushing seas, air full of birds and suchlike pleasurable things—to redeem and save and sanctify. So Mr. Tagore's book loses grip as we read on.

[In the summer of 1913, they went to live at Mr.
Masefield's house, 13, Well Walk, Hampstead, for a few
months. Edith could no longer walk, and lay on her
couch in the drawing-room, where she loved to receive
visits from her friends.]

The evening wears on. Tommy is to bring the Ben-
galese Poet, Rabindranath Tagore, to see me—and be
seen of me for a few moments. Nine o'clock! I give
them up, as Tommy knows nine is my bed hour. A
ring! Josephine reports that Tommy and Tagore are
images of each other—" one in silver, one in copper,"
I add—and they enter so solemnly, she would be afraid
of the two out at night. Michael soon brings me in
the Hindoo. He seems to hang in his loose European [1]
clothes, as if he were hung in their wardrobe. The hair
and long beard have a handsome, designed crinkle in
them, darker in tone than the dark silver of both. There
is in the face something of the patient and quiet beauty
of a lustrous-eyed animal. He, himself, is full of rumina-
tion, affability, and his smile is a jewel—the particular
jewel of his soul. The leanness of his body attains
elegance in the sway of his hands, swaying as water
plants do. He speaks little : his voice is childish in
timbre and picks its way in English. I am aware when
he has left me that I have done most of the talking. I
make a central plunge, " It is happy to meet one who

[1] Many mistook Tagore's long unlapelled caftan, a purely
Eastern garment, for a clergyman's coat, from which the latter is
descended. When he discovered this mistake was so easily made,
he changed the colour from black to brown.

esteems pain as much as you do.   All my friends, even
Mr. Sturge Moore, regret it for me—and it has been the
' holiest experience of my life.'   I am a Catholic, only
Catholics, in the West, understand what pain means !
It is so holy, a cloister is built round it.   Yes, it is
cloistral."   The hands begin to move.   " I have just
been suffering pain.   It is a great solitude.   And I have
been able to think of things with a quietness I would
not have lost."   And he smiles as honey poured into
a brown pot and settling.

I speak to him of the *Poems* about a child and its
mother he will give us at Christmas.   He is pleased in a
quite humble and ever-smiling way, that I find him able
to really understand a child.   Pain is so real it may even
be a key to the fresh motions of childhood.   It makes all
things new, and childhood is so novel.

We speak of Rothenstein.   The eyes before me take
possession of their friend, as the gods used to take
possession of those they loved, in a deep cloud.   The
possessive darkness of Tagore's eyes, as he speaks of
Rothenstein, would sweep away the cynicism from
Heavenly Dog—a strain that jars often with his veritable
Oriental abstraction from unreality.

Rothenstein has been England to Tagore—welcome,
fame, introduction to friendships, with their ideas, aims,
the zeal of the West, its active discursions, its practical
publication.   He has gently, humbly enjoyed being published.   He is going to France, to find friends there and
visit them.   I tell him it is only in the home one catches
the veritable spirit of a country, if we can stay in the
country only a short time.   Then he sails to Bengal and

takes up his school and lives again among his boys, who
are pining for him.

" Will you hope to come back to England ? "

" Oh, yes—I must."

The smile melts into breadth and fixes into a seal,
stamped with, " I must."

Then Michael comes in and we part.

Late on Friday evening, Mr. Salter comes (Gurney
Salter, his friend name), to find us quite disenchanted
with Hampstead—grateful but resigned. He brings
more Synge volumes. With the sting of his fresh face,
he rallies us. The fine, proudly closed lips would
be sarcastic, but they have been sent to service with
Admetus, as Apollo was, gently to tend sheep and
make kindly speech to men. We are devoted to our
executor—one of the good gifts so divinely given to
us.

I am reading Synge. How I remember the yellow
eyes of the man in his Dublin Art Gallery portrait—eyes
that haunt rather like Ferrer's [their wolf-hound], watchful, cruel, almost pathetically inhuman and covetous of
an ideality they do not observe. The plays are brilliant,
hieroglyphic, brief yet large in design, the dialogue " tast-
ing of the country green." Rich in the native savour,
though limited in what it expresses in a very strange
way, you come to realise after you have read these four
plays. The taste of the plays is not good—there is
infamy in them, the special Irish infamy that does not
respect the human in a creature, that is impious to God
the Father's image in man, and therefore can be infamous

to a father and speak of him with poisoned impiousness, as the Playboy does of his " Da." The humour of the dialogue is salient—but it revolts us and therefore throws a lassoo round our laughter!

CHAPTER TWENTY-SEVEN

DEATH COMES HOME

[1] In the evening comes the faithful Francis.[2] He was with us just before we went to Hampstead, and now he comes at the passing of the melancholy dream. Dear, faithful Francis! Still, though we had much of the peaceful, gently humorous talk that wins welcome to François, we have no touch of the great days of old. Well, on Friday evening it is moved that I read from *Wild Honey*. . . . The great days begin, glorious things are spoken by the bee-circled book.[3] And I am moved to read to Francis (I believe it is only to him I could read what is so thrilling and sacred to my heart)—I am moved to read Michael's poems to me.—*Old Ivories—The Dear Temptation of Her Face—Atthis, my darling of Long Ago*—the loveliest nocturne of love ever created, *Palimpsest*—to say by heart

> " A girl
> Her soul a deep wave pearl."

I am moved to show him triumph and joy in this lovely praise, and in showing him my so often guarded mood before my glory, I also let my Love understand what

[1] Edith.
[2] Prof. Francis Brookes, their cousin and intimate friend.
[3] The cover design by Ricketts.

her poet's gift has been to me—her poet-lover's gift. Think of it ! She has often read these lovely poems to me, she has not heard them tender but high-voiced from my lips. It is Paradise between us. When we're together eternally, our spirits will be inter-penetrated with our loves and our art under the benison of the Vision of God.

For it wants another. There was need of Francis to listen to *Wild Honey* ; there will be need of God to assure the immortal oneness of Love with Love, of praise and being praised and the response of the praised, casting all joy into union with the poet-lover. God drive the time along ! It was an evening of such infinite promises. The rarest evening of a lifetime. Francis, dazzled and mystified, bade me good night, with a face under an ancient spell and impress on it of ancient acknowledgement of Power.

[1] It is Francis' last night. How spend it ? I find I am listening to Henry's voice—Hennie reading my love poems to her, aloud to Francis. Of course I have never listened to them before—she read the famous sonnet *A window full of ancient things*, also *Atthis* and others.

For a little while I am in Paradise. It is infinitely soft between us. Warm buds open. I feel at least I have merited gems of passionate love.

And Francis, who has loved me so well, listens to the singing amid the boughs, that is not for him— listening as he would to a nightingale overhead. It is an intense moment. A moment not of memory—but of

[1] Katherine.

creation. A moment never to be forgotten of Francis or of me.

[A later entry.] [1] I can remember nothing. Sometimes impressions float up, gleam awhile—sink.

Oct. 21st, 1913. At last, my dear Father Goscannon comes forth, from much travel and much trial with nerves and insomnia, and I rejoice in a visit I had not dared to hope for. He is back in his little cure, with a stalwart missionary priest to help for two months ; he has a new and bright little housekeeper. He looks very brown and settled into middle-age, with its serious proportions—but oh, how precious a sight, the sweet and holy eyes—the double stars that led me through such spaces of wonder and fear. My life confessor has been the confessor I needed—who broke me in and trained me. Father Vincent challenges and he enlightens, but Goss lashed me with Catholic realities—told me I had pride up to the top of the mould, made me shake with tears of shame and humiliation, and then from the secrecy of the intimate truth of my being, known to him, won me to toil at my soul, to offer the dire things of the past, purgatorially and with sacramental passion to God, dwelling with his beloved ones on the Altar.

All this comes over me and I speak of it very simply— the brown face and averted eyes seem to grow more intense and so respond. I have never taken up the threads of friendship so naturally, with the tenderness of inter-communication. And I have wondered

[1] Edith.

whether he were lost to me, in a cloud of utter nerve collapse.

I give thanks from the flooded fountain of my heart to our dear Lord and Redeemer.

October 27. It is early morning of my own Love's birthday. How dear she is to me—how the sweetness and clench of love grow pain and joy as I look at her, and receive her little wreath of kisses in my withered hair. We have the bond of our art, precious, precious. We have had the bond of race, with the delicious adventure of the stranger nature, introduced by the beloved father; we have had the bond of life, deep set in the years; and now we have the bond of the Faith and the bond—different from any other bond—of threatened death.

November 25th. To think how long it is since I wrote in the White Book. I have been very ill, very drowsy with the worst dreaded of my enemies, the dropsy, and with the needs of a very active heart. I realised yesterday, when Dr. Lishman had been and had rejoiced to find my brain so much brighter than when he punctured, and felt the intellectual need of each stab for me, how my real, deepest physical sorrow is the dropsy. I was speaking to Josephine of Dr. Lishman's joy, when suddenly I hear a sound like that of a dove that fights against choking corn. I had to realise it came from my throat and that other spasms were there to choke me, till I let their strange noise grind themselves out. But I do not think our dear Lord will let me drowse into death when it comes. I have been allowed to offer poppy [1] to Him, that I may keep my brain and will clear. He will remember and drive away hebetude at the end.

My Love and I are growing closer and closer in spirit. She comes down every night in a fleece of silver blue, with twisted golden cord, strange softness of pain and charm on her face and coming from under her hair. And she reads to me *Lord Clifford* and *Dion*, *The Affliction of Margaret* and *Ruth* and other wonderful, deathless gems old Wordsworth wrought, or else reads odes in which Keats dethrones every poet. Sometimes she has read some of Thomas Hardy's stories in *A Changed Man*, stories full of arresting genius in spite of their monotony.

December 4th. " Swift ! Thy tablets, memory ! " For my memory has so few. . . . Father Prior has just been in to help and strengthen me. Before he helped me against the rebellion that, through my own order, I should have been restricted in the help given by the Blessed Sacrament. Now it is a much more central rebellion he has to meet—against the Prince, the Bridegroom himself—spaces of temptation far more dangerous —" far more." It is rebellion of far deeper weakness and can only be met by elements of strength—sheer strength : By the Frontal Attack.

How is this to be done ?

(1) By giving Thanks. You cannot have an insecure moment when you give active thanks. Why and how give thanks in my present case ? That, all through my

---

[1] She had refused the alleviation of opiates.

time of special prayer, for cleanness of mind up to the end—all through my little sacrifice of the help of poppy, that I might not be shattered in will like poor Francis Thompson—I had received already such marked and amazing response.·

(2) That I had learnt a tremendous secret of the spiritual life, that I must offer during the hours of strength, what in hours of weakness I could not. The hours capable of offering beforehand must be sacerdotal. . . .

(3) Then again I must remember that I am setting up a little gift of my own to be remembered and that this is not a spiritual motion of the soul.

The wonderful thing to realise is that Christ may give me, at the end, something of His own Holy End, " My God, My God," of Calvary and the previous joy, " I have longed for this hour," in the Supper Room of the Blessed Sacrament. Never till Father Prior and I have had this talk had he realised the place of the Eucharist in the death and immortality of the Lord.

Again we pray we may love God with all our heart and mind. Sometimes we have to give the mind wholly to Him—as we give Him the heart to do what He likes with. We must remember we don't give to dictate but to delight. The dry Sacrament of Thanksgiving precedes in His precious death the blood-drenched weaknesses and merely mortal atmosphere of dereliction that God himself endured when dying.

[So ends Edith's last entry in *Works and Days*. She died on Dec. 13th, 1913.]

[1] Christmas Eve. O Hennie, Hennie, but a little blue nun has been with me in the river room, dressing a wound in my breast—cancer—O Hennie, my Blue Bird, my Beloved—and this woe was shown to me in the octave of Corpus Christi.

I have been a bad nurse—this little extra offering I have been able to make clean for thee. Two days after thou wert gone, bleeding came—God's quiet sign that I must open my secret.

But I write of Christmas Eve. Last Night-Eve, I could not go to the Midnight Mass, to-night I go alone. And is it my last Midnight Mass?

She sang to me *Adeste Fideles* and *The Nativity Ode*, then we loved best the lines of the stars:

> Bending one weightier precious influencé,

To-night it is the lines:

> When such music sweet,
> Their heart's desire did greet,
> As never was by mortal fingers struck.

> Now is the time of the Baby Jesus!

And the virginal heart breaks in its tenderness. How lovely is the room, how soft! I think this room would inspire me to write. At once, Hennie's devotion to Beauty sways this Irish heart. She notes too, lovingly, my hair, gray and curly against my veil. The favour of me pleasures her—and oh, to hear the loving, soft accents—Mrs. Court comes in. I have rung for her, feeling very lonely. She gives me a new memory,

[1] Katherine.

" Good night and good-bye," she said to Mrs. Court, as she went away on Friday evening. That same evening she avowed to Mrs. Court, " I feel so like Christmas." My Beloved.

Twelve months ago what a year of suffering was before her ! And now she is her crisp, delicious, gay and gamesome Ariel spirit of old.

The Annunciation picture of an Angel, Mary gave her, I have had put under glass. It comes this morning. But, oh Henry, I am growing blind of thee, my memory is growing blind. I cannot see—only conjure. . . . It is Henry I want. The fragrance of Henry seems fainter in Paragon. . . .

FADING

Nay, I have lost thee, and I cannot find !
No image of thee wavers in my mind,
My memory is growing blind.

I utter my past knowledge of thee—fond,
I leave thee as a book that I have conned,
Thine eyes were dusk as alder-shadowed pond.

Thy face, how full of augur, hidden will,
When thou wert silent, dreaming, very still,
Some of the whitest mischief to fulfil.

The little happenings to thy voice, the drop,
As when the warblings of the linnets stop,
While tiny sounds from twig to twig still hop.

In the old accents I will sing, my glory, my delight,
In the old accents tipped with flame before we knew the right,
True way of singing with reserve. O love, with pagan might.

White in our steeds, and white too in our armour let us ride
Immortal, white, triumphing, flashing downward side by side
To where our friends the Argonauts are fighting with the tide.

Let us draw calm to them, Beloved, the souls on heavenly voyage
    bound,
Saluting as one presence—great disaster, were it found,
If one with half-fed lambency, should halt and flicker round.

O friends, so fondly loving, so beloved, look up to us,
In constellation breathing on your errand arduous,
O Argonauts !
              Now, faded from their sight
We cling and joy. It was thy intercession gave me right
My fellow, to this fellowship—O Henry, my delight !

Father Gray comes. We have solemn talk. I open
up my grief at the Church's action—first speaking of my
Love as among the Angels ; then, after a few weeks, in
Purgatory. I tell him how this has checked me and use
the simile of Henry landing in Australia and enjoying the
kangaroos, and Henry still tossed on unknown seas.
" Michael," he says, " you must accept this paradox."
He always thinks of a dead friend as with God. The
awful thing is for it to become possible to God, to have
His desire and to be able to admit man into His presence.
Father Gray makes me feel how awful God's task is.
Yes : what I feel about Henry's being gone is aridity :
it happens. He commands me to be sure, whatever
suffering is before me, sufficient grace will be with me

to meet that suffering. " But, Father Gray, do you think I am going to die ? "

" Not unless a miracle happens, Michael, you have not the allure." This is one of Father Gray's greatest sayings.

At Wincanton Convent. St. Theresa, I call on you to help ! Oh, my beloved, come and comfort me ! My intercessors, stand round and bless me !

Paragon Cottage ! [1] Thank God ! Sep. 18th, 1914. All night, sister Carmel says, I lay smiling. This morning I was saved the cruel torture of being carried and tossed, wheeled into church ; receiving the immense charity—though so much ashamed of myself—I must offer a Mass in thanksgiving. And I am striving now to write a bit. The Fathers are in retreat, which makes it so hard for me. They are merciful and charitable. God take my offering.

[So ends the last entry in *Works and Days*. Michael died on September 26th.]

---

[1] Michael went to Leicester to be near Father Vincent MacNab ; at first he was in uncomfortable quarters and then moved to a cottage near Hawksyard Priory. Miss E. Fortey, her devoted friend, tells me that Michael was delighted with her new surroundings, and though the place was usually referred to as the Cottage, there is no doubt that she rechristened it.

INDEX TO PROPER NAMES

Made and Printed in Great Britain by Butler & Tanner Ltd., Frome and London